GW01086999

Law and Gospel in the theology of Andrew Fuller

George M. Ella

Go Publications

Go Publications
The Cairn, Hill Top, Eggleston, Co. Durham, DL12 0AU, England

© Go Publications 1996
First published 1996

British Library Cataloguing in Publication Data available

ISBN 0 9527074 1 1

Printed and bound in Great Britain by
Creative Print & Design Group (Wales), Ebbw Vale

Fullerism

A main error of Mr Fuller — and perhaps it was that in which his system and the arguments by which he defended it originated — consisted in the excessive and antiscriptural ideas he formed of the accountableness of man. He attached obligations to him as a free agent, which, in fact never developed upon him by any law of his Creator; and invested him with a responsibility for talents which he never possessed. Because man is naturally obligated as a creature to love and obey God, according to the extensive purity and requirements of the divine law, he maintained that the same reason in which his natural obligations as a *creature* was founded obliged him also, as a *sinner*, to believe in the Lord Jesus Christ for salvation upon his having the Gospel revelation. Independent of the absurdity of representing faith in Jesus in a light which classes it with the works of the law, I call this an excessive and extravagant idea of human responsibility. Accountability, if it relates to anything, must relate to some *service* to be performed according to the measure of ability with which the Creator originally endows us, or to some *trust* with which he has charged us, that we may employ it for all purposes of his righteous will; or to some *talents* which he has given, that we may improve them, and return to him that revenue of praise to which he is entitled — but *accountability can have no place in the reception of gifts and benefits which he communicates, with an absolute sovereignty of will,* to whom he pleases. How can anyone be responsible for the gifts of a benefactor which he never received, or account for property with which he was never entrusted? A peasant is bound to observe allegiance to the sovereign and the government under which he lives, and to behave himself peaceably and justly towards every member of the community. If he violates the law, he is answerable for the offense at the bar of his country. But whoever imagined that a peasant is culpable and entitled to punishment for a capital crime because he has not advanced himself to the rank of a peer in the realm, and secured to himself a pension for life from the king's treasury? A proceeding of such a kind is absurd in supposition, because at variance with all the known principles and rules of equity and justice, yet such a proceeding actually takes place under the divine government, according to Mr Fuller's notion of accountability, which obliges a servant under the Gospel to receive salvation by faith under pain of death, because he is obliged by the *law* to obey the divine will.

Of all the benefits and blessings of grace, which is it that the possession or enjoyment thereof hinges upon the accountability of man, or rather, the *responsibility of a dead sinner*? Is it *election*? (Rom. viii. 29, 30); ix.; xi. 5. 6; Eph. i. 3, 4); *Redemption*? (Rom. v. 6, 8); *Reconciliation*? (Rom. v. 10); *Justification*? (Rom. iii. 21, 28; viii. 3, 4; x. 4); *Faith*? (Eph. i. 19; ii. 8; Phil. i. 29; Col. ii. 12; John vi. 29; Acts xiii. 48; xiv. 27); *or even personal and practical holiness and obedience*? (Ezek. xvi. 60, 63; xxxvi. 25, 27; Jer. xxxii. 38, 40). Search these and other Scriptures of a similar import, and compare them with the work of God in your personal experience, and you will see indeed that you must put the crown of salvation where you delight to see it — on the head, not of human accountableness, but the sovereignty of Jehovah's grace.

Under this view, I am sure you will join with me in the most unfeigned abhorrence of a system that robs God of his glory, and enhances the condemnation of the guilty to an immeasurable degree by increasing their responsibility.

George Wright
Reprinted by courtesy of *The Gospel Magazine*, vol. xii, 1877, p. 343.

This work is dedicated to John and Gwen Sarson who, under God, prompted me to examine more closely the practical outworking of the imputed righteousness of Christ in the believer contrasted with Andrew Fuller's theory of figurative imputation.

Contents

Part IV
Andrew Fuller and the gospel's evangelistic witness

Foreword

In many ways this book may be viewed as a companion volume to two recent excellent biographies by George Ella which have caused no little stir in certain parts of the religious press. I refer to *William Huntington: Pastor of Providence* and *John Gill and the Cause of God and Truth*. Although these are principally biographical studies Dr Ella does also defend the doctrinal positions of these Gospel ministers and Christian leaders from the past. However, what we have here is even more theological than biographical as Dr Ella's chief concern is simply to give us the pure and unadulterated Word of God. It is just the sort of book that is needed at present because the evangelical and Reformed establishment would tell us that Andrew Fuller is by far to be preferred to Gill and Huntington, because it reckons that his teaching stands in the tradition of mainline Calvinism and therefore represents historic Reformed Christianity. The implication is that whereas Fullerism is orthodox, the doctrines associated with Gill and Huntington are an aberration of the truths of sovereign grace. In fact it is suggested that these men taught the worst forms of Hyper-Calvinism and Antinomianism.

A few years ago in reading the life and some of the works of Fuller I came to the conclusion that the man's experience was better than his doctrine. Although his conversion seemed to be real I saw that he was inclined in his writings to indulge in speculative philosophy when considering the relationship between divine sovereignty and human accountability. In contrast there is a consistency between Huntington's experience and doctrine, as the one is firmly grounded in the other. The truth of God's absolute sovereignty was burnt deep into his soul in conversion, he learnt the doctrine of eternal election experimentally. As the sovereignty of divine grace was the first saving truth that God revealed to him Huntington felt himself obliged to defend and enforce it. He thus became a great lover of and contender for the five points of Calvinism. The same can be said of John Gill. In his theological works he gives an unanswerable defence of the doctrines of free grace. And he was clearly as Calvinistic in his preaching as he was in his doctrine, as witness his published sermons.

Today a different Calvinism is in vogue. Those who advocate this popular religion profess to believe in divine predestination and the doctrine of particular redemption, but they also constantly affirm their notion of God's universal redeeming love. They say that God really wants to save everybody, and this is to be demonstrated in an indiscriminate offer of salvation to all in preaching. Such men appeal to Fuller as a champion of their views. Many, as they halt between particularism on the one hand and universalism on the other hand, are getting entangled in the web being woven by these modern day Fullerites. However in biblical Calvinism the purpose of the Father is seen to be co-extensive with the purchase of the Son which is in perfect harmony with the regenerating work of the Holy Spirit. Thus God is seen to be triune in salvation as well as in subsistence. Joseph Hart expresses it so beautifully:

> But all true Christians this may boast
> (A truth from nature never learned)
> That Father, Son and Holy Ghost
> To save our souls are all concerned

It is really this Trinitarian salvation that is destroyed in Fuller's teaching.

The following pages contain a thorough analysis and a faithful exposure of this whole system of theology, which is shown to be even more pernicious than one might first think. As he faithfully contends for the truth Dr Ella not only demonstrates that Fullerism is an attack on particular redemption or definite atonement, but he also reveals Fuller as, in many respects, the forerunner of that liberal theology that has spread like poison through so many churches over the last 150 years. I count it a privilege to be once again associated with my friend George Ella, in writing this foreword to a work which I believe will, under God, do much noble service for the cause of Christ's gospel and the purity of it.

Henry Sant
Pastor, Salem Strict & Particular Baptist Chapel
Portsmouth, England

Part I
The church awake and asleep: which is which?

1. Preface: The path of life and the ways of all flesh

I do not presume to have sounded the death knell of Fullerism with this little book. That mock-gospel has been dead all along. Its adherents still live, however, on its carnage, but this is the way of all flesh. As Fuller says when he hyper-critically views the doctrines of grace, 'There must needs be heresies, that they who are approved may be made manifest.'[1] The design of this book has not so much been to rescue Fullerites from their worldly philosophy, worthy though this objective might be, but rather to help Zion's pilgrims who are tempted to stray from well-charted Bible paths by the hawkers and peddlers of inaccurate maps printed by Messrs. Andrew Fuller & Co., of no fixed spiritual abode.

When one examines the charts and charters of these dealers in false goods one quickly finds out that they have no cartographic authority from the Royal Government of the Heavenly City and the re-planning and re-routing of the roads to the Celestial Realms which they are trying to enforce by appealing to man's free agency in true democratic spirit are completely contrary to the Royal Law. Indeed, in a last, panicky move to distract the pilgrim from his true path before their firm goes bankrupt, Fuller & Co. have decided to bring out a special 'free offer'. An offer free of the grace of the King of Kings and free of the will of His Majesty. An offer which abounds in the revolutionary, rationalistic politics of free-willism and free agency to determine one's own destiny and freedom to tread whatever paths one is inclined to take. This offer denies the King's promise that He has called a free amnesty for His very own people and devised a means whereby all of them will become eternal citizens of His Kingdom and none shall be lost. Reader, may this book help you to discern the Royal preacher from the pirate peddler.

2. The clarion call of revival and the blast of heresy's own trumpet

The age of reason
Historians call the 18th century the Century of Reason because it was greatly influenced by thinkers such as Sir Isaac Newton (1642-1727) and John Locke (1632-1704) who taught that the workings of the known world and the ways of the unknown God could all be demonstrated by logical deduction. Men of letters such as Beattie and Blair in Scotland and Lessing in Germany taught that following the paths of logic was akin to following in the footsteps of God. Lessing even went so far as to say that Christ had the right use of reason in mind when He promised that the Holy Spirit would come. In his *Education of the Human Race*, Lessing pointed out that by the aid of reason, man would go on to perfection and finally reach a state of being Christ-like. Many Christians accepted this philosophy, arguing that as it issued from the pens of practising Christians, it could not be wrong.

A reformation of manners
The 18th century also brought with it a strong desire to reform public manners. The previous, so-called Restoration period, which raised a play-boy King to the throne and brought literature and language down to the bawdy-house floor was not to be tolerated long by Providence. Writers such as Addison and Young began to clean up the English language and the Church of England responded with a best-selling book called *The Whole Duty of Man* which taught the necessity of good conduct and respectability for right living. High moral principles were put forward as the mark of a godly life but there was no Gospel in the book but rather a latent teaching of righteousness according to works. Now the moral law, not reason, was emphasised as the measure of all things. This emphasis on duty to the moral law as opposed to the Mosaic Law, brought with it an upsurge in Neonomianism and Amyraldism. Sincere obedience to moral precepts became the new gospel.

The Latitudinarians and the Cambridge Platonists
This was the heyday of Latitudinarian theology. On the more positive side, it was a move to curb the spiritual apathy of the church, pull down the barriers between the Church of England and Dissenters and reform church

order and worship, returning to the basic beliefs which all Christians have in common. It was an outgoing movement, eager to encourage a missionary spirit, especially in the growing colonies. On the very negative side its most famous contenders and those who climbed highest in church ranks such as Cudworth and Tillotson, left the orthodoxy of the Reformation, overtook the theology of the Arminians and settled down, theologically speaking, somewhere between Arminianism and Socinianism or plain Deism. Performing one's natural duty to God became one of the key items in their agenda.

The Latitudinarians were closely connected to the Cambridge Platonists who tended to trace their spiritual ancestry to the Puritans but departed from them in making their religion more a moral philosophy concerning God's moral government of the world rather than the system of law and grace found in the Scriptures. The movement was anti-materialistic, emphasising the triumph of reason and rationality in religion. Though they spoke much of the Spirit of God, it was really, as their name suggested, the spirit of Plato whom they worshipped. Their teaching was summed up by the Earl of Shaftesbury as, 'Religion is being as much like God as man can be like him.' John Smith (1618-1652) defined the aim of religion as 'by a contemplation of our own souls, we can climb up to an understanding of the Deity.' Just as the Latitudinarians emphasised duty-faith, so the Cambridge Platonists emphasised the presence of unfallen abilities in man which could point and lead man to God. Both these elements were to be subdued in the churches due to the Evangelical Revival of the 18th century but returned with renewed vigour and with an even more proselytising force almost a century later.

Archbishop Tillotson (1630-1698) is seen as one of the most learned and influential of the Latitudinarians. Of his works, George Whitefield wrote: 'Any spiritual man who reads them may easily see that the Archbishop knew of no other than a bare historical faith; and as to the method of our acceptance before God, and our justification by faith alone (which is the doctrine of the Scripture and of the Church of England), he certainly was as ignorant as Mohamet himself.'[2]

Tillotson outlines his duty-faith teaching in a sermon entitled *The Wisdom of Being Religious*, in which he argues that the knowledge of duty is the image of God in man. Of this natural awareness of duty, he says:

> For to know our duty, is to know what it is to be like God in *goodness*, and *pity*, and *patience*, and *clemency*, in *pardoning injuries*, and *passing by provocations*; in *justice and righteousness*, in *truth* and *faithfulness*,[3] and in hatred and detestation of

the contrary of these: In a word, it is to know what is the good and acceptable will of God, what it is that he loves and delights in, and is pleased withal, and would have us to do in order to our perfection and our happiness.[4]

Tillotson defined 'religion' as a coming to God through obeying one's duty. Whether one 'came' or not indicated whether one was dutiful or not. Tillotson argued in this way because he believed that one could find the full Gospel in the Law and if one obeyed the Law, one automatically obeyed the Gospel. Here Tillotson has lost sight of the fall and the need for justification through faith which is a gift of God who approaches man by grace. He sees duty-faith rather as a matter of natural religion and within the scope of man's natural powers.

The Governmentalists
Influential, too, amongst the less Reformed leaders of the Church of England was the teaching of rationalist and anti-Calvinist Hugo Grotius (1583-1645). He popularised his radical theology by composing songs and ditties which became the 17th century equivalent of 'Top of the Pops' and were sung by farmers, soldiers and especially sailors. Grotius was a vowed opponent of the English Puritans and Dissenters and wished to live as if the Reformation had never taken place, building his church on the more speculative philosophies of the first five centuries AD. He thus scorned *sola scriptura* and idealised the *pia antiquitas*. His call was back to the piety of antiquity and thus his major interest lay in the Roman Catholic Church and Eastern Orthodoxy.

Though Grotius was a statesman of note, he is known best amongst church historians and theologians for his Moral Government Theory. Influenced strongly by Abelard (1079-1142) via the Socinians, Grotius believed that natural law as a part of divine law may be deduced *a priori* from the conception of human nature, and *a posteriori* from the fact of its universal acceptation. Thus the moral law is seen as an inherent part of human nature and is authoritative because it is created by God. The aim of preaching the gospel is thus first to make the hearer conscious of his natural ability to know and understand what God requires of him and secondly to appeal to his sense of duty which this is thought to kindle. The theory denies that the justice of God necessarily demands that all the requirements of the Law be met. The atonement is thus merely a *nominal* display on God's part, not a *real* atonement. The sufferings of Christ are to be seen as a moral deterrent which becomes efficacious when it works. Thus the act of atonement is not seen in the work of Christ but in the response of the human agent to the appeal Christ's sufferings make on him. In this way the sinner is frightened off committing future sins but there is no retribution for past sins, God merely relaxing His standards. Indeed, man is not so much reconciled to God as to a right view of himself leading to the correct sentiments for acceptance with God. Grotius wished by this theory to distance himself from the Socinians with whom he was accused of agreeing. In this he was completely unsuccessful. In full agreement with the Socinians, Grotius denies that the satisfaction of Christ was required by the nature and attributes of God and was thus a full equivalent of the penalty of sin.

Writing at the end of last century, Benjamin B. Warfield argues that Grotianism became the standard doctrine of European Arminians who had been influenced by the Socinians. He sees it as entering America when New England Puritanism began to break down, rejecting the satisfaction doctrine of the atonement for the rectoral view.[5] Warfield viewed Grotianism as dead and gone in his day but it is now spreading rapidly amongst former Reformed men and one can no longer call it an Arminian or Socinian doctrine. Nowadays, it is being traded as 'Evangelical Calvinism' and has stormed and almost conquered most of the former Five Point strongholds, especially in the English-speaking world.

The Great Awakening
However, just as it seemed that Latitudinarian and moral governmental ideas were swamping Britain and Cotton Mather was protesting in New England that their missionaries were not working for *The Society for Propagating the Gospel in Foreign Parts* but *The Society for the Molestation of the Gospel,* God in His mercy began to pour out His Spirit on Europe, the British Isles and the American colonies. Men were raised up such as Spener, Franke and Untereyck on the Continent and Hervey, Gill, Brine, Toplady, Romaine and Huntington in Britain. Mighty preachers such as Frelinghuysen of Holland/Germany, Tennet of Ireland and Whitefield of England commuted backwards and forwards across the Atlantic planting the Word of God wherever they came. These men, though men of learning, logic and highly moral lives, had found something greater. They believed in preaching the righteousness of Christ imputed to elect sinners through the free grace of God. Works-faith and works-righteousness were shown to be the sham gospels they were as free redemption, faith, reconciliation and justification by means of Christ's redeeming and atoning, vicarious death became the gospel worthy of the God who had called it into being.

On the Continent and in Britain thousands flocked to places of worship which they had scorned before. Both state church and Dissenting pastors were now preaching Christ as the fulfilment of the Law for His elect. The American colonies were ablaze with the light of the gospel. Research done at the Elias-Schrenk Institute in Germany shows that in 1700 only five per cent of the Colonists attended a place of worship, by 1775, it had risen to twenty per cent.[6] Some of the major pioneers in the work of 18th century gospel outreach were staunch British Baptists such as John Gill and that class of men who became famous as 'Gillites' in both continents. Particular Baptist John Ryland Senior, no mean evangelist himself, could say in 1777,

> At present blessed be God, we believe there is no apparent apostasy in our ministers and people from the glorious principles we profess.' He goes on to say, 'Much of the credit for this unswerving allegiance to the doctrine of Scripture, under God, must be attributed to John Gill, known affectionately as Dr. Voluminous.[7]

Pioneers of the Awakening in Britain such as James Hervey and preachers of righteousness such as Augustus Toplady enriched the work of the Anglican church by the teaching they gained sitting at the feet of this Baptist stalwart whom they called their Master in Israel.

The Counter-Awakening
As the harvesting time of the Calvinistic Awakening began to end towards the 1780s, the winnowing time came with such preachers as William Huntington who were used of God to build up the churches and sift the wheat from the chaff. It was during this time that the Counter-Awakening emerged in the same way as the Counter-Reformation had raised its ugly head to try and smother the work of Luther and Calvin. The teaching of Grotius, Tillotson and his Cambridge Platonist friends re-entered the churches with great proselytising fervour. The date 1785 thus stands as a turning point in the work of the Evangelical Awakening. It is the publishing date of a book by a former Particular Baptist[8] pastor named Andrew Fuller (1754-1815) called *The Gospel Worthy of All Acceptation* that put the clock back almost a hundred years.[9]

According to Fuller's followers, there was no awakening in the 18th century amongst Baptists up to the publishing of Fuller's notoriously controversial book. 'It was Fuller who fanned the smoking wick into a blaze.'[10] They believe also that it had been a time of spiritual death for the Anglicans and the Scottish Presbyterians as they had preached that God justified sinners as sinners and that Christ had literally died in their stead and literally bore their sins and the salvation of Christ's Bride and hers alone was wrought out in the atonement. They had also preached the total inability of man to comprehend spiritual things. Gentle James Hervey was now looked upon as an arch heretic as he taught that faith was a gift of God and not a dutiful response to a Gospel invitation.[11] For the Counter-Awakening all these doctrines failed to do justice, in their eyes, to man's agency in salvation and therefore did not demonstrate God's purpose with man correctly. Thus the major break-through of the true gospel came, they believe, on the publication of Fuller's book. Indeed 1785 is likened to 1517 by Fullerites as they devotedly believe that Fuller's book succeeded in England to do that which Luther had aimed to do in Germany by the nailing up of his ninety-five theses to the door of the Schloßkirche in Wittenberg.[12] Indeed the laudation which Fuller receives from his followers is of a surprising intensity and conviction, as if they really believe that Christianity had been in a state of permanent hibernation before Fuller 'sounded the awakening alarm to these sleeping churches in his epochal treatise, *The Gospel Worthy of All Acceptation.*'[13] Indeed, modern critics of traditional Calvinism have raised Andrew Fuller unashamedly to the status of a prophet, a prophet of what they call 'Evangelical Calvinism'.[14] True to all sects who raise a Guru in the Saviour's stead, the writings of such antichrists are claimed as life-givers by their devotees. Thus E. F. Clipsham calls Ernest Payne's adulation 'well-described' when that Baptist Union official pronounces *The Gospel Worthy of All Acceptation* 'an epoch making, life giving book.'[15]

Putting back the clock
Thus, in spite of the huge spread of the Awakening in the 18th century which was there for all to see, the Fullerites play the part of human ostriches and boast that nothing had really happened of spiritual value before 'the shot heard around the world in this spiritual offensive was fired from the pen of Andrew Fuller.'[16] Up to then, Fuller's biographers tell us, the system of doctrine which had prevailed amongst believers was 'to a considerable extent a caricature of Calvinism, exercising under some of its forms a peculiarly degrading and pernicious influence'.[17] Clipsham tells us that the days immediately before the publication of Fuller's prophetic work were 'the dark days of hyper-Calvinism' during which few 'refused to bow the knee to Gill and Brine'.[18] This was also the opinion of Fuller who could write, fully convinced of his own importance as a pioneer: 'When I first published my treatise on the nature of faith, and the duty of all men to believe it, the Christian profession had sunk into contempt amongst us;

insomuch that had matters gone on but a few years longer, the Baptists would have become a perfect dunghill in society.'[19] Such was his opinion, it would seem, of stalwart Baptists of the calibre of Bunyan, Kiffin, Knollys, Noble, Brine, Skepp, the Wallins, Wilson, the Stennetts, Beddome, Booth, Kinghorn, Gill and Brine, the like of which has scarcely been seen since Fullerism emerged. Fuller was particularly eager to challenge the theological credentials of his Baptist fathers in the faith who stood close to Gill and Brine whom he accused of being 'High Calvinists,' 'Hyper-Calvinists' or 'False Calvinists' and of having a false view of the Law, the Gospel and redemption. In fact, when Fuller is finished firing his furious guns at his orthodox Baptist brethren past and present and fellow ministers in England, Scotland and North America and aiming many a salvo at Anglicans, Presbyterians, and Congregationalists, he believes he has cleared the entire evangelical field of all but his own trusty band of Fullerite followers.

Annus calamitosus

1785 was a bad year for truth, sound sense, moral integrity and Gospel theology. This little book seeks to show how Andrew Fuller returned to the follies of his pre-Awakening Latitudinarian fathers and left the beaten track trod by saints who were justified and sanctified by free-grace. He chose to return to the rational doctrines of moral duties and works-righteousness of more darkened times. It will be shown that Andrew Fuller had a faulty view of man, a faulty view of God, a faulty view of the Law, a faulty view of the Gospel, a faulty view of redemption and a faulty view of Christ's Church. To crown it all, it will be shown that Fullerism, despite its boast of being the only true means of evangelism, is not in any way conducive to preaching the gospel of free grace to sinners. In its essential features, it is a gospel for Fullerite believers only.

Pointing out Fuller's theological follies is no easy task. This is because Fuller delights in using a meta-language of his own invention to describe traditional theological concepts. He also uses such terminologies to camouflage the fact that he is using worldly philosophical conceptions to explain Biblical truths. This is nowhere more evident than when Fuller is speaking of virtue, disinterested benevolence, the pursuit of happiness, the nature and fitness of things, free-agency, justice, natural and moral ability, the letter and spirit of the law and moral and positive obedience. Anyone trying to follow Fuller's use of words must invariable lose his meaning at some time or other. Thus this writer does not presume to have understood Fuller completely. Anyone who claims that almost every phrase and utterance he makes concerning Bible doctrines is to be understood figuratively, is bound to be misunderstood, especially as Fuller rarely explains what he means by his metaphors. Whenever I caught myself feeling that I had quite understood Fuller's explanations, I found that he was, in reality, explaining metaphors by metaphors and explaining Bible truths by explaining them away.

Joseph Belcher, Fuller's editor and compiler, tells the story of how Fuller sought to gain entrance to the pulpits of eastern England which were opposed to him. He thus hatched a plot of deception and arranged to take the place of a friend anonymously at an association meeting, with no previous announcement of the clandestine operation being made. Apparently, after the sermon, all were convinced that the unknown preacher had destroyed every argument of Fullerism and proclaimed the truth. Great was the surprise when it was announced who the anonymous speaker was. Belcher concludes his anecdote by saying, 'Several of them were convinced of the truth of the system he advocated; and all opened their pulpits, that he might plead the cause of the mission.'[20] Such a conclusion is not at all surprising as Fuller obviously preached, using the 'language of Zion', i.e. terms which the hearers took to be a sign of orthodoxy. Equally obvious is the fact that Fuller did not explain in his sermon that he meant a completely different thing by almost every orthodox term he used. Typical, too, of what we learn from Belcher is that Fuller did not preach to evangelise eastern England but to gain interest in and raise money for the Baptist Missionary Society's work in India.

The bulk of Fuller's writings arose out of fierce controversy with Booth, Taylor, Button, Martin, Beddome, McLean, Vidler, Belsham, Kentish and Toulmin, men of very varied doctrinal beliefs. They were also planned as criticism of Fuller's more orthodox Baptist forerunners such as John Gill and John Brine. Such writing rarely encourages cool thinking. As criticism poured in from within and without the evangelical fold, Fuller's highly defensive and strongly controversial essays poured out. Thus it is as difficult to organise and analyse his theology systematically as it is to understand its meaning. Much of it is simply taken up with his trying to clean himself of the miry clay he fell into through leaving the rock of Biblical Calvinism and the plain meaning of Scripture. He accuses his numerous critics of misunderstanding him and reading into his words concepts which were far from his mind. He believed, however, that this was proof that such critics were Hyper-Calvinists and Antinomians as his arguments were as clear as day to himself and the only yardstick for orthodoxy possible. He never seems to have suspected that the presence of so much 'misunderstanding' amongst many saintly men was a clear sign that something was wrong with his own arguments. Surprisingly, the closer those whom Fuller marked out for criticism were to orthodox Calvinism, the harsher was Fuller's language against them.

A juggler of words

Fuller is in his element when juggling with words. He loves to boil down words to what he calls their 'proper meaning' which he believes is their secular 'dictionary' meaning. This often leaves him with theological concepts quite robbed of their theological content. This is nowhere more clear than when Fuller is dealing with sin, the fall and the atonement. We thus are often surprised to find Fuller taking a normal Biblical word and paraphrasing it in high-sounding philosophical terms which completely clouds its meaning for the normal intelligent reader. This caused Abraham Booth (1734-1806) and the Olney Independent minister Samuel Greatheed (d. 1823) to say that Fuller tried to explain Biblical concepts with language borrowed from pagans instead of using the plain language of the Bible. In fact Fuller obviously disdains the plain language of the common man and strives to lift his language above conceptions which may be understood by the less-educated. This is because he feels that it is the uneducated man who has been mostly influenced by the Calvinism of his forefathers which has produced, he feels, High-Calvinism and Antinomianism in them.[21] This seems to be Fuller's attempt to jump over his own shadow as he himself had very little education to boast of. Indeed, it seems to be an ingrained feature of Fullerite criticism to believe that traditional Calvinism is the religion of the Christian of average to greatly less than average intelligence and the Christian who is lacking in education. Thinking of men such as Dr John Gill of all people in his book *The Emergence of Hyper-Calvinism in English Nonconformity*, Peter Toon argues that Hyper-Calvinists 'were sincere men of *average* intelligence, but they *lacked* a prophetic and discerning spirit'. In an *Evangelical Quarterly* article,[22] referring to another of these 'average intelligent' men, i.e. the nigh genius Thomas Goodwin, Toon claims that Goodwin's ideas are 'a dangerous mode of thought in the hands of less intelligent men.' On the whole, High-Calvinists, he argues, were, 'the poorly educated Independents and Baptists.'[23] The numerous tirades appearing from 1988-1995 in the Banner of Truth Magazine stress until it becomes obnoxious how uneducated and vulgar were preachers of righteousness such as William Huntington and his like who dared to travel in a coach, preach the gospel etc. although they were of the lowest social class.

A love of re-defining terms

Then there is Fuller's frustrating habit of using terms such as redemption, imputation, sin, being made sin, punishment, debt, guilt, wrath, justification, substitution, satisfaction in his writings and dialogues in a way acceptable to the normal Christian reader, then he will suddenly redefine their meanings and argue that they were 'improperly' or 'metaphorically' used in the Bible. Fuller's use of redemptive language is a puzzle indeed. He obviously feels that the inspired writers could have chosen a better terminology but uses the words though he rejects their meaning. Fullerites are apparently not at all put off by this tongue-in-cheek approach to the language of Scripture. Tom J. Nettles, in his adulation of Fuller says:

> Though he *derided* [24] what he characterised as a 'commercial' view of the atonement, he saw some merit in it and at times spoke that language so as to make his belief in the absolute efficacy of Christ's death as clear as possible. [25]

This is quite an extraordinary statement in view of the normal meaning of the word 'deride' i.e. 'laugh to scorn.' Here we have a picture of the prophet of evangelical Calvinism laughing to scorn the descriptions of Christ's purchased possessions in the Scriptures. Yet he still finds 'some merit' in the Bible's use of the words to enable him to use such language in making his belief in the absolute efficacy of Christ's death as clear as possible. One can only wonder how conceptions worthy of being ridiculed can have any limited merit in expressing anything absolute, especially when speaking of the most holy things. If this is the kind of clarity of expression Fuller offers his readers, then it is no wonder that he is so often misunderstood. Equally amazing is Nettles' statement that Fuller believed in the absolute efficacy of Christ's death. Fuller's basic doctrine is that though Christ's death was for all, it was only eventually applied to a particular few. As the word 'efficacy' means 'producing the desired effect' one wonders how effectual Fuller's atonement can be judged when it is made as much for a Paul as it is a Judas but only the former is efficaciously saved.

Then there is Fuller's condescending way of so often telling his readers that he is quite favourable to traditional Reformed doctrine but differs merely regarding the explanations given to it. This would seem to be either Fuller's idea of a theological joke or an honest confession that he accepts traditional theological terminology but not its meaning. Fuller's method of arguing is thus most confusing, particularly as he re-defines words as he goes along, apparently not realising that, at the end, he is using them with a different meaning to the one with which he started. Thus when writing on the sin of Adam, the fall and imputation, one finds Fuller apparently changing his mind at will, though not renouncing his previous views. Especially when outlining his highly rational view of holiness, we find Fuller, for instance, at times adopting the philosophical view of 'disinterested benevolence', normally attributed to Jonathan Edwards, but in the same work claiming agreement with the New Divinity School which left Edwards' view to stress that all holy motives are towards personal happiness.[26] Again, Nettles comes to Fuller's defence here stating that those who see a gradual changing of Fuller's Calvinism towards, say, Baxterism have misunderstood him. Fuller, he tells us, could not even read Baxter without making himself ill.[27] This is no defence whatsoever as it will be shown that Fuller stood at the other side of Baxter to Calvinism, so there is little wonder that he thought the 'Reformed Pastor' was lukewarm. Furthermore, Warfield's cool and scholarly denunciation of the New Divinity School reveals how far that system, and thus Fuller's, was from believing the faith once delivered to the saints.[28]

Use of false premises and antitheses
Another, most off-putting feature of Fuller's dialectic is his use of false premises and antitheses to prove his case which break the bounds of all logic. Typical of such false reasoning is when he tells his readers that there are only two possibilities of understanding the atonement. Either one believes that God paid Satan to drop his claim on sinners or one accepts his idea of the atonement as a demonstration of God's rectoral or executive power.[29] The correct Reformed doctrine of a substitutive expiation is thus either cunningly or naively side-stepped and the doctrines of the ontological necessity of the atonement and its judicial efficacy as a satisfaction for sin are ignored or interpreted figuratively. Fuller often condemns the arguments of his opponents and then appears to argue in the self same way before he tells them that he is giving a different meaning to his words. Most off-putting are his dialogues in which he takes on the role of a rather supercilious James correcting the Calvinism of Peter and John and always succeeding masterfully in talking them into accepting his interpretations as the real thing. James' aim in life is apparently to prove that nothing in the Bible is as it appears to be. It is also off-putting to find Fuller often taking a critic to task for using words wrongly, only to find he uses the words in just the same way himself.[30] Most damaging for Fuller's theology is that he redefines gifts of grace as the duties of the graceless and actually teaches that the graceless have the ability to use these gifts. Never was there such an example of Lewis Carroll's Humpty Dumpty saying that he made words mean what he wanted them to mean!

William Rushton's remarks on Fuller's tendency to confuse his readers
These observances reveal nothing new in Fuller's methods, indeed, they

have been complained of many times before. They must be stressed, however, as modern Fullerites present Fuller as a cornucopia of lucidity and clarity of thought and explanation, thus quite suppressing the fact that he was quite the opposite. As long ago as 1831, William Rushton wrote in his excellent work *Particular Redemption*:

> The extracts to which I have called your attention are very ingeniously written. But the very ingenuity is suspicious, because truth requires none. Such are the obscurity and artfulness which run through them, that of the many persons who have read Mr. Fuller's Dialogues, etc., very few fully understand them. Some imagine he held the doctrine of particular redemption, because he sometimes speaks of Christ dying for His people. Others suppose he teaches universal redemption; but many, though they do not altogether understand him, plainly perceive that he favours their predisposition to Arminianism, and therefore they approve of his system. In some instances, no doubt, Mr. Fuller has been misunderstood from inattention, but this has not always been the case. There is an uncommon degree of subtlety in his statements, attended with much speciousness: palpable inconsistencies are hid with great ingenuity, and the difference between him and his opponents is so artfully lessened, that it appears to many readers to be of little importance. He evidently wishes not to be considered an opponent of particular redemption; yet he neither agrees with the Particular Baptists on the one side, nor asserts boldly, with the General Baptists, that Christ died equally for every man; but maintains a kind of metaphysical medium which is as far removed from the simplicity that is in Christ, as it is from the gospel which is hid from the wise and prudent.[31]

Wearing false feathers

Fuller loves to clothe himself in the apparel of orthodoxy which makes him avow that the staunchest Puritans are his closest allies. He claims this unity of thought even when arguing that his views may not tie up very well with the doctrines of grace. Thus he claims that Calvin agrees with him on imputation, Witsius on an open atonement, Owen on the universal offer and Edwards on the natural and moral capacities of man. This effort to try on false feathers for size has so baffled students of Fuller's works that they have great difficulty in assessing the sources of his theology. Arthur Kirkby, for instance, argues convincingly that Edward's influence was far less on Fuller than supposed, yet he finds Fuller quoting Calvin almost verbatim on many occasions.[32] E. Clipsham rejects this argument, seeking to prove that Fuller could have found his material seemingly anywhere, but claims that Edwards was the major influence in Fuller's life.[33] Michael Haykin is much nearer the mark when he claims that the New Divinity School was the greatest influence on Fuller and his circle but he confuses this teaching with that of Edwards and feels it is all orthodox Calvinism.[34]

Stress on rational and natural abilities

The essential feature of Fullerism is the stress laid on man's rational capacity to realise his own state before God and use his natural abilities in co-operation with God to accept the gospel and believe savingly in Christ. Though Fullerites would not deny that from God's side, salvation is all of grace; they would add that in preaching they are warranted to offer this grace to every sinner as his for the asking as he is fully equipped and fully capable of seeing his own need of salvation and, if he is but willing, he is able to partake of it.[35] Where Scripture says that man is dead and thus blind to spiritual truths and void of any spiritual discernment, Fullerism says that man is alive to them and can perceive them. His sole fault is that he does not want to use his abilities in this direction. Whereas the New Testament and our Reformers tell us that fallen man will not trust in Christ because he cannot, Fuller tells us that man can trust if he wishes but he does not want to. It is as if all men are untried Adams who have absolute freedom of the will and all their faculties intact but, even when they say no to God, their fall remains only in the realms of making a negative choice, or, in Fullerite jargon, making the wrong moral choice. The theological conception of sin and the fall as revealed in the Bible, as will be shown, is unknown to the Fullerites. Indeed, this basic misconception of Fuller's is a good starting point for an analysis of his system. One's view of sin automatically influences one's view of the law and one's view of the law, in turn, colours one's view of the gospel.

---

[1] *Works*, vol. III, p. 838. This is Fuller's conclusion on reviewing William Huntington's gospel preaching.

[2] Tyerman, *Whitefield*, vol. I, pp 360-1.

[3] Tillotson's emphasis.

[4] Taken from *The Works of the Most Reverend Dr. John Tillotson*, London, 1704, p. 5.

[5] See *Atonement*, vol. IX, Warfield's *Works*.

[6] Paulus Scharpff, *Geschichte der Evangelisation*, p. 58.

[7] John Collet Ryland, *The Beauty of Social Religion*, circular letter, Northamptonshire Baptist Association, 1777, p. 7.

[8] Some readers may object to the word 'former' here and argue that Fuller always claimed to be a Particular Baptist. This was a false claim as Fuller did not hold to those doctrines which make a Baptist 'Particular' i.e. a particular atonement securing a particular redemption for a particular people.

[9] This is the publishing date usually given but others vary from 1781 to 1786 for the first edition. Pastor J. A. Jones claimed in the *Earthan Vessel* of Sep. 2, 1861 that he had a first edition copy, printed in 1781 entitled *The Gospel of Christ worthy of all acceptation*. The slight difference in the title could suggest an earlier version.

[10] E. Clipsham, *Andrew Fuller and Fullerism: A Study in Evangelical Calvinism*, BQ, 4. p. 268

[11] *The Gospel Worthy of All Acceptation*, *Works*, Vol. II, p. 335.

[12] Tom J. Nettles, Preface, *Works*, vol. I, Sprinkle Publications reprint, 1988,

[13] Kenneth Good, *Are Baptists Calvinists?*, p. 106.

[14] E. Clipsham, *Andrew Fuller and Fullerism*, 4, p. 268.

[15] *Andrew Fuller and Fullerism*, 3. BQ, p. 214.

[16] Tom J. Nettles, Preface, *Works*, vol. I, Sprinkle Publications reprint, 1988,

[17] Andrew Gunton Fuller, *Memoir*, vol. I, p.1.

[18] Op. sit., p. 268.

[19] *Memoirs of the Life and Writings of the Rev. Andrew Fuller*, John Webster Morris, 1816, p. 269.

[20] *Works*, vol. I, p. 82, note.

[21] See his essay *Memoirs of the Life and Writings of the Rev. Andrew Fuller*, *Works*, vol. II, p. 737 ff.

[22] *The Growth of a Supralapsarian Christology*, XXIX, 1967, p. 25,

[23] See the section entitled *The Factor Involved in the Change from High to Hyper-Calvinism*, p. 146 ff.

[24] My emphasis.

[25] *Preface to the New Edition, Works*, vol. I, p. 6? Preface pages are unnumbered in my Sprinkle Publications, 1988 edition.

[26] See *Works*, vol. II, *The Holy Nature of the Christian Religion Contrasted with the Immorality of Deism* where both views are used alternately, especially pp. 52-56. See also p. 344 for a statement of typical New Divinity theology.

[27] Ibid, p. 6? (Pages not numbered in *Preface to the New Edition*.)

[28] See Warfield's essays on *Edwards and the New Divinity School, Atonement* and *Modern Theories of the Atonement*, vol. IX, *Works*.

[29] Fuller emphasises God's *moral* government but his view of what is moral is not that of traditional orthodoxy. Actually Fuller uses the term more in the sense of rectoral rather than spiritual rule.

[30] See vol II, *Conversation on Imputation*, p. 683, Vol. III, *Proper and Improper Use of Terms*, p. 681. It is interesting to note that Fuller describes almost all the central doctrines of the Bible as being worded in 'improper' or 'metaphorical' language but when he comes to the word βαπτιζω (I baptise) he argues for only one possible 'proper' literal meaning.

[31] P. 23.

[32] Arthur Kirkby, *The Theology of Andrew Fuller and its relation to Calvinism*, Ph.D., Edin., 1956.

[33] *Andrew Fuller and Fullerism* 1-4, BQ, XX, 1963.

[34] *One Heart and One Soul*, EP, 1995.

[35] John Sutcliff did not quite agree with Fuller here. Though he accepted his moral-natural distinction, he looked upon man as also fallen in his natural abilities. Nettles in the above mentioned preface quotes Sutcliff at length to prove what Fuller believed. This falsely colours Nettles' presentation of Fuller's true view which is that man is only fallen in his moral capacities and not fully fallen in those, either.

Part II
The letter law and the spirit law

1. Sin and its consequences

No debts accrued, no debts paid

Sin in Fuller's reasoning, outlined in his *Conversation on Substitution*,[1] is not debt to the righteous Law as an affront to God's natural and eternal nature. It is a mere metaphorical, moral term indicating that one thinks negatively of God. It is a disinclination to believe. Thus Fuller cannot accept the vicarious, debt-paying, sin-bearing sacrifice of Christ. He says debts are transferable to others, but sin is not a debt, it is a metaphor to express crimes and crimes are not transferable.[2] Thus by changing the meaning of sin, Fuller changes the meaning of the atonement. Sin, according to Scripture is debt accrued through disobeying God's Law which reflects God's holy and eternal character. This debt is paid off for us by our Redeemer Jesus Christ paying the price for our sins and suffering their penalties. Where we ought to have been punished, Christ was punished in our stead.

This is all unacceptable to Fuller who believes 'that many important mistakes have arisen from considering the interposition of Christ under the notion of paying a debt.' The latter term, if taken literally 'may lead us into many errors'. Satisfaction for sin, Fuller argues, is required to be made, 'not on pecuniary but on moral principles.'[3] Furthermore Fuller argues that it is impossible for Christ to become a debtor to the Law as each man alone is accountable for his own deserts, a third person cannot step in and take them over.[4] Thus Fuller lays his axe to the roots of the most fundamental doctrines of the Bible; that Christ became what we are, that we may become what He is, namely righteous before God.

Fuller's extraordinary stubbornness in not accepting the Biblical doctrine of redemption shows on what a shaky foundation his whole system is built. He argues in the section on *Particular Redemption* in *The Gospel Worthy of All Acceptation* that if he could believe that the atonement of Christ were a literal payment of debt he would admit that it was inconsistent with his system. He cannot believe this - though it is stated plainly in Scripture - because he feels it would be inconsistent with free forgiveness and would cause man to approach God as a claimant and not as a supplicant. Again, Fuller's reasoning gets in the way of his theological thinking. Like Felix he is almost there but cannot make the right step! His natural abilities have blinded him. He cannot see that the Scriptures do not regard the elect as either claimants or supplicants in the work of redemption but as recipients of grace. They become such recipients because they have been bought free from their bondage to the Law and to its curse. How wonderful it is to turn the pages of Hebrews and to find that Christ is our surety in God's better testament (Hebrews 7:22)! How gracious it is of God to forgive us our debts, i.e. remove them, as the Lord's Prayer instructs us! How marvellous to know that we are bought with a price (1 Corinthians 20)! How blessed our state when we hear that, 'we were not redeemed with corruptible things, as silver and gold, from our vain conversation . . . but with the precious blood of Christ, as a lamb and without spot.' The Law claimed the highest price and, thanks be to God, Christ paid it!

Fulfilling the spirit whilst ignoring the letter
Thus, according to Fuller, we must not look on the Biblical account of the atonement as a literal story, explaining how obedience to every jot and tittle of the *letter* of the Law was carried out in Christ on our behalf but we are to take it as a moral account showing how Christ performed a mere moral satisfaction to law and justice according to their *spirit*. This did not in any way oblige Christ to put Himself under the Law on the sinner's behalf.

Fuller does not leave the question open whether one can obey the *spirit* of the Law through some token propitiation without obeying its *letter*. He is convinced that this is possible and was indeed performed by Christ. To prove the 'principle' of what he is saying, he departs from the Bible account to tell one of his usual inappropriate secular stories to illustrate his version of Scriptural truths, thus clouding the issue. This is the story of Zaleucus,[5] the Grecian lawgiver whose son was condemned to have both eyes put out for breaking the law. Zaleucus offered one of his eyes that his son might keep one of his, thus combining justice and mercy in one act. Both father and son lost an eye and thus, according to Fuller, proved that the law can be fulfilled without adhering to its letter.

The story, moving as it is, still shows how far Fuller's theology has gone astray from the Bible account of redemption. This would mean he leaves a man only half redeemed and a Christ only half punished. Indeed, this is quite in accordance with Fuller's general theology which speaks of a reconciling of man's agency with God's purpose by token displays of the spirit of moral justice and mercy which are acceptable to God *as if they were the real thing*. This, of course, has nothing to do with redemption from sin and is a completely different gospel to the all-of-grace message of the Bible. In his theology, Fuller overlooks the whole account of redemption given by Paul in Romans 5 where he stresses that it was disobedience to the Law that brought on man's death and it was redemption by the vicarious death of One who was obedient to the Law that brought eternal life to the dead. Nothing is, however, real in Fuller's metaphorical gospel and one wearies of reading through him in an effort to find what lies behind the metaphor and his strange extra-Biblical stories which seem to totally ignore the gospel point.

No real and proper punishment for sin

Whilst telling Zaleucus' story, Fuller is careful not to use the word *punishment* to describe the half-justice and half-mercy given to Zaleucus' son, which, of course, is thus neither proper justice nor proper mercy. Although Fuller does use this word sparingly at times concerning Christ's atonement, he does not use the word at its face value. What Fuller thinks of Christ's bearing the sinner's punishment is outlined in a dialogue in which he takes the position of James talking with Peter and John whom he gradually coaxes away from orthodox Christianity into his own brand of Grotian-like 'Fullerism':

> **Peter**: Do you consider Christ as having been *punished, really* and *properly* PUNISHED?[6]
> **James**: I should think I do not. But what do you mean by punishment?
> **Peter**: An innocent person may *suffer*, but, properly speaking, he cannot be *punished*. Punishment necessarily supposes *criminality*.
> **James**: Just so; and therefore, as I do not believe that Jesus was in any way criminal, I cannot say he was really and properly punished.[7]

Now if Christ were not 'really and properly punished' on our behalf, and as Christ's death took away the punishment due to His Church, no punishment for sin was meted out at all by God. Neither the elect, nor Christ were punished. This would mean that though salvation was accomplished in mercy the claims of the Law were not met. Justice, then for Fuller, does not come into the history of salvation at all!

Fuller fights shy of accepting that God could be vindictive and show wrath i.e. punishment for sin in the sense of being wrathful against the sinner or against the sin-bearer. This is because he sees wrath as being 'punishment for the pleasure of punishing' and God is never 'unamiable'. This is one of the many ways in which Fuller dodges a difficult word by re-defining it. Nobody would dream of arguing that God found pleasure in punishment, argues Fuller, so the wrath of God must be struck off the evangelical agenda![8] It would be very difficult for Fuller to show that the hundreds of references to God's wrath in the Bible are all 'amiable'. What would he make, for instance, of Romans 9:22, 'What if God, willing to show his wrath, and to make his power known, endured with much long-suffering the vessels of wrath fitted to destruction?' Fullerites are at least consistent when they argue that even this destruction is 'amiable' as it places those who have not used their natural abilities to believe savingly in Christ in hell where they have abundant time for 'recollection and reflection'.[9] How condemned sinners are to profit from this eternity of recollection and reflection, we are not told! However, the Fullerite doctrine of an amiable hell must be quite unique in Christian theology.

Christ being made sin is a mere figure of speech

One of the fundamental Biblical texts dealing with the removal of man's sin is 2 Corinthians 5:21, 'For he hath made him to be sin for us, who knew no sin; that we might be made the righteousness of God in him.' As Bultmann of recent years sought to 'demythologise' the key conceptions of Christianity, so 18th century Fuller with his very similar instrument to 'demetaphorise' Scripture goes to work on this text. He argues that the word 'made' in both 'made sin' and 'made righteous' 'is not to be taken literally'.[10] He explains in his usual way that the true meaning behind all this is that Christ's suffering was a mere token satisfaction for sin (i.e. crimes), which revealed the *spirit* of God's 'displeasure' at sin and not His demand that the *letter* of the Law be carried out. This is in keeping with Fuller's standard method of de-theologising sin and making it a mere moral problem. Moral problems do not need penal and vicarious death to put them right but merely a moral demonstration of God's displeasure. Fuller puts it rather more sophistically and says: 'The sufferings of Christ in our stead, therefore, are not a punishment inflicted in the ordinary course of distributive justice, but an extraordinary interposition of infinite wisdom and love; not contrary to, but rather above the law, deviating from the letter, but more than preserving the spirit of it. Such brethren, as well as I am able to explain them, are my views of the substitution of Christ.'[11]

Fuller is actually expecting us to believe that God sent His Son on an arbitrary journey of suffering and death merely to perform an equally arbitrary sacrificial ceremony as a token to appease His arbitrary will so that He can tell man that He is perfectly satisfied with what has happened and hopes Christ's death will be registered in the sinners' minds as a moral deterrent. The claims of the Law are therefore not met in Christ's death but this does not matter to Fuller who teaches that the Law has no claims on anyone on a 'do this and live, break this and die'[12] basis as God has annulled the covenant of works for believer and sinner alike irrespective of Christ's sacrifice. Strictly speaking, to Fullerites, Christ's sacrifice was not at all necessary. God could have used any other means whatsoever.

If Christ were made sin, Fuller argues, He would be the subject of moral evil; He would have become a criminal and would thus deserve the punishment He received for His own sake. As Christ 'knew no sin' when He became sin, this cannot mean that He was a criminal.[13] This is proof enough for Fuller that we are dealing with highly figurative language. What then is the reality behind the figurative word 'sin' in this passage? In his essay *Conversation on Imputation* Fuller explains that the passage does not refer directly to sin in conjunction with Christ but to a sin-offering.[14] Even here, Fuller qualifies what he means by a sin-offering by saying he does not mean a sacrifice for sin but merely the fact that the sins of the people were imputed to an animal by the laying on of hands of the priest and it was *counted*, in the Divine administration, *as if the animal had been* the sinner, and the only sinner of the nation.'[15] Fuller tells us that in the case of the animal, it was a mere shadow but Christ really took away sin. If, however, Christ did not virtually bear our sins in his body on the cross and was not virtually punished in our stead, then there is no difference between Christ's death on the cross and the Old Testament sin-offering. Both would be mere shadows of the real thing. Indeed, Christ's sacrifice would be less than the old sin-offering as hands were placed on the head of the bullock to represent the transfer of sins to the bullock. Fuller, however, argues that in the case of Christ, no transfer of sin was made. Again, the old scapegoat received the sins of the people and they were carried away into the wilderness, but no such carrying away and reception of sin is attributed to Christ in Fuller's fight with the letter of Scripture so that his idea of its spirit may be seen as the true Gospel. Such ideas, Benjamin Warfield argues, 'fall so far short of the Biblical doctrine of the nature and effect of Christ's sacrifice as to seem little else than travesties of it.' Warfield does not equate such a theory with any form of Calvinism but says it is an 'ordinary Remonstrant theory.'[16]

The fact that Fuller claims that Christ became sin only in a metaphorical sense, must have the same consequence when applied to our being made righteous. Just as our sins were not transferred to Christ, so Christ's righteousness can never be transferred to us. Man is not actually made righteous. The elect still bear their own sins and guilt and no punishment has been effected. Indeed, as Fuller made it quite clear in his controversy with Abraham Booth, he cannot accept the Christian doctrine that saved souls can approach the Throne of Grace with boldness and stand guiltless before God. For Fuller, the correct token sufferings have been performed; God is satisfied that His moral government of the world has been maintained and He now pardons and excuses man for Christ's sake - but leaves him in his sin and in his guilt and without any righteousness. This would mean to Bible-believing Christians, that believers in Christ are still fallen, unrighteous sinners. This is not, of course, how Fuller sees man's post-salvation predicament. Even the fall, in his view, as will be shown, is not to be taken literally. Instead he puts forward a view that runs completely contrary to the teaching of both Reformed and Arminian teaching.

God's justice separated from His righteousness
Just as Fuller explains away the theological meaning of sin on man's part by calling it a crime, he also takes away the theological meaning of sin on Christ's part by saying that Christ did not actually become sin but He performed a token expiation for sin. Again, this would be an expiation according to the shadows and types of the Old Testament but not the real redemption in the Lamb of God who takes away the sins of the world. If Christ did not have our sins put on him, in the way Peter tells us that He did, one wonders how He can be said to have borne them.

1 Peter 2:24 reads, 'Who his own self bare our sins in his own body on the tree, that we, being dead to sins, should live unto righteousness: by whose stripes we were healed.' This text can only mean what it clearly says; that Christ bore our guilt and punishment so that we might be judged truly guiltless and go free. This is utterly wrong, says Fuller. Our guilt remains as it was never borne by Christ. Guilt, as punishment, is not transferable.[17] Christ bore the effects of sin in his obedient token suffering and because of this, God is satisfied and we receive the effects of Christ's obedience, God's pardon. God's justice has nothing to do with the matter.

Fuller cannot accept the Biblical teaching of sin and Christ as the sin-bearer as he explains that God accepted Christ's sufferings in mercy as being an adequate satisfaction. Christ did not need to go the whole way of justice. When it really comes to the point, He did not even have to go half way like Zaleucus. Fuller always stresses that mercy triumphs over justice whereas Scripture stresses that the merciful way in which God saves us is according to His justice. God's righteousness cannot be separated from His justice as the fundamental idea of righteousness in the Scriptures is that it is a strict adherence to the Law which reveals God's character. God demands of man 'Be ye holy, for I am holy'.[18] As 2 Timothy 4:8 tells us, God is the 'Righteous Judge'. This identification of righteousness with justice in God means that He is bound by His own nature to punish evil and claim that the full penalty be paid.

Man fell but remained standing on his feet

As sin is not taken seriously by Fuller, how do Fullerites view the Fall? Again Fuller resorts to re-defining terms. There is a difference, he argues, between a moral fall, and a total fall of all man's natural and spiritual capacities. To him the Fall is 'wholly of the moral, and therefore of the criminal kind'. This fall is, according to him, not total as man is not 'totally unable' or 'unable in every respect' to believe in Christ.[19] Fullerites indeed tend to take the doctrine of man's total fall and total inability to understand spiritual things as the doctrine of Antinomians because they feel this is a mere excuse for Christians not to live according to the Law.[20] As sin is a mere metaphor to Fuller, one will not be surprised to find that the Fall is also understood to be figurative and in no way means that sin marred all man's abilities and capabilities. Andrew Gunten Fuller, Andrew Fuller's son, taking up the Scriptural teaching that man is totally unable to respond to God, argues that this would take away the universal obligation to exercise faith in Christ, thus it just cannot be true. He thus argues that his father shows: 'this inability is in no way represented in Scripture as of a *proper* or *physical*, but of a *figurative* or *moral* kind.'[21] Anxious that the reader will understand the true significance of these words, he adds in a footnote words of his father which claim, 'All such terms as *necessary, cannot, impossible*, &c., when applied to these subjects, are used improperly.' The word 'improperly' being Fuller's pet-name for 'figuratively'. We have thus figurative sins, figurative debts, a figurative sin-bearer and a figurative fall. Fuller is always taking about finding the spirit behind the letter but how does one find the reality behind the figure?

The reality behind the metaphor

What do words which, on their face value, appear to denote a total fall, *really* mean to Fuller? His son and biographer continues to quote him as saying, 'They always denote, in strict propriety of speech, an obstruction arising from something distinct from the state of the will.' This un-biblical, non-theological explanation is Fuller's definition of the Fall and one can only ask, what does he seek to prove by such a vague explanation of what traditional Christianity has always understood in most certain terms? Fuller explains that this view, 'represents man as not only possessing great advantages, but *as able to comply with everything that God requires at his hand*; and that all his misery arises from his *voluntary* abuse of mercy, and his *wilful* rebellion against God. It is not want of *ability*, but of *inclination*, that proves his ruin.' Fallen man could be forgiven for believing that Fuller is in fact saying that the Fall brought nothing negative to man apart from his inclinations regarding God. As man rebelled against God to be rid of Him, it would stand to reason that man won the rebellion with no lasting damage.

Man's depravity in not coming to Christ for life viewed figuratively by Fuller

But does not Christ point out in John 5 that man will not come to Christ because he cannot hear God and has not the Word of God abiding in him and this is why he will not seek Christ and find life? Is it not true that man is unable to seek Christ of himself because he is fallen? Does not total depravity imply total ignorance and unawareness of spiritual things? Not in the least, says Fuller yet hides behind a smoke screen of words that might be, for the unwary, interpreted as orthodox. He says, '*The degree of this depravity is such as that, figuratively speaking, men cannot come to Christ for life.*'[22] Note again, however, Fuller is viewing man's need and Christ's work merely *figuratively*. We must not suppose, he argues, that this means that man could not come to Christ if he so chose. He then resorts to his famous language game concerning what is a 'proper' meaning of a word and what is a metaphorical or 'improper' meaning. If we say, he argues, Ahijah *could not* see, by reason of his age; this is a 'proper' use of the words. When the Bible says man *cannot* do anything with reference to pleasing God, ceasing from sin or believing in Christ, we cannot take this literally as it would be a contradiction in terms to say that as man cannot believe, he will not. 'Cannot' thus must be understood as 'does not want to.' This is why Arthur Kirkby summed up Andrew Fuller's doctrine of man and the Fall succinctly in the sentence 'He could if he would'.[23] Fuller is quite shocked that there are those who call themselves Christians who cannot accept what 'every person of common understanding, whether he will or not' must see. In fact, in his letters from Crispus to Gaius on *The Total Depravity of Human Nature*. Letter I, Fuller accuses those who cannot and therefore will not agree with him of having a 'confused and superficial view of things'. He even goes so far as to suspect them of 'criminal indolence' as well as 'meanness' and says they prefer 'to sip muddy waters from any puddle that presents itself', rather than draw from his deep well.[24] It would strike humble-minded Christians that pride always goes before a fall and as Fuller denies the Fall, he has only sinful pride left.

The real natural and physical symptoms of the Fall ignored
In stressing that the Fall is a mere volitional matter of inclinations, the physical results of the Fall are fully ignored by Fuller. For instance, the fact that God told Adam that he would die if he disobeyed his Creator, seems to have escaped him. Genesis 3 cannot possibly mean that when God mentioned 'death', He was merely using a metaphor to express moral disinclination. Immediately on sinning, man experienced physical and spiritual weakness and did, in fact, die *physically* because of his sin. Otherwise Adam would be still alive and well on the earth today. Yet Fuller denies time and time again that the Fall had anything to do with man's physical and natural constitution. The Bible stresses that the Fall brought with it dire physical consequences. Paul in Romans 5.12 is most definite about this when he says, 'Wherefore, as by one man sin entered into the world, and *death* by sin; and so *death* passed upon all men, for that all have sinned.' The solemn words of Romans 6:23 also pronounce this truth, 'The wages of sin is *death*.' He seems, too, to have forgotten the physical agony of Christ whose perfectly beautiful face was marred as He bled and died on the cross, crying, 'My God, My God. Why hast thou forsaken me.' Here Christ is obviously suffering the Fall bodily in His own person. To be forsaken by God is to be forsaken in body, soul and spirit.

Man's reason is not affected by the Fall, but his reasoning may be wrong
Fuller teaches that the image of God in man is of two kinds: the natural and the moral. The former, consists of man's reason, conscience, natural freedom and immortality[25] and is not fallen, the latter is. Fuller lays great store on the right use of reason or 'right reason' as he calls it. The word reason signifies to Fuller '*the fitness of things*'. This is the way, he argues, the apostles used it when they said, 'It is not *reason* that we should leave the word of God, and serve tables;'[26] that is, it is not fit or proper.' Right reason, Fuller tells us, 'is perfect and immutable, remaining always the same.' 'No Divine truth can disagree' with it. Such reason may, however, 'be above and contrary to' man's reasoning which is shattered by sin, blindness and prejudice. Fuller, however, in stressing that right reason may not of necessity contradict man's reasoning, obviously feels that man is somehow capable

of using right reason. In fact, for Fuller, the practical use of right reason distinguishes New Testament teaching from the Old which was law-bound.[27] The Old hindered man from using his reason whereas the New encourages it. Fuller gives an example of such 'proper' reason used by an educated man in conversation with one less endowed. 'A philosopher, for instance, tells an unlettered countryman that it is generally thought that the earth turns round, every day, upon its own axis, and not the sun round the earth. The countryman replies, 'I don't believe it.' 'Very likely,' says the philosopher; 'but why not?' 'It is contrary to my *reason*.' 'Contrary to *your* reason? that may be; but I hope you do not think that every thing contrary to your reason is contrary to *right* reason!' It would seem that the philosopher not only possessed right reason but he trusted that he could persuade the unlettered countryman to drop his shattered reasoning for it.[28]

Man's reason, i.e. the ability to see the fitness of things, together with his conscience, are not only not fallen in Fuller's view but they are the very capacities which make man accountable before God. If he had no reason and no conscience, he would not be accountable. It will be shown, when dealing with Fuller's view of the law that man's ability to see 'the fitness of things' is the human agency through which God works His purpose out and which enables man to see the spirit in the law as opposed to the letter.

Even man's moral powers are seen as not truly fallen
Though Fuller stresses that the Fall was limited to the moral sphere, he nevertheless goes to great length to explain that even this moral fall was only of a figurative kind and in no way took away man's virtual or 'proper' moral abilities. This explains why Fuller believes that exercising faith in Christ is a proper moral duty for fallen sinners. Man, to him, is aware of his proper moral duties and obligations to Christ, irrespective of the figurative fall. By nature, he can see the fitness of things. In fact, he argues that 'man has the same power, strictly speaking, before they are wrought upon by the Holy Spirit, as after; and before conversion as after; that the work of the Spirit endows us with no rational powers, nor any powers that are necessary to moral agency.'[29] Indeed, Fuller argues that man is not dead in trespasses and sins as God could not speak to a dead man. He only speaks to one capable of hearing and responding. This is why Fuller argues in his *The Gospel Worthy of All Acceptation*, 'Or if the inability of sinners to believe in Christ were of the same nature as that of a dead body in a grave to rise up and walk, it were absurd to suppose that they would on this account fall under the Divine censure. No man is reproved for not doing that which is naturally impossible; but sinners are reproved for not believing,

and given to understand that it is solely owing to their criminal ignorance, pride, dishonesty of heart, and aversion from God.'[30] The figurative fall then to Fuller is not physical and spiritual death, nor even moral inability, but merely an 'unwillingness to believe'. The *real* fall, according to Fuller, comes when Christ is rejected on hearing the gospel because man then refuses to use his inherent capabilities to believe in Christ savingly.

argumentum ex silentio
The audacity of Fuller's philosophy is seen when he calls upon the Church Fathers, the Reformers and the Puritans to vouch for his teaching. He uses the dangerous but well-trod path of *argumentum ex silentio* and affirms:

> Neither Augustine, nor Calvin, who each in his day defended predestination, and the other doctrines connected with it, ever appear to have thought of denying it to be the duty of every sinner who has heard the gospel to repent, and believe in Jesus Christ. Neither did the other Reformers, nor the Puritans of the sixteenth century, nor the divines of the Synod of Dort, who opposed Arminius, nor any of the nonconformists of the seventeenth century.

Thus, as these Old School Christian stalwarts of by-gone years did not foresee the New School[31] Reformation which was to come through the humanistic and rationalistic theorising of Andrew Fuller, that gentleman found all his views backed up by those very people with whom he most disagreed. Typical of Fuller's confusing, if not chaotic way of arguing, is that immediately after writing the above, he adds, 'I allow that the principles here defended may be inconsistent with the doctrines of grace.'[32] Never was a truer word spoken!

This argument from silence is also applied to Fuller's contemporaries in an equally illogical manner, though more critically. One who stood very close to Fuller, yet was often severely reproached by him, was Abraham Booth (1734-1806). After reviving the rationalistic Latitudinarian teaching on duty-faith in Part I of his *The Gospel Worthy of All Acceptation*, Fuller closes with a broadside against Booth, scolding him for not giving support to his arguments and stating that though Booth remains silent on the question, his works indicate that he secretly believes the doctrine. Fuller thus writes, 'Mr Booth has (to all appearance, designedly) avoided the question, Whether faith in Christ be the *duty* of the ungodly? The leading principle of the former part of his work, however, cannot stand on any other ground.' Fuller's reason for claiming that Booth silently agrees with him and ought to affirm this, is because Booth believed in preaching the gospel to all and inviting all to partake of its benefits. Fuller concludes quite unbiblically that if this is so, and one does not believe that sinners are duty bound to accept the gospel, then their rejection of the gospel must be guiltless.

Fuller's criticism of Booth lays open his own great theological weakness. In holding that man is not truly fallen, he believes that he is fully able to believe in Christ and is condemned for not using his natural, unfallen insights when he rejects Christ. This is the true fall for Fuller. The Bible teaches, however, that man is a law-breaker from his conception on, yet is fully responsible for breaking that law. He is already dead in trespasses and sins before he hears the gospel. With the gospel, however, comes the Spirit of God to awaken the elect from their deadness and give them new life in Christ Jesus. Those who do not receive Christ at that time, either because their time has not come or they are not of the elect, are still responsible before God because they are fallen creatures who have broken His law.

2. Antinomianism considered

Who are the Antinomians?

Though enough evidence has been given to indicate that Andrew Fuller had a very low view of the law of God and of sin and the Fall, he nevertheless was extremely verbose in condemning as Antinomians those on all sides who disagreed with him. This word often drops from his lips and his pen and it soon becomes clear that Fuller regards anyone as an Antinomian who cannot accept his high view of man and his extremely low view of God's justice. Admittedly, the Bible teaches that the letter of the law kills but the spirit brings life, yet the Bible is just as clear in showing how important the killing letter of the law is in salvation. If one ignores the letter that kills, one can never understand the need for the spirit to bring life, nor can one see God's purpose in salvation. Seemingly oblivious to such problems of his own design, Fuller goes to verbal war against the 'Antinomians' in his essay on a *Picture of an Antinomian*,[33] in his *Dialogues and Letters Between Crispus and Gaius*,[34] in his review of *The Voice of Years concerning the late W. Huntington, S. S*[35] and in his book *Antinomianism Contrasted with the Religion Taught and Exemplified in Holy Scriptures*.[36] These works are marked by an almost entire lack of Biblical analysis, an arrogant display of prejudice and a style which drops to the level of vicious gossip.

The vulgar meridian

In the more lengthy work *Antinomianism Contrasted with the Religion Taught and Exemplified in Holy Scriptures,* Fuller, a man of very humble circumstances himself, starts his definition of Antinomianism by showing in which social class Antinomianisms are to be found. He complains that 'the vulgar meridian' or 'the illiterate part of professing Christians' are a breeding ground, in general, for heresies. It soon becomes obvious what special working-class heresy common Christians are guilty of. It is Antinomianism, alias Selfishness. Antinomianism is thus the poor, uneducated man's religion according to Fuller and not the religion of the better classes. This is probably why, Fuller, again forgetting his own humble origins, made a special issue of weeding out William Huntington as an Antinomian. Here was a man who dared to enter the pulpit and preach, though he was school-wise completely uneducated.

No reconciliation for the unconverted

Fuller's next point is that this religion of the vulgar does not teach the unconverted to be reconciled with God. This is a rather bold statement for Fuller to make on three counts. He still has not said what Antinomianism really is as opposed to his own teaching on the law; he has given no proof that poor people tend towards Antinomianism and the rich do not and, as it is clearly demonstrable from his works, he himself does not accept a reconciliation of the unconverted but a reconciliation that comes when the believer grasps it. Furthermore, there is no literal doctrine of reconciliation in Fuller's works as he interprets the Biblical doctrine merely figuratively, as will be demonstrated in Part II of this book. As will also be shown, Fuller teaches that justification and righteousness are also given after faith is exercised.

No prayers for sinners

We learn furthermore that these unintelligent Antinomians do not pray for sinners because they might be reprobates. One would like to know who these 'Christians' are who do not pray for their families, friends and even strangers so that they might be saved, be it God's will. Again, this is a sweeping statement which Fuller leaves entirely unexplained and unverified. Perhaps here Fuller's own theology is colouring his prejudice. Fuller did not distinguish between reprobates and the elect, viewing all as sheep until some of those sheep emerged as goats on rejecting Christ. He also taught that the atonement was theoretically there for an Esau as it was for a Jacob; there for a Peter as it was for a Judas. Perhaps the Calvinist position that reprobation is prior to a rejection of Christ has coloured Fuller's view of this 'vulgar meridian' and 'illiterate part'. In his controversy with Dan Taylor,[37] however, Fuller makes it clear that the full gospel, including what Zanchius calls the comforting elements i.e. predestination and election, can only be taught to believers and is only for believers. We presume then that Fuller also did not pray, as he ought to have done according to his own criticism of 'Antinomians', for God to give all the unsaved what he believed He had reserved for the elect. Again, Fuller seems to have forgotten that he also accuses those whom he calls Antinomians of teaching that God justifies sinners whilst they are ungodly but Fuller says God justifies believers only. Sinners, whether reprobate or not, have no part whatsoever in the full gospel. In fact, if his complaints against Philanthropos are a true demonstration of his mind, when compared with *The Gospel Worthy of All Acceptation*, we see that Fuller just could not make up his own mind whether the full gospel was for believers only or for all mankind.[38] His doctrine seems to be that God, when exercising love, wishes to save all men and has made such a salvation possible but when He thinks in terms of justice, He allows this to force Him to compromise. The God of Love thus becomes, for Fuller, a God of Caprice of whom he says, 'However difficult it may appear to us, it is proper for God to exhort and invite men to duties with which he has not determined to give them a moral ability, or a heart, to comply; and for which compliance he has made no effectual provision by the death of his Son.'[39] Fuller is not speaking of the 'thou shalt' and 'thou shalt not' of the law here; he is speaking of saving duties relating to faith. Fuller's picture of God is a being who binds men's arms, tells them He loves them and expects them to exercise duty-faith savingly and invites and exhorts them to do so with the proviso that he is not jolly well going to let them. It seems that this is not only the teaching of one who stands far from an understanding of Christ's redemptive work in relation to a God's Holy Law but of a veritable misanthrope!

Oddly enough, Fuller applies this very reasoning to those he energetically opposes. In his arguments against Booth, who after hearing of Fuller's fall into Liberalism told him he was lost, Fuller states:

> If there were not a sufficiency in the atonement for the salvation of sinners, and yet they were invited to be reconciled to God, they must be invited to what is *naturally impossible*.[40] The message of the gospel would in this case be as if the servants who went forth to bid the guests had said, 'Come', though, in fact, nothing was ready if many of them had come.[41]

Here, of course, Fuller artificially distinguishes between 'moral' and 'natural' abilities, which, as he believes that the image of God in man is not lost in the Fall, he ought not to do. Fuller's orthodox antagonists do not, however, maintain that God calls to the wedding feast according to either natural or moral abilities. That is not the divine criterion as no such abilities are there. God's effectual call is concentrated on those to whom He has given the correct robe, as the Biblical account makes clear in Matthew 22: 9-14. This, orthodox men believe, is the robe of Christ's righteousness which is placed on His own people. God does not therefore invite to anything which requires man's agency. He chooses His guests carefully and calls them effectually. They are certainly invited to that which is naturally and morally impossible for man but whom the Lord calls, He also equips (Romans 8:30).

Having said that, it is obvious from Scripture that indiscriminate prayer is as little called for as indiscriminate preaching. The Puritans prayed and preached as the Spirit led. John Gill whom Fuller placed very near the Antinomian fold, prayed for the unsaved, taught that all sinners had a duty to love God who had made them and also taught that the unsaved should pray. Prayer is a highly selective exercise which God, in His divine sovereignty has commanded as a means of furthering His will. Prayer must thus be exercised within the guidance and unction of the Holy Spirit. We must pray, as we preach, in the Spirit. The Scriptures provide us with abundant examples of discriminating prayer, not the least being Christ's High-Priestly prayer outlined in John 17. Thus if Fuller can demonstrate that others do not pray as he does, this may not reflect negatively on either party as the Lord places different burdens in prayer on different people. If, however, Fuller deduces that his 'Antinomians' pray amiss because they do not pray for the spread of the kind of gospel he represents and in the way he wishes, there are no grounds for concluding that his judgement is correct. Fuller's naming of Huntington as the proto-type of his Antinomians, however, suggests that he is quite wrong in his judgement. Huntington always pointed out that no one knows who are reprobate and who are not so that we must pray even for those who persecute us as there may be a persecuting Saul amongst them who will, by God's grace turn into a Paul. Even, however, when no signs of turning are there, we must pray for obvious non-Christians because, 'many of the saints' prayers have been heard in behalf of persons that never will be saved; as when prayers have been put up for people sick, afflicted, or in poverty: God has raised them up, delivered, and relieved them. The whole ship's crew that sailed with Paul reaped the benefit of his prayers, and so did many sick in the isle of Malta.'[42]

Huntington adds that there are none so merciful as those who have obtained God's mercy, none so loving as those who have obtained God's love and those love the most who have been most forgiven. The belief that prayer was 'the most glorious of all privileges'[43] influenced the Huntingtonians' prayer life immensely, seeing souls who had been won by their ministry under God as 'trophies of prayer'.[44]

The opportunity of emphasising the pioneering role of so-called Antinomians in evangelistic prayer activity must not be allowed to pass here. It was William Romaine and James Hervey, both labelled Antinomians by modern Fullerites, who sparked off a nation-wide call to prayer in the 1750s. Such a call was taken up by Fuller and his friends some 30 years later! Modern Fullerites boast that the Fullerite call to pray was the beginning of true evangelistic activity. This author prefers the evangelistic activity of the New Testament apostles and gospel worthies of all ages who have preached the full gospel to the whole man as witnessed by Romaine's and Hervey's lives and testimonies.

Sending people to hell with glee

Fuller tells us, without evidence, that his Antinomians can talk of people going to hell with calmness and indeed with glee. They cry, 'I wish they were in hell: every one should be in his own place, and the sooner the better!' Again, it is a pity that Fuller neither names these monsters or gives us the necessary details to judge the circumstances of such wrathful words. Such strong claims must be verified. However, this very shocking passage was also apparently written in all calmness and Fuller adds concerning his morally dubious statement made to Philanthropos above 'I have the *happiness* to reason from principles which, I suppose, P. will allow.' Even Fuller's record of anonymous Antinomians gloating over the hell-bound is not quite foreign to Fuller's own position. 'Gloat' is the very word which describes his own treatment of his opponents whether orthodox or 'Antinomian'. This is, of course, when he is not calling them criminals, mud-drinkers etc.. On 21st December, 1801, Fuller relates how he was asked to write on spiritual pride. He replied, 'I feel myself much more capable of depicting *Antinomian*[45] pride, than the other. For this purpose I have procured Huntington's works. But, in reading them, I am stopped for a time. I have eight or nine volumes! I never read anything more void of true religion. I do not think of naming him, or his works, or those of any other person; but merely to *draw pictures*,[46] and let the reader judge who they are like.'[47] Fuller then painted his highly discoloured *Picture of an Antinomian* which is one of the most vulgar pieces of libel ever penned against a man of God who was praised amongst the denominations as

Whitefield's successor. Echoing these thoughts in his appreciative review
of that scandalous book *The Voice of Years,*[48] Fuller rejects any sign
whatsoever of a work of grace in Huntington for his defence of the doctrines
of grace and places him out of the bounds of Christianity. If condemning
one's fellow evangelicals is a sign of Antinomianism, then Fuller was in no
position to throw the first stone.

The Antinomians and party attachment

Fuller goes on to describe an Antinomian as one who stresses party
attachment, loving those who love him. Such is the attachment of publicans
and heathens, says Fuller. Again Fuller is forgetting how insular he is
himself in his displays of affection, which in no way went out to those with
whom he did not agree. Even when he agreed with people closely on many
issues, such as with John Wesley, he was still hyper-critical of him. Writing
to William Ward in 1809, Fuller says he doubts whether Wesley is a 'good
man' and approves of those who considered him a 'dishonest man' and a
'crafty Jesuit'.[49] When one reads through his works, very few Christian
writers in any denomination, even those who were very close to him such
as Abraham Booth, escape the sharpness and sulking criticism of his pen.
It was not always safe to be Fuller's friend as the Serampore Trio found out
when they founded a Church without Fuller's absent-Bishop approval.[50] It
was terrible to be his enemy, as Huntington and many another Five-Point
man experienced.

Antinomians take their sins too seriously according to Fuller

Oddly enough, Fuller rails against the Antinomians because of their
sensitive consciences. Instead of trusting confidently in Christ, he finds
they complain of 'temptations, or the workings of unbelief, and supposes
that the enemy of souls wants to rob him of his enjoyments.' Fuller has
apparently no room in his own 'party attachment' for men who feel their
vileness and are ashamed when they live below the level of their heavenly
calling. He also seems to feel that a life of triumph in Christ has nothing to
do with fighting the Devil and all his works. Fuller appears here to have
forgotten Romans 7. Moreover, one would have thought that those who
take their own sin seriously were anything but Antinomians and one who
ridicules their mortification must be an Antinomian indeed. Indeed, Fuller's
statements against these poor suffering souls who, like Job, are chastened
and tried become positively cruel. He maintains that their 'terror on account
of the consequence of sin' is merely selfish and a mere concern for their
own safety. At other times he believes their sorrows are all self-delusions.
A *real* Christian, he argues, experiences 'an ingenuous grief for having

sinned', but finds, though the right symptoms are there, the motives of his 'Antinomians' must be false as they do not agree with his version of holiness! Fuller is arguing within his own narrow circle of subjective judgement and prejudice. One begins to feel sorry for these so-called Antinomians on whom Fuller vents his wrath and one feels that he is stretching his point far too far. It seems that Fuller is merely unlawfully slandering his brethren in Christ whose faces he does not like. With these thoughts, Fuller is still only half way through his *Introduction* and there are still another twenty-one pages of this kind of verbal, highly emotive defamation to come. Indeed, a systematic Biblical analysis of the Law and what causes man to be anti-law, i.e. Antinomian, is spared the reader.

The false nature of Fuller's view of his orthodox brethren whom he terms Antinomians is shown by many a letter of Huntington's to those struggling with the old man. Such letters may be hempen home-spun in their language, but they are in gospel tones that lead a soul to union with their Lord. Writing as an elderly man to an elderly sister who is feeling the purifying chastisement of God, the Coalheaver says:

Be honest, my dear friend, and act truly and uprightly with thine own soul, and suffer conscience to magnify her office. 'Search me, and try me,' said David; who was willing to know the worst; he did not desire to have his wounds healed slightly, with a cry of 'Peace, peace.' Whatever wild terrors, horrors, alarms, frights, and fears, hypocrites like Cain, Esau, Saul, and Judas, may have had, be assured of this, that none know and feel the plague of their own hearts but God's elect - the churches, not the world. 'All the churches shall know that I am he that searcheth the reins and the hearts,' Rev. 2:23. Therefore submit, and be willing to have the worst laid open. It is the true light which discovers the depths of the human heart; it is the omniscience of God that makes manifest the counsels, workings, conceptions, and productions, of inbred corruptions; and it is the life of God that gives all our longings, cravings, hungerings, and thirstings, after the provisions of Zion. God, my friend, is in all these works, 'I wound and I heal; I bring low, and I lift up.' Yea, he killeth by the law, and maketh alive by the Spirit; 'he bringeth down to the grave and bringeth up.' These are the sick which need the great Physician; and not the whole, the sound, nor the healthy.

None know the depth of man's fall, nor the foulness and filth, the uncleanness, the infidelity and enmity, hardness and impenitency, the rebellion and atheism, of our inbred corruptions, but those who are taught of God; and none but such will ever embrace, adore, and admire the Saviour. Of all the spectres, ghosts, beasts or devils, whether in earth or hell, whether real or imaginary; not one ever appeared half so fearful, terrific, or dreadful to me as myself, when exposed by the application of the law! No free will, self-confidence, daring presumption, false hopes, or head notions, can live, or maintain their standing, on this ground: and I bless God for their destruction; for when we are thus withered God revives us, and under his reviving a better crop is produced; faith and hope, fear and peace, love and joy, light and life, spring up; and this fruit shall never fade, wither, or die away.

Come, old girl, pluck up, take heart, be of good courage, and 'he that shall come will come.' The old man has got the dagger in him, and die he must. And Satan has lost the fort royal of thine affections, and shall never regain it more.[51]

Apart from the extraordinary high standard of pastoral guidance revealed in such letters, Huntington shows the true nature of besetting sin and the true nature of law to point its condemning finger at it so that the burdened soul is forced into the arms of the Spirit for help. Those who have a lighter view of sin invariably have a lighter view of the Law which deals with that sin. Those who do not experience the vileness of sin cannot appreciate the holiness of the Law.

The causes of Antinomianism 1: The doctrine of total inability

In Part I, Fuller argues that there are two causes of Antinomianism. The first is that Antinomians emphasise the total inability of fallen man to believe the gospel. This is a surprise, indeed. One would have thought that this was hardly an Antinomian trend as the Bible teaches clearly that the soul that sins shall die and that all men have disobeyed the Law and thus all are dead in trespasses and sins. One cannot expect much spiritual, or, as Fuller will have it, much moral ability, in a dead man, not to mention his fallen physical status as part of the whole creation which groans under sin because of his Fall. True to Fuller's practice, he uses the term 'total inability' in an apparently orthodox way at first, suggesting that such a doctrine 'if properly understood, is of great account in true religion.' Here we must be wary of Fuller's remark as when he uses the word 'properly', he usually means he is thinking in non-theological terms and when he uses the word 'improperly' he is thinking theologically but using pure metaphor, so that whether a thing is proper or not, we can never get a true, concrete theological statement out of him. Sure enough, it pays to be wary in this case, too. Fuller believes that those who understand the term 'improperly' of sinners believe that it 'serves to keep them easy in their sins,' and even serves to 'excuse the sinner in his sins.' Antinomians, Fuller argues, use the term 'total inability' improperly because they feel it envelopes all, thus they deceive the sinner by telling him he has no abilities at all to get himself out of his mess and thus cannot be made responsible for his own sin. Thus Antinomians are such because they believe that the law slays the sinner fully and he must wait to see whether God in His mercy will save him, having no agency in himself to provoke such an action on God's part. It is beginning to appear as if Fuller's Antinomians are really the real law-abiders whom Fuller is striving to cloth with false feathers.

The causes of Antinomianism 2: The liberty and privileges of the gospel
The second definition of Antinomianism that Fuller gives is, if it were possible, even more surprising. Antinomians, he tells us, stress 'the liberty and privileges of the gospel.' This leads them, we read, 'to cherish in them spiritual pride, slothfulness, and presumption.' Again Fuller tells us that his second ground for suspicion against Antinomians is 'a truth full of the richest consolation, that those who believe in Jesus are freed, not only from the ceremonial yoke of the Mosaic dispensation, but from the condemning power of the law considered as moral.'[52] Why then does he use this truth as an argument against his supposed Antinomians who uphold it? Fuller argues that his Antinomian opponents mean by 'the liberty and privileges of the gospel' that 'they are no longer under obligation to love God with all their heart, soul, mind and strength, or their neighbour as themselves.'

Here again, it would seem that Fuller is in grave danger of giving himself spiritual airs and professing that whereas he is eager to conform to the precepts of Christ in summing up the law, those professing Christians whom he labels Antinomians are not. His presumption may be based on fact but these facts are not given the reader. All Fuller does to prove his case is labour on the presumed cunning, Pharisaism and hypocrisy of those he obviously hates with a burning hatred but grounds this solely in his sheer prejudice and, at times, haughty arrogance. There may well have been such men who felt that they need neither love God nor their neighbour but these would not only be worthy of the name of Antinomian but also of the epithet 'totally pagan'. Fuller, however, is not confuting such people. Indeed, what makes Fuller's accusations so odd is that he affirms concerning his 'Antinomians', 'strange that it may appear, there is scarcely any people who speak of their sins in such exaggerated language, or who make use of such degrading epithets concerning their character, as they.'

It would seem to an impartial enquirer that Fuller is contradicting himself. People who are very conscious of their sins must be very conscious of the Law and the will of Christ that condemns such sin. Without the Law, they had not known sin. Without Christ they would have no idea of righteousness. Such people can hardly be called Antinomians. Indeed, Fuller argues time and time again that his Antinomians have joined hands with the self-righteous Pharisees. At best, if his undocumented opinion were taken as evidence, this would point to extreme legalism but Fuller is eager to show just the opposite. He is seeking to prove that his Antinomians are guilty of an extreme distaste of having anything to do with the Law or Christ's precepts. He is saying that they misuse 'the liberty and privileges of the gospel', which he interprets as meaning that they do not place themselves under the Law.

Those who cunningly profess their vileness
All that one can conclude from Fuller's tirades about the supposed Antinomians is that when they struggle with their sin or show repentance, they do so, he tells us, 'with a cunning smile in their countenances, profess to be as bad as Satan himself; manifestly with the design of being thought deep Christians, thoroughly acquainted with the plague of their own heart.' Here, Fuller is calling his brethren hypocrites, because he cannot understand their kind of piety. He is not willing for a moment to exercise that love to his brethren that his moral law exhorts him to practise. He seems to be upbraiding his neighbours for feeling that they are the chief of sinners and vile in God's sight when clothed in their own righteousness. Such men of the law and gospel as William Huntington, Fuller's Arch-Antinomian, were suspicious of accepting the testimony of any 'professor of the faith' if that person had not tasted his own vileness. Unless that way was gone, they believed, no one could taste and see that the Lord is good. Placing an acute consciousness of sin in a soul is the way the Holy Spirit converts sinners and builds up believers.

On the other hand, what Christian would deny that we are not legally under the Law as a covenant of works, nor even in its Mosaic form, nor in any form for that matter. We are under the Law to Christ which is a rule of grace according to the eternal standards of God, shown in the Law and which Christ has kept in our stead and is working out in us. Thus it is now 'God which worketh in you both to will and do of his good pleasure (Philippians 2:13) and through the blood of the everlasting covenant the God of peace makes us 'perfect in every good work to do his will, working in you that which is well-pleasing in his sight, through Jesus Christ; to whom be glory for ever.' (Hebrews 13:20-21).

Fuller's doctrinal case against his supposed Antinomians 1: Election
In Part II, the final part of his treatise against Antinomians, Fuller begins at
last to develop a doctrinal case to back up his arguments showing which
doctrines are 'perverted' by Antinomians. The first doctrine Fuller examines
is election. His Antinomians, i.e. those who have 'a fleshly mind,' he
believes, cling too much to the idea of a gift of God and ask critically, 'How
can these things be? How can predestination be made to comport with
human agency and accountableness?' Fuller's answer is, 'But a truly
humble Christian, finding both in the Bible, will believe both, though he
may be unable fully to conceive of their consistency; and will find in the
one (i.e. human agency) a motive to depend on God, and in the other
(man's accountability)[53] a caution against slothfulness and a presumptuous
neglect of duty.' Fuller is here classifying those who believe election and
predestination are matters of grace alone as having fleshly minds. Surely
the fleshly mind is the very opposite. One who, like Fuller, argues that
'motives to depend upon God' are to be found in the sinner's own agency
and 'cautions against the sinner's slothness and a presumptuous neglect
of duty' are part and parcel of his sense of accountability must have a
fleshly mind indeed as these do not signify works of grace but works of
human merit. Again Fuller is arguing that leopards have at least the basic
tools for changing their spots, even if they need outside help to alter them.

Nevertheless, Fuller goes on to argue, obviously rather unsure of his
subject, 'But, whatever this doctrine is in itself it may be held in such a
manner as to become a source of pride, bitterness, slothfulness, and
presumption.' Fuller adds that such people who see predestination as
'only so it was and so it must be' are guilty of 'conceiving the love of God
as a capricious fondness.' They thus react like 'a flattered female, who,
while she affects to decline the compliments paid her, is in reality so
intoxicated with the idea of her own importance, as to look down with
contempt on all her former companions.' They also 'excite contemptuous
feelings towards all who are not its adherents, considering them as graceless
sinners, strangers to the liberty of the Gospel, Pharisees, Hagarenes,
children of the bond-woman, and the like: towards whom the most malignant
bitterness is Christian faithfulness.' All this, needless to say, Fuller has
argued without giving a single Scriptural, historical or contemporary proof
for his position. What is clear is that all the malice he accuses his
Antinomians of having because of their emphasis on 'all of grace' is both
shown and used in his own merciless way of treating them. It is little use
Fuller calling his neighbours 'Pharisees' because they allegedly call others
by such names if no evidence is forthcoming other than one's own hyper-
critical presumption and prejudice.

Fuller at last produces a text from Scripture

To round off his emotive outburst concerning election and predestination, Fuller at last gives a Scriptural reference, Deuteronomy 7:7, 9:1-6 though he neither quotes the verses nor expounds them. Obviously Fuller believes no exposition is necessary as the verses clearly illustrate what he has been saying. This they do not do. Deuteronomy 7:7 reads 'The Lord did not set his love upon you, nor choose you, because ye were more numerous than any people; for ye were the fewest of all people.' This, of all texts, shows that election is 'only so it was, and so it must be.' Yet Fuller has been arguing all along that he wants his Bible truths both ways, they must be consistent with reason and consistent with grace. They must be consistent with man's agency and with God's purpose. In arguing this way, Fuller is turning away from the truth of the very text he quotes.

Deuteronomy 9:1-6 is the story of God's promise to the Jews that they shall defeat the Anakims but ought not to look to themselves as in any way worthy of the Lord's care as, though God's own people, they were 'stiff-necked'. Here again, this text should lead Fuller to disown any human agency in salvation. He does not use, however, the text to this positive end but merely to illustrate how 'the Jews in our Saviour's time turned their national election into another kind of doctrine, full of flattery towards themselves, and of the most intolerable contempt and malignity towards others.' Anyone, not realising that Fuller claimed to be a Calvinist, could only believe that he was arguing against election. Again, in comparing those under his criticism with the Jews who felt themselves better than the rest, he is criticising them in the very way he claims is the method of Antinomians. How refreshing it is to turn to John Gill's commentary on these very texts, showing how they affirm God's sovereign love in election and instil in the believer that all is of grace and none of the elect has the tiniest reason to boast. How refreshing it is, too, to see how positive Gill views these words and does not use them as a sounding-board to rail at others.[54]

Fuller's doctrinal case against his supposed Antinomians 2: The atonement

Next, Fuller claims that his Antinomians have a faulty view of the atonement. He tells us 'The principles of the Divine interposition are set forth in the Scriptures in divers forms; but probably in none so fully as in the substitutional sacrifices, which, from the fall to the coming of Christ, formed a conspicuous part of instituted worship.' The 'nature and tendency of the Christian doctrine of atonement,' Fuller explains, is illustrated in 'the sacrifice of Job, on behalf of his three friends.' Here, Fuller expounds his

moral government theory, or moral deterrent theory, of the atonement which
emphasises not so much the objective nature of what is accomplished but
the 'sentiments it was calculated to inspire.' Fuller illustrates and comments
on the atonement by means of a story taken from the book of Job.

> The Lord said to Eliphaz the Temanite, My wrath is kindled
> against thee, and against thy two friends; for ye have not spoken
> of me the thing that is right, as my servant Job hath. Therefore take
> unto you now seven bullocks and seven rams, and go to my servant
> Job, and offer up for your selves a burnt-offering; and my servant
> Job shall pray for you, for him will I accept; lest I deal with you
> after your folly, in that ye have not spoken of me the thing that is
> right, like my servant Job.'[55] This reproof and direction would, if
> rightly taken, excite the deepest repentance and self-abasement.
> To be told that they had sinned, that the wrath of Heaven was
> kindled against them, that an offering, and even a petition for
> mercy, would not be accepted at their hands, that it must be
> presented by a mediator, and that this mediator should be the very
> person whom they had despised and condemned as smitten of
> God and afflicted, was altogether so humiliating, that had they
> been unbelievers, and left to their own spirit, they would have
> rejected it with a sullen scorn, equal to that which many in our day
> reject the mediation of Jesus Christ. But they were good men and
> followed the Divine direction, humiliating as it was, with implicit
> obedience. 'They did as the Lord commanded them: the Lord also
> accepted Job.' To them, therefore, this direction must have imparted
> a new set of views and feelings; as full of humility, thankfulness,
> conciliation, and brotherly love, as their speeches had been of
> pride, folly, and bitterness. Such is the nature and tendency of the
> Christian doctrine of atonement.

It is interesting to note that whenever Fuller deals with Christ's atonement,
he deals with it in relation to Old Testament figures and shadows of it and
not with the real New Testament accomplishment which these figures and
shadows foretell. Fuller, in fact, sees no essential difference in the Old
Testament symbols and Christ's sacrifice, as everything is to be interpreted
figuratively. For Fuller, Christ's sacrifice is not different to the Old Testament
sacrifices in nature but only in degree. It is not so much what was objectively
accomplished in the atonement but what effect the knowledge of such a
sacrifice imparts on the believer, prompting him to respond with 'a new set
of views and feelings.' This is all in keeping with Fuller's refusal to regard

the atonement in its strictly physical, penal, and redemptive aspects, points which will be dealt with when considering more fully, Fuller's figurative view of redemption. It is sufficient at this stage to point out that Fuller accepts only a moral interpretation of the atonement, encouraging man to take up the moral duties of 'humility, thankfulness, conciliation and brotherly love.' The atonement is thus neutral in our salvation. It is not what it *is* that ensures our salvation but what it inspires us *to do*.

Salvation not a matter of essential justice

Though Fuller often uses the word 'justice' in relation to the atonement, it is obvious that the idea of justice does not arise directly from the atonement, in his opinion, as no debt has been paid, no punishment has been executed, no sins have been expiated and no justification has been wrought. This all comes with the believer's acceptance of the moral principles supposedly involved. Thus Fuller argues that salvation is not required by justice but is, nevertheless as God so wills, consistent with it.[56]

After discussing Fuller's figurative doctrine of sin and the fall and after viewing his equally figurative doctrine of imputed righteousness which will be discussed below, Fuller's condemnations of his brethren who take sin seriously in a different way, need to be severely modified if not rejected fully. Justice in Fuller's system, is not objectively brought into relationship with the punishment that Christ bore on the sinner's behalf. Thus Fuller teaches, 'Every one that knows anything of the gospel, knows that one of its grand peculiarities is, that it harmonises the justice and mercy of God in the forgiveness of sins.' Justice is always other than mercy in Fuller's view and salvation is attained by their both meeting half-way as in the case of Zaleucus who had his son's eye put out and one of his own to make justice and mercy meet. Actually, again we see that mercy triumphs over justice in Fuller's system as it is not justice being satisfied in the atonement that is central to salvation but the forgiveness of sin - one might add, however this may be accomplished. The means to the end is unimportant. The Reformed Faith, however, rests on the fact that sins can be forgiven because justice has been done. The Biblical doctrine of God's choosing a way to exercise real and complete justice in harmony with real and complete mercy does not come into Fuller's system as this would incur what he calls 'commercial language', i.e. the language of redemption, which Fuller rejects. Thus we find Fuller saying, 'I am far from thinking that every one who has pleaded for salvation as a matter required by essential justice is an Antinomian; but such may be the tendency of the principle notwithstanding.'

A false antithesis
It is here that Fuller provides us with one of his false antitheses which he
constantly uses to prove his case. Either we believe his theory of moral
deterrence and inspiration or we believe that God made a pact with the
devil to buy us back. Satisfaction would be then made, not to the Law
which was conquered, but to Satan. Either we accept Fullerism or believe
that the Law is not holy and just but an oppressive curse. Either sinner and
saint alike put themselves gladly under God's Law as a rule of duty,
motivated to this by Christ's moral example or they 'represent the
redemption of Christ as delivering us from a tyrannical yoke,' i.e. make
Antinomians of themselves. Fuller thus can argue that, humbling as his
doctrine of moral inspiration is, other people's doctrine of redemption:

> may be so perverted as to become quite another thing, and
> productive of an opposite effect. If God as a lawgiver be held up as
> an Egyptian taskmaster, and the mercy of the Saviour be magnified
> at his expense - if his atonement be considered rather as a victory
> over the law than as an honour due to it - if his enduring the curse be
> supposed to exonerate us from obeying the precepts - if, in
> consequence of his having laid down his life, we think more lightly
> of sin, and imagine it to be a less dangerous evil - finally, if, from the
> full satisfaction which he has made to divine justice, we reckon
> ourselves to be freed not only from punishment, but from the *desert*
> of it, and warranted not merely to implore mercy in his name, but to
> *claim it as a right* - we are in possession of a scheme abhorrent to
> the gospel, and not a little productive of spiritual pride. Such views
> of the atonement excite an irreverent familiarity with God, and in
> some cases, a daring boldness in approaching him; yet such is the
> strength of the delusion, it passes for intimate communion with him!

Now here, Fuller has ensnared himself in a real theological tangle. He
cannot possibly accept the plain Scriptural teaching that Christ died as a
ransom for many, paying the debts and wages of sin on behalf of His Bride.
He therefore has to revert to an either / or alternative, both sides of which
have little to do with the true Biblical doctrine of the atonement. They have
also little to do with those whom Fuller castigates as being Antinomian.
This can be clearly shown using William Huntington as an example. For
Fuller, he was the contemporary leader of the Antinomians and a man who
reaped his full and complete hatred. Huntington, for Fuller was typical of
the 'vulgar meridian' which was the breeding ground of Antinomianism.
Indeed, he was the *Picture of an Antinomian*, a 'low wit' who used the

language of Billingsgate[57] and should have stayed a day-labourer rather than become a preacher.[58] Acknowledging that crowds flocked to hear Huntington preach, he yet denounces those crowds of appreciative hushed and awed hearers as being 'affected with delusion'. Perhaps a more humble man, seeing how thrilled and blessed the crowd was at Huntington's preaching, might have asked himself if he, being quite alone in his rebellion against what he had heard, were not the deluded one.

According to Fuller, Huntington ought to despise the Law as being an evil destroyed in the atonement so that the Christian could live a life of lasciviousness. Let us thus listen to the Old Coalheaver writing to his dear friend J. Jenkins in 1796, over ten years after Fuller's notorious book *The Gospel Worthy of All Acceptation* had fired a broadside against such piety as that of the Huntingtonians. It was a broadside that never hit its mark. Here, in stark contrast to Fuller's anti-Huntington gossip, the true Biblical work of an evangelist is outlined:

> I have no doubt but thy aims are right, for I am sure that that preacher that exposes the vileness of human nature, and preaches the purity, spirituality, and unlimited demands of the law; that sets forth the sinner's need of a Saviour, the suitableness and the worth of him, and that debases the creature; and who enforces the necessity of regeneration, spiritual fruitfulness, spiritual service, and a life and walk in faith, shall not err in these things.

Listen to Huntington's bibline words concerning the contrite sinner, longing for righteousness:

> Such a soul, hungering and thirsting after righteousness; fixing his longing eyes upon Jesus; mourning, sighing, and praying to him, with sincere and honest confessions; pleading the promises; loathing himself in his own sight; acknowledging his guilt before God; pleading the blood and righteousness of Christ; covered with shame and confusion; driven on by a sense of want, and encouraged by the kind invitations in the Word of God; such a soul, I say, is an army with banners.

Such a contrite soul, however, is derided on page after page of Fuller's anti-Antinomian tirades as he cannot accept such a fine Christian testimony. A testimony built on a literal blood and righteousness theology, a literal redemptive theology and a literal belief that Christ washed away all the sin of His Bride on the cross. This is a religion that Fuller cannot and will not stomach. It is thus all hypocrisy and sham to him. It does not fit into his view of 'the fitness of things'.

Fuller maintains that Antinomians are ever claiming their rights before the Throne of Grace, fully oblivious to their own true nature. Huntington, Fuller's Arch-Antinomian, however, writes of the old Adam in the new man which prevents any believer from thinking he is more than Christ has made him:

> God has left in all his children the old crop, to remind us of our base origin, to hide pride from our eyes, to exclude boasting from our lips, and to keep us from putting any confidence in the flesh. It is to exercise our grace, especially patience; to make us watchful, to make us sensible of the depth of man's fall, and, finally, to exalt the grace of God; to make us sick of self, and sick of the world, sick of sin, and to make us to prize the great Physician, and to make us long for that perfect rest which remaineth to the people of God.[59]

In such teaching, there is no speculative talk about human agency but the depth and totality of man's fall is revealed to man through God's holy Word. Those who know that sin goes deep and that repentance must go as deep, know that, by God's elective love, forgiveness goes deep and this deep work of grace is always before them. To stop Huntington in his tracts and tell him that he talks too much of God's purpose in man and too little of human agency, would be to make a mockery of the gospel of salvation. It is just this, however, that Fuller strives to do. His law is far weaker than that of the supposed Antinomians he derides and thus his gospel is all the less effective. In Huntington's eyes, it was not merely those who belittled the Mosaic Law that were Antinomians but those also who weakened the power and the extent of the gospel.[60]

We may also rightly protest at Fuller's condemnation of those children of God who believe they have claims on their heavenly Father in the sense that they can stand with boldness in His presence. Fuller does not recognise the Biblical doctrine of sons and servants. All children know their duties to their earthly father, he argues, therefore all sinners know their duty to exercise faith savingly in their heavenly Father.[61] This is a clear denial of Galatians 4 and its teaching that the Holy Spirit is put into the hearts of adopted sons to make them such and to make them aware of their relationship to their Father. According to Scripture, true sons have free access to their Father's mansions and are at home in His presence. They are not in bondage like the servants but have been adopted by One who tells them to come boldly to the Throne of Grace and enables them to boldly say, 'The Lord is my helper, and I will not fear what men shall do unto me.' (Hebrews 4:16, 13:6). This boldness has been given them by the redemptive blood of Jesus which has purchased them for their Father (Hebrews 10:19). They may even stand before God in boldness on the Day of Judgement, thanks be to Christ whose blood has redeemed them! (1 John 4:17).

3. Fuller's antinomianism behind the mask

The common beliefs of Wesley and Fuller

Shortly before James Hervey died, John Wesley accused him of Antinomianism on the grounds that he believed the charges of the Law are all answered in Christ on our behalf. Wesley argued that if this were so, then neither God nor man need bother to exercise obedience to the Law. This, he claimed, was 'Antinomianism without a mask.'[62] It is clear to a Reformed mind that anyone, like Wesley, who denies that Christ answered all the charges of the Law on our behalf, must have a very low view of the Law and also a low view of the extent to which Christ went to secure our salvation. Arminians and Fullerites, of course, deny that Christ's obedience to the Law was so complete that He secured the salvation of His flock in the atonement. They believe that Christ's relation to the Law merely enabled Him to declare that His work on the cross, enhanced and complemented by human agency, might save whosoever avails himself of the opportunity to try it out.

Reading through Wesley's long letter to Hervey[63] on the subject, one is made immediately aware that Wesley's errors are very similar to those made by Fuller. Indeed the eleven letters in which Hervey defends the doctrines of grace against Wesley's erroneous views are equally a masterful refutation of Andrew Fuller. Hervey is especially keen to show up Wesley's error concerning the atonement and its allegedly merely becoming efficacious on being applied to whosoever might ask for it. He demonstrates that the atonement is efficacious in itself, it first secures faith, righteousness and justification for God's people and then applies them. We are made righteous, then accounted as what we are. Wesley reversed this order. He believed that God merely accounted us as righteous (here we have Fuller's 'as if' theology) and then through sincere obedience the believer was made righteous.

Accounting sinners righteous

Hervey takes up Wesley's whim by saying: 'God, through him (Christ), first accounts, and then makes us righteous. How! does God account us righteous, before he makes us so? Then his judgement is not according to truth; then he reckons us to be righteous, when we are really otherwise. Is this not the language of your doctrine? this the unavoidable consequence of your notion? But how harsh, if not horrid, does it sound in every ear! Is not this absolutely irreconcilable with our ideas of the Supreme Being, and equally incompatible with the dictates of Scripture? There we are taught that God "justifieth the ungodly". Mark the words: "The ungodly" are the objects of the divine justification. But can he account the ungodly righteous? Impossible! How then does he act? He first makes them righteous. After what manner? By imputing to them the righteousness of his dear Son. Then he pronounces them righteous, and most truly; he treats them as righteous, and most justly. In short, then he absolves them from the guilt, adopts them for his children, and makes them heirs of his eternal kingdom. In the grand transaction, thus regulated, mercy and truth meet together; all proceeds in the most harmonious and beautiful consistency with the several attributes of God, with his whole revealed will, and with all his righteous law.'

This can all be applied to Fuller who shared Wesley's weak view of the atonement and belief that God justifies believers on their acceptance of the gospel and then makes them righteous. Wesley, however, always comes off best in a direct comparison with Fuller. The latter is not as Biblical as Wesley who, for all his Arminianism, still believed that the demands of the Law must be fulfilled to the letter. This is all irrelevant to Fuller as he does not believe that God need trouble Himself about fulfilling the letter of His own standards. Hervey, however maintains that the yardstick to which a belief must tally or be judged as Antinomian is, 'The claims of the Law, as a covenant of works; as being the condition of life and glory; the claims of the law, as requiring perfect obedience on pain of eternal death - these claims are all satisfied by our most blessed and gracious Surety: If not, they are still incumbent upon us, and upon every child of man. A burden this, which neither "we nor our fathers were able to bear"; which, heavier than the sands of the sea, would have sunk us into the nethermost hell. This doctrine, therefore is not "Antinomianism without a mask", but it is the doctrine of "righteousness without works", Rom. 4:6, and of justification "without the deeds of the law", Rom. 3:28.'[64]

An Antinomian proper
Hervey gives Wesley this list of fundamental doctrines because they are at the heart of the Reformed Faith which Wesley, being an Arminian, calls Antinomianism. These can also be used as a yardstick to measure Fuller's orthodoxy. When applied to Fuller, this yardstick shows that his views

coincide with Wesley's concerning what is Antinomian. Needless to say, such views are contrary to the doctrines of the Reformers regarding the Law, indeed, they are contrary to the plain teaching of Scripture. Thus that which any Reformed man must suspect on reading Fuller can be proved, i.e. that his views are Antinomian and thus he is *real* Antinomian.

First: The covenant of works.
This is a central teaching of the Reformation, though denied by Arminians. It is based on God's decree revealed to Adam in Genesis 2:17 concerning punishment for disobedience to His will by eating the forbidden fruit. 'In the day that thou eatest thereof, thou shalt surely die.' The covenant was outlined in full in the Mosaic Law, committing man to full obedience, otherwise the broken law would be used as evidence against the sinner, condemning him to judgement and perdition. Arminians claim that when Adam broke the covenant, God dropped it, too, because fallen man was not in a position to keep it. Where there is no compact, they argue, there can be no obligation. It would thus be contrary to God's character to demand a perfect holy life of man, when He knew man could not live up to His demands.[65] The Reformed position is that though the Covenant of Works is annulled for believers, who come under the Covenant of Grace, it is not annulled for unbelievers who are still responsible to God for their obedience, even to the point of loving Him, and still under the broken Law's curse and thus under God's wrath and punishment. Paul makes this succinctly clear in Romans 2:32-3:1, 'Who knowing the judgement of God, that they which commit such things are worthy of death, not only do the same, but have pleasure in them that do them. Therefore thou art inexcusable, O man, whosoever thou art.' The great Reformed theologian Herman Witsius (1636-1708) can thus conclude in his two-volume work on the Covenants, 'The covenant of works . . . is in no account abolished.'[66] This is because 'There is a plain passage, Gal. 5:3 which confirms, that even by the promulgation of the new gospel covenant, the breakers of the covenant who are without Christ, are not set free from that obligation of the law, which demands perfect obedience, but continue debtors to do the whole law.'[67]

What is Fuller's attitude to the covenant of works? As now probably suspected, Fuller uses the term at times but when it comes to the pinch, explains it away. Indeed, when writing under the heading *Of Sinners Being Under the Covenant of Works* in his controversial treatise against the Reformed Faith which he calls provokingly, *The Gospel Worthy of All Acceptation,* he denies outright that the Covenant still stands, giving exactly the same Antinomian reasons as the Arminians. Here Fuller states:

'Strictly speaking, men are not now under the covenant of works, but under the curse for having broken it. God is not in covenant with them, nor they with him.'[68] There is, however, a major difference between the Arminians' argument and Fuller's concerning man's fall. Arminians argue that as man is dead in trespasses and sin, the covenant of works does not apply as you cannot have a covenant with a dead man. Fuller is even less Biblical. He argues that the idea of viewing sinful man as dead is wrong. He is very much alive and kicking, physically and morally. There are no 'cannots' in man, merely 'will nots'. He can serve God, but he will not. He is only fallen in his inclinations. This is all that the 'curse' implies for Fuller. Thus the covenant of works is done away with because fallen man is directly addressable and responsive to the gospel of grace and understands that He must love Christ as if he had never apostatised. In other words, the Arminian, with all his being at variance with Scripture, still accepts the doctrine of man's total depravity because of his breaking the Law of God, but Fuller will not accept this doctrine which is fundamental to a right understanding of the Law. From a Reformed point of view, Fuller is clearly an Antinomian and from an Arminian point of view, he is an Antinomian, too. His system can be placed at the other side of Arminianism to the theology of the Reformation. The true Biblical view of fallen man is that he is totally unable to comprehend anything spiritual - and it is his own fault. 'But the natural man receiveth not the things of the spirit of God: for they are foolishness unto him: neither can he know them, because they are spiritually discerned.' (1 Corinthians 2:14).

Second: The law as a condition of life and glory.
If Adam had stood the test and obeyed God, it is obvious that he would not have died but have lived on for eternity. He died solely because he had sinned. The Mosaic Law was thus established as an eternal demonstration by God of what entails holy life-giving obedience. Those who live according to the Law are worthy of eternal life. This was what the Jews were told whilst the Mosaic Law was being given. 'Ye shall therefore keep my statutes and judgements: which if a man do, he shall live in them: I am the Lord.' (Leviticus 10:28). Paul in the New Testament tells his hearers the very same thing, 'For Moses describeth the righteousness which is of the law, That the man which doeth those things shall live by them.' (Romans 10:5).[69] Paul says, however, that 'The commandment which was ordained to life, I found to be unto death.' (Romans 7:10). This was because man when faced with God's standards, experiences that he has no righteousness of His own. This is the work of the Law in the heart of man. The work of the covenant

of grace is to show Him that the Law can be fulfilled in him through the righteousness of Another. But what does Fuller say to all this?

Criticising John Brine who believed that God makes unconverted sinners duty-bound to obey the Law 'as a rule of life or as a covenant', Fuller argues either in ignorance of the Scripture just quoted or plainly deciding to ignore them, that we cannot say of the Law 'Do and live!' because 'God requires nothing of fallen creatures as a term of life'.[70] Thus, again, Fuller sides with Wesley and puts himself outside of the Biblical doctrine of the Mosaic Law. He thus sides with the Antinomians.

Third: The claims of the Law require perfect obedience on pain of eternal death.

Hervey explains that anyone who tampers in any way with this doctrine, disclaims God's justice and, in view of Christ's fulfilling the Law absolutely, rejects God's mercy. It is here that Fuller is at his most radical and allows his own search for the spirit behind the letter of the Law to draw him far from the Reformed doctrine of the Law as a reflection of God's eternal character which is lived out and therefore fulfilled in Christ. Salvation is won for man, according to Fuller, on an 'as if' basis; not only with regards to man but also with regards to Christ. Both parties stand before a Law which is never literally propitiated and vindicated. No true punishment is dealt out and no true guilt is removed. The moral truth behind the atonement is not that Christ exercised perfect obedience to all the claims of the Law, as is commonly understood in Reformed theology, but that He provided a token 'as if' sacrifice which was morally acceptable to God. There was thus no necessity whatsoever in the atonement and no necessity whatsoever in keeping the Law. The atonement was not right because there was no other way, it was right because God arbitrarily willed it so. It was not the means but the end that was significant. It is not the fall which ultimately condemns man, according to Fuller, but the non-acceptance of the moral deterrent exercised in Christ's suffering. This is the heinous sin of sins in Fuller's eyes. Duty-faith, or rather duty-to-faith, is Fuller's parole, not duty to the Law. The Law as a means of life never existed. It never even existed for Christ. It was an anachronism before it was instigated. Moral slavery has nothing to do with moral inability but with sheer unwillingness.[71] Thus a law-work in man to lead him to Christ is quite superfluous in the work of an evangelist because one can appeal directly to him to love God savingly.[72]

If such a view does not lead to rank Antinomianism, it is difficult to understand what does. Huntington and all truly Reformed men see in

Fuller's abuse of the Law nothing but the most blatant Antinomianism. This, however, is far from admitted by modern Fullerites who are very vociferous in magazines such as the British *Banner of Truth* in condemning those of Huntington's persuasions as being Antinomians themselves. We must thus look closely at Fuller's doctrine of God's Law and his principle of 'the fitness of things' which regulates a right understanding of it.

4. The nature and fitness of things

God's 'lovely' and 'amiable' wrath

It has been shown when dealing with the fall that Fuller adhered to a great degree to the Cambridge Platonist and Latitudinarian doctrine of what they called 'the nature and fitness of things.' Thus, after failing to find enough evidence in Scripture for his view that God's justice is always 'amiable' and aimed at 'the good of the community' rather than God's own honour and ignoring that God will have vengeance on whom he will have vengeance as outlined in Scripture, we find Fuller turning to reason and claiming 'As to the nature and fitness of things, we cannot draw any conclusion thence against the loveliness of vindictive justice, as a Divine attribute, unless the thing itself can be proved to be unlovely. But this is contrary to the common sense and practice of mankind.' He goes on to argue how his view of a 'lovely', wrathless vengeance and an amiable vindication is commonly accepted among the nations and concludes: 'Now if vindictive justice may be glorious in a human government, there is no reason to be drawn from the nature and fitness of things why it would not be the same in the Divine administration.'[73]

This method of understanding the Divine by examining the human is used by Fuller throughout his system and is typical of the 'Divine sagacity' of the Cambridge Platonists and Latitudinarians. It is also Hugo Grotius' *a posteriori* argument from rational deduction.

Latitudinarian 'fitness' teaching

A brief look at the history of the Latitudinarian sect will be advantageous in understanding correctly what Fuller means by 'the fitness of things'. Gilbert Burnet (1643-1715) describes his fellow Latitudinarian adherents such as Cudworth, More, Stillingfleet (who later changed his views) and Tillotson in the words:

> All these, and those who were formed under them, studied to examine farther into the nature of things than had been done formerly.

They declared against superstition on the one hand, and enthusiasm on the other. They loved the Constitution of the Church and the liturgy, and could well live under them: but they did not think it unlawful to live under another form. They wished that things might have been carried with more moderation. And they continued to keep a good correspondence with those who had differed from them in opinion, and allowed a great freedom in philosophy and divinity: from whence they were called men of latitude. And upon this men of narrower thoughts and fiercer tempers fastened upon them the name Latitudinarians. They read Episcopius much. And the making out the reasons of things being a main part of their studies, their enemies called them Socinians. They were all very zealous against popery. And so, they becoming soon very considerable, the papists set themselves against them to decry them as atheists, deists or at best Socinians.[74]

The Cambridge Platonists, or New Sect or New Philosophy as they were also called, believed that Truth comes in natural and revealed forms and reason is the faculty which apprehends and judges them to be what they are. Their maxim was 'Our reason is not confounded by our Religion, but awakened, excited, employed, directed, and improved.'[75]

The appealing idea of truth recognisable by reason
On the surface, the idea that Truth is recognisable by reason is appealing and, indeed, comforting. However, it soon became apparent to the Latitudinarians that the application of reason in discerning natural and revealed truth was greatly discriminating concerning the Word of God. While it was accepted that God revealed Himself in Nature as a benevolent being, the Latitudinarians' reason began to argue that, when viewing Scripture, the essentials must be separated from the inessentials. The spirit must be discovered where the letter conceals. It was as if they believed God had wrapped up his heavenly revelation in mere carnal coverings so that the reason of the rationalists could become 'more excited, employed, directed and improved.' God, however, was given credit for this gift of 'Divine sagacity' which enabled man to be a sure judge of what was essential in Scripture. Such 'Divine sagacity', which the Latitudinarians believed they possessed, was looked upon as the presence of God in the soul. Just as the inspired authors of Scripture were God-indwelt so God indwells our reason to make the Scriptures plain. These Latitudinarians had great trouble with the Calvinists on one side and the Arminians on the other. It was obvious to them, however, that their opponents had not

discovered this Divine principle within themselves. They did not reason differently; they were classified as unreasonable.

The essential law of nature or nature deified
A further development was that the essentials found in revealed religion, were thought to be a reflection of what was clearly to be seen in Nature or Natural Religion. Thus the work of the Scriptures was regarded as pointing to the excellencies of Natural Religion. In their controversy with the teachings of Descartes, the Cambridge Platonists developed the idea that the difference between right and wrong was not revealed through God's will but was basic to man's physical constitution in understanding the eternal nature of things or law of the ideal world. This was understood as a law essential to nature, rather than an arbitrary product of nature. Here, the Cambridge Platonists came very near to deifying nature or at least giving nature an existence independent of God's will. This suspicion must be seen as valid when one reads that these lovers of reason believed the law of the ideal world to be antecedent to God's will in the world He had created.

One does not have to read far into Andrew Fuller's works to find that he uses ideas, concepts and phraseology which are very much reminiscent of what came to be called the New Philosophy. These ideas had been exported to the New World and become dominant in the teaching of the New England School after Jonathan Edwards influence had ceased. This movement, probably influenced by the idea of a more theological emphasis than the Latitudinarians' New Philosophy, began to call themselves the New Divinity School. It is from New England that these views probably returned to Britain to take hold of Fuller's imaginative reason there. This would explain why Fuller was even more radical than the Latitudinarians in seeing God's will as being arbitrary rather than essential where he found it did not tie up with Natural Law. His view reflects Grotian influence, which, again, Fuller probably obtained via the New Divinity School which was a gathering place of European theological aberrations of all kinds.

Chandlerism compared with Fullerism
It would seem strange that Andrew Fuller, a convinced Dissenter, would adopt views of philosophers who were so very Anglican in their love for the teachings of the classical writers, the Early Church Fathers and philosophical speculation. These views, however had already breached British Dissenting strongholds in a more radical form through the teaching of the Semi-Arian Presbyterian minister Samuel Chandler (1693-1766). John Gill had adequately refuted this writer's heretical views in his masterly

work *The Moral Nature and Fitness of Things Considered Occasioned by Some Passages in the Rev. Mr. Samuel Chandler's Sermon, lately preached to the Societies for the Reformation of Manners*. As Fuller regarded Gill with great suspicion, he was probably not familiar with this work which might have put him on better paths.

Gill's view of 'the nature and fitness of things'

Gill starts his criticism of the nature and fitness of things theory by affirming that the phrase was on all lips as a sign of 'this enlightened age, this age of politeness, reason and good sense'. He suspects, however, that the phrase is used to camouflage the need for revelation and as a retreat when faced with the superior force of sound theological argument. Gill argues that one only needs to ask these common sense enthusiasts what nature are they talking about and what are 'things' and what is fit about them and most who use this fashionable phrase 'are at once silenced and confounded.'

Gill continues concerning Chandler:

> This Gentleman, not content to assert that the difference between moral good and evil is certain and immutable, which will be readily granted; further affirms that, 'this arises from the nature of things; is strictly and properly eternal; is prior to the will of God, and independent of it; is the invariable and eternal rule of the divine conduct, by which God himself regulates and determines his own will and conduct to his creatures; the great reason and measure of all his actions towards them, and is the supreme, original, universal and most perfect rule of action to all reasonable beings whatsoever: and that there are certain fitnesses and unfitnesses of things arising from hence, which are of the same nature with this distinction; and that this difference, and these fitnesses and unfitnesses are as easily discerned by mankind, as the differences between any natural and sensible objects whatever.'

Fuller more radical than even Chandler

This statement of Chandler's shows that though Fullerism is greeted as the new philosophy which put the Baptists back on the evangelical map, it is an old pseudo-intellectual heresy that was aired by Fuller's Dissenting predecessors and equally unmasked and refuted by the very men such as Gill on whose theology Fuller so misguidedly turned his back. It will be shown that Fuller followed Chandler's rationalism fairly closely but where he departed from Chandler, it was to emphasise that God did not even adhere closely to the eternal nature and fitness of things but added His own, strictly arbitrary revealed will to it in the Scriptures, complicating the simple matter of exercising one's reason no end.

Gill refutes Chandlerism as having nothing to do with the religion of the Bible as it postulates the nature and fitness of things as a deity who deserves the name of God more than the god who organises his ways by its rule. Thus we ought to worship this god rather than the God of Abraham, Isaac and Jacob. Before we start bowing before this all-recognisable god, Gill tells us to observe certain points. 1. Who gives us ideas of morals, God or nature? Every good and perfect gift comes from God who created heaven and earth and they reflect the moral perfections of His eternal nature. It is this nature that determines what is evil and what is good and the believer is exhorted to take this Divine nature as his standard. Evil is thus, not older than the good will of God but that which sets itself up against it. Man has no idea about what is good or evil apart from the revealed will of God. 2. Nothing is strictly and properly eternal but God. Thus any eternal nature and fitness of things must be found in God, in His nature. 3. God thus wills and commands right and fit things because they are, in themselves, fit and proper, just and good. They are not so simply because He commands them, though whatever God commands would be good and proper as He does not act outside of His good and proper nature. God cannot deny himself.

Gill finds Chandler most confusing in his arguments as he, at times, seems to be arguing that God is independent of Natural Law and at times subject to it. This dilemma is also Fuller's who feels, however, he can solve the problem by postulating two wills of God, the eternal and the temporary. The first being right because it agrees with the nature and fitness of things, the second is right merely as long as God requires it to be. Often he likens the eternal law to God's secret will and the temporary law to God's revealed will. Thus Fuller postulates a god who is often in conflict with His own will. He has a god who denies himself. This is nowhere more apparent than in Fuller's teaching on the law and the gospel.

Fuller shares Chandler's high view of fallen man

Chandler's view of man is very similar to Fuller's as he believes, 'nature itself hath seemed to have been friendly to mankind in this respect, which hath implanted a kind of constitutional abhorrence of vice in their mind, an instinctive prejudice against it, and fear to commit it.' Here is Fuller's theory of a knowledge of absolute goodness in man and a natural pursuit of happiness which he knows can be fulfilled in exercising his duties savingly. Against this Gill points out that:

man is shapen in iniquity, and conceived in sin; he is a transgressor from the womb; the carnal mind is enmity against God, and all that is good; and is not subject to the law of God, nor can it be; there is none that doeth good, no not one; nor is there any fear of God before their eyes. In how many instances has it appeared, that the imagination of the thoughts of man's heart is evil, and that continually? such who are renewed by the grace of God, and are enabled to live sober and religious lives, yet were sometimes foolish, disobedient, deceived; serving divers lusts and pleasures; living in malice and envy, hateful, and hating one another. Before their conversion, they walked according to the course of this world, according to the prince of the power of the air, the spirit that now worketh in the children of disobedience; among whom they all had their conversation in times past, in the lusts of their flesh, fulfilling the desires of the flesh, and of the mind; and were by nature children of wrath, even as others.[76]

Chandlerism is Antinomianism

For Gill, Chandlerism was absolute Antinomianism and he was careful to point out that it was such as Chandler who pointed the finger of accusation at such as Gill, calling him an Antinomian. So Gill can say: 'If the moral nature and fitness of things is the supreme, original, universal, and most perfect rule of action to all reasonable beings whatsoever, prior to, and independent of the will of God, then what need is there of the law of God? or, what regard should be paid, to it? Since, as it is said, "It is impossible that there can be a rule of action more excellent in itself, or more worthy the regard of reasonable beings." Now, to set aside, and disregard the law of God, as a rule of life and conversation or action, is strictly and properly Antinomianism.'

In spite of having such a wise Baptist father in the faith, indeed Master in Israel, to keep him on the straight and narrow path, Fuller chose Chandlerism and thus Antinomianism as his guide. To Fuller the great difference between the Old Testament dispensation and that of the New Testament is that members of the former felt they had to adhere slavishly to the Mosaic Law, whereas members of the latter are ruled by 'the nature and fitness of things'. Fuller is apparently not aware of any self-contradiction in his arguments in assuming that what is fully evident as pertaining to the nature and fitness of things to a Christian of his day was less evident to all those prior to Christ. This is because Fuller's moral deterrent philosophy actually deters only those who live after the pseudo-atonement declaration of moral justice took place at the death of Christ. It also appears that Fuller never developed a doctrine of the Old Testament Church. The enigma, however, remains. Actually, for Fuller, the gospel brings nothing new to the teaching of the Old Testament but merely provides the keys to unlock its secrets and separate what he calls the moral from the positive or the essential from the carnalities.

The Old Testament was law-bound, the New Testament founded on reason
Comparing the post New Testament Church with its Old Testament counterpart in his essay on *The Principle of Church Discipline,*[77] Fuller maintains:

> The form and order of the Christian church, much more than that of the Jewish church, are founded on *the reason and fitness of things*. Under the former dispensation, the duties of religion were mostly *positive*; and were of course prescribed with the nicest precision, and in the most exact minuteness. Under the gospel they are chiefly *moral*, and consequently, require only the suggestion of general principles. In conforming to the one, it was necessary that men should keep their eye incessantly upon the rule; but, in complying with the other, there is more occasion for fixing it upon the *end*.[78]

In the context Fuller is arguing that there is 'a want of fitness' in church life which 'impedes the growth of the spiritual Temple'. He thus stresses, in highly non-Scriptural and un-theological language, that, whereas the Jewish church was governed by *positive* rules and means, the New Testament Church is governed by a *moral* awareness of the natural harmony of the world i.e. the fitness of things, which needs a mere 'suggestion of general principles' to guide the believer, or rather the rationalist, to the right ends. But what on earth does this mean? Whatever it does mean, it is obviously not working as Fuller, in the context laments. His 'fitness of things' seems to be all theory and no practice. What are positive rules and what are moral ends? Is Fuller arguing that the Jews were expected to exercise a concrete, absolute righteous life but Christians have a much easier task, obeying mere 'suggestions' and 'general principles' in their life of holiness? Is this Neonomianism's 'easier way'? Why does Fuller use terms that are foreign to normal evangelical usage and which, when they emerged in the early part of the century, they were rightly severely criticised by the very Baptist leaders that Fuller accused of making the churches respectless and a 'dunghill in society'?

The questions such a radical view poses are endless as, if Fuller is correct, it would appear that all the orthodox saints up to his appearing were completely wrong about the Mosaic Law and the apostles themselves misunderstood their own task in relation to the Old Testament. In order to tackle these questions, it is necessary to make another rather laborious detour to consider more closely the second major philosophical source constituent in Fullerism. This is the teaching of Hugo Grotius.

5. Moral and positive obedience

Grotian influence on Fuller observed more fully

In Fuller's work *On Moral and Positive Obedience*, in which he explains his view of the triumph of the nature and fitness of things over the Mosaic Law, thus reaching gospel ends through its innate power, we have a frank and candid confession on Fuller's part, that he has adopted the teaching of the Grotian school. This taught that there are eternals such as the order of nature and temporals such as God's Law and revelations to man which are entirely arbitrary. The latter are right only because God commanded them and have no relation to the intrinsic nature of God's own character, nor to the 'fitness of things'.

This influence on Fuller by Grotian thinking has been denied consistently by Fullerites since Fuller started to teach the Grotian system openly in the 1780s. They were just not willing to admit that their idol had based his teachings on those of a man almost violently opposed to the Reformation. Nor were they willing to view the Holy Law as the eternal standard of God's Holy character and the yardstick of acceptance which He demanded of His Son in order to fulfil all righteousness. Now Fullerites, who have stormed and captured the citadels of the evangelical Establishment, confident of their stranglehold on the faith once committed to the saints, are making a clean breast of it. It has now become openly fashionable to define 'evangelical Calvinism' in terms of Grotianism. Nothing could be a greater insult to the truth. There was not a shred of gospel preaching in Grotius as he believed that man could basically understand the 'fitness of things' in the moral law and he outdid the Remonstrants in their hatred towards Calvinism. Nevertheless, we now find Prof. Michael Haykin, in a recently published work, arguing with obvious approval that one of the greatest factors which led Andrew Fuller and his closest associates away from what the author terms 'False Calvinism', was the teaching of the New Divinity School, influenced by the Grotian Moral Government Theory.[79] This theory denies that the Law is a reflection of God's essential nature, that Christ was the Sin-Bearer, that the atonement of Christ is a necessary revelation of the righteousness of God, that Christ's death was the penalty of a broken Law and a sacrifice through which God is reconciled to the sinner. It sees the entire work of redemption as a gigantic metaphor or sham demonstration of justice to serve as a moral deterrent. This view is more in keeping with Socinianism than with the Reformed Faith and indeed, Grotius propagated it to serve as a demarcation border between the two areas. Modern Grotians use it as a bridge to make it appear as if the opposite banks are in the very same country. Grotianism uses typical Reformed vocabulary such as 'substitution' and 'satisfaction' which make it appear orthodox to the unwary. On deeper examination, one finds that Grotian substitution is neither vicariously penal, nor redemptive but a figurative substitution for both truths and the term satisfaction refers to the airy-fairy doctrine of a 'satisfaction of benevolence', whatever that may be.

Michael Haykin in praise of the Grotian system
Haykin, in his book *One Heart and One Soul* discusses the influence of Jonathan Edwards and Joseph Bellamy on Fuller, Ryland and Sutcliff but does not distinguish between Edwards' and the New Divinity School's theology. It seems that he links them together for repectability's sake to give the impression that Bellamy was one with Edwards and both were Grotians. Though Edwards in his philosophical works viewed the fall as being a moral action alone, thus confusing the theological issue, he nevertheless held firmly to the Scriptural doctrine of the penal, vicarious, substitutionary death of Christ. Bellamy stressed that as man was only fallen morally, his salvation need only occur in the realm of morals. He thus began to teach the Grotianism that had so influenced the English Deists and Latitudinarians a century before him. As a corollary, he rejected penal substitution and the Reformed doctrine of imputation emphasising that Christ's death was a mere moral deterrent. As is clear from Fuller's quotes and arguments in *The Gospel Worthy of All Acceptation*, his teaching is based on Bellamy's and not Edward's.[80] Thus the Grotian doctrine that man's natural abilities, including his reason, are all intact and salvation comes through making the best use of them is the foundation on which Fullerism and modern Liberalism is built. It is now time to look closer at the way Grotianism has crept into Fullerism and changed the rules of law, faith and Christ maintained in the Scriptures to the rule of reason and an unseared conscience.

'Give me understanding and I shall keep thy law'
David's plea in Psalm 119 becomes very relevant when faced with Andrew

Fuller's analysis of the Law of God. In order to understand Fuller we must go back in time to 1625 when Grotius was writing his *The Rights of War and Peace*. In this work, Grotius deals with God's laws arguing that the primary law is the Law of Nature which is unchangeable and unalterable, even by God Himself. God is fully subject to it. This unchanging law can be seen *a priori* as it agrees with 'a reasonable and social nature' and *a posteriori* as it can be shown that the more civilised nations accept it. There is another kind of right or law which is 'voluntary right' derived from the will of either man or God. That derived from God's will is divine right or divine law. Now though Natural Law is eternally binding, the law arising from God's will is not. God's will, unlike the eternal law, is changeable. It is also, as it is not the same as Natural Law, arbitrary. It is not that God wills a thing because it is right. That would mean that God wills Natural Law, which He cannot do because it is there already. Divine law is right or binding, according to God's will, merely because He wills it. It is not right, therefore He wills it but it is right to Him because he arbitrarily wills it. Thus, though the Law of Nature never changes, divine law can, must and does. Thus divine law (written without capitals to distinguish it from the Law of Nature) is neither perfect nor faultless. It thus stands to reason that obeying the divine will to the very letter will never enable the sinner to get behind the arbitrary and temporary in order to understand the Eternal. He must use his natural, rational *a priori* and *a posteriori* capacities to see the spirit of the thing beyond the letter. This may seem more like Greek philosophy than Christian Divinity but it is possible to follow the reasoning, pagan as it may be. Grotius, however, complicates matters by often calling the Law of Nature divine because it is the law that rules God. Thus it is always difficult to find out, when Grotius is speaking in religious terms, whether he is speaking of the divine voluntary law or the Law of Nature which is Divine. He gives an example. The commandment regarding the Sabbath is, he believes, temporary, that is, it is a divine law. The spirit, however, behind it is that man should devote not less than a seventh of his time to divine worship. This is Natural Law. The day itself is not part of Natural Law. This is the very example Fuller also uses in his pastoral letter on moral and positive obedience mentioned in detail below. If one had asked Grotius how one could be sure that his interpretation of the Eternal Law was the spirit and the commandment the mere letter, he would have said, 'Use your natural reason.'

Sola scriptura rejected

With ideas like this, it is no wonder that Grotius gave up *sola scriptura* for the belief that the Church Fathers should be approached as the authoritative voice in judging what is an eternal truth and what is a mere temporary manifestation. It is also no wonder that if one approaches a modern Reformed theologian in Holland who bases his faith in the truths of Scripture and asks him his opinion of the Dutch theologian Grotius, he will answer, 'Grotius was a humanistic philosopher and not a theologian.' British, American and Canadian Fullerites, however, are of a different opinion and recent works show how they are backing Grotius against the supposed 'false Calvinism' of John Gill, James Hervey etc. i.e. against theologians of great note and spirituality. We notice, however, that Psalm 119 does not say, 'I have understanding and I shall keep the law. It says, 'Give me understanding'. David knew that common sense in fallen man was far from common. Grotius looked to man's power of reasoning to guide him in spiritual matters. David wanted the eternal mind of God on the matter. The mind of a God who never changes and has issued a Law that reflects His own sovereign unchangeable nature.

What has this to do with Andrew Fuller? Much indeed. This is also Fuller's basic view of Natural Law and divine law, though he complicates the matter even more than Grotius, adding his own 'evangelical' flair. This also explains why Fuller believes that all theology is based on natural theology which has still a positive, saving effect on fallen man. It also explains why he refuses to believe that both natural theology and the Mosaic Law work in a condemning way regarding man in telling him that he is both lost and without excuse. It is because of natural theology, revealing Natural Law, according to Fuller, that the revealed will of God built on it ought to be, and can be, understood.

Depraved men's duties

In his book *The Gospel Worthy of All Acceptation*, Fuller explains his theory of natural theology which departs radically from the theology behind Romans 1:20. Paul taught that nature points to a Creator and stops there. Fuller builds on this, saying, 'And the same law that obliged them (Adam, Moses and Israel) to love him in these discoveries of himself obliges us to love him in other discoveries, by which he has since more gloriously appeared, as *saving sinners through the death of his Son*.[81] To suppose that we are obliged to love God as manifesting himself in the works of creation and providence, but not in the work of redemption, is to suppose that in the highest and most glorious display he deserves no regard. The same perfections which appear in all his other works, and render him lovely, appear in this with a ten-fold lustre; to be obliged to love him on account of the one, and not the other, is not a little extraordinary.'[82] Fuller is speaking here of what the sinner has a duty to see 'notwithstanding the depravity of his nature'!

Astounding claims concerning natural theology
Fuller's claims for natural theology and man's abilities to recognise God
through it are truly astounding. The Bible teaches clearly that the Heavens
declare God's glory (Psalm 19:1) and Paul is quite explicit in teaching that
God's eternal power is seen in creation. However, neither David nor Paul
teach that through contemplating nature a man who is fallen is obliged or
even enabled to love God in a saving way. Fuller teaches that love
engendered through natural revelation produces spiritual discernment.
Paul's argument in Romans shows the opposite. Fallen man, faced with
natural revelation has changed its truth's into lies and can only see lies in
creation. Creation is dead to him as a means of revelation. God has thus
dealt mercifully with man in giving him what he desired. He has left man in
his ignorance, an ignorance which can only be removed when Christ comes
into his life. Fuller's argument, however, right through his book is that
what is discernible rationally is also discernible spiritually. 'He that loves
God for any excellency, as manifested in one form, must of necessity love
him for that excellency, let it be manifested in what form it may.'[83] Here, it
seems, Fuller is contradicting himself as he elsewhere argues so strongly
that there are no necessities in religion. Such passages refer, however, to
the necessity of being condemned whereas in this passage taken from his
Gospel Worthy of All Acceptation, he is talking about natural theology
and man's logical abilities. Fuller, because of his high view of man, does
not accept that God is not recognisable in any form by man. The only god
man recognises according to Philippians 3:19 is his belly, i.e. his own
selfish self. This does not trouble Fuller in any way, however, as he believes
the natural desires of the human 'belly' are for the common good. He is
thus open to any revelation which is given either through natural revelation
or the revealed will of God which is to be interpreted through it.

Natural operations of love to God extinct in fallen man
Fuller speaks much of the 'natural operation of love to God' but this is
absolutely extinct in fallen man. Adam exercised such love, but Adam fell.
We love, says the Scriptures, because Christ first loved us. Any love to
God, according to the Bible, reflects God's own natural love in thanksgiving
after God has given His own love to man through salvation in Jesus Christ.
True love, is shown in Christ's voluntary will in saving His flock by fulfilling
the law on their behalf and writing His commandments i.e. the law he
fulfilled, on their hearts. This is, a contrary gospel to Fuller's, however, as
he does not see any absolute authority in the Biblical Law as it is God's
voluntary will which has hidden its light or spirit under the bushel of the
letter which is to be rejected.

Fuller thus remains blind and stubborn, arguing that there are laws of natural religion which prompt a man to love God. He can thus argue, quoting 'an able writer', 'If a sinner, therefore, who hears the gospel have these suitable affections of love to God and hatred of sin, to which he is obliged by the laws of natural religion, these things cannot be separated from a real complacency in that redemption and grace which are proposed in revealed religion.'[84] Huntington summed up Fuller's faith by saying his 'points of thought' were his 'points of faith' in order to stress that Fuller's gospel was all in the mind and not in the Scriptures.

Now we are in a position to understand why Fuller emphasises so much that fallen man experiences a duty to love God on hearing the gospel. Though he is cursed by the Mosaic Law, indeed, slain by it, and is thus dead in trespasses and sins, there is another law which is stronger than the Mosaic Law i.e. 'the law of natural religion' which opens a man's eyes to the love of God. He is thus enabled to see the nature and fitness of things by means of this Natural Law.

Men with the same powers to believe as to disbelieve
It is obvious that Fuller cannot accept the total depravity of man as he does not view what he calls man's 'moral inability' to believe as pervading his total nature. Apart from in the field of morals, fallen 'men have the same natural powers to love Christ,' he tells us, 'as to hate him, to believe as to disbelieve'.[85] He is actually saying that just as fallen man is free and able to hate Christ, he is also free and able to believe in him. The only thing that is stopping him, is not his completely fallen nature but his lack of moral principles. Man *could* believe if he *would*! If this is not a total denial of man's total depravity, it is difficult to imagine what is. This is reducing man's fall to one aspect of his nature only. The Bible teaches that not only man as man but the entire creation in all its aspects is groaning and travailing under sin. As Cowper the poet puts it, 'Sin marr'd all'. The very blood and bones, body, soul and spirit of man is fallen. There is nothing in him which works 'normally'. He is fully scarred by the wages of sin and even the elect must bear their physical and mental deficiencies, not merely moral inabilities, with them to the grave. Man has no natural, nor rational powers to believe in Christ because sin permeates his very being. Fuller begs to differ.

Fuller revealed his Chandler-Grotian view of law in his 1807 pastoral circular letter to the churches of the Northamptonshire Association entitled *On Moral and Positive Obedience*. Though the topic, one would think, is highly philosophical and completely unfitting for a pastoral address, Fuller makes no apologies but argues that the topics of moral and positive obedience are the 'most discriminating principles' of religion. In other words, those who abide by them are marked off as true Christians.

The essentiality of distinguishing between two fully different laws of God emphasised

When viewing the revealed will of God in whatever form it is delivered and which must be obeyed, Fuller argues, we must distinguish between the moral and the positive. This is far from being a novel distinction, Fuller explains and if we do not understand this, he argues, we cannot possibly understand the Scriptures. Concerning this crucial and vital distinction, Fuller says:

> Without it, we should confound the eternal standard of right and wrong given to Israel at Sinai (the sum of which is love to God and our neighbour) with the body of 'carnal ordinances imposed upon them until the time of reformation.' We should also confound those precepts and examples of the New Testament which arise from the relations we stand in to God and to one another, with positive institutions which arise merely from the sovereign will of the Lawgiver, and could never have been known had he not expressly enjoined them.

Anyone familiar with the Latitudinarian, Cambridge-Platonistic and Grotian theories which were swept away by the pioneering teaching of John Gill, and the Calvinistic Awakening will now begin to grow rather suspicious. Is Fuller advocating Grotianism? Is he saying that moral precepts are natural and eternal whereas positive laws which 'arise merely from the sovereign will of the Lawgiver' are temporary, a mere carnal imposition to reform us into seeing the true spiritual light of reason i.e. once we see the relationship we stand in to God and to one another, they are dispensable? This would seem to be the case as Fuller goes on to affirm:

> Concerning the former, an inspired writer does not scruple to refer the primitive Christians to that sense of right and wrong which is implanted in the minds of men in general; saying, 'Whatsoever things are *true*, whatsoever things are *honest*, whatsoever things are *just*, whatsoever things are *pure*, whatsoever things *lovely*, whatsoever things are of *good report*; if there be any virtue, and if there be any praise, think on these things.' But concerning the latter, he directs their whole attention to Christ, and to those who acted under his authority. 'Be ye followers of me as I also am of Christ.' - 'Now I praise you, brethren, that ye remember me in all things, and keep the *ordinances* as I delivered them to you.' The one is commanded because it is right; the other is right because it

is commanded. The great principles of the former are of perpetual obligation, and know no other variety than that which arises from the varying of relations and conditions; but those of the latter may be binding at one period of time, and utterly abolished at another.

Grotianism pure and unadulterated

This is Grotianism served up pure and unadulterated. Men in general know what is true, honest, just, pure, lovely and of good report and these are eternals but the commands of Holy Writ and the ordinances of Christ are as the chaff blown by the wind. Here today and gone tomorrow. Fuller is advising his readers to follow their sense of right and wrong which will eternally guide them but following Christ through the inspired word of the Apostles will provide them with but a temporary solution to their problems. Such are mere carnal ordinances which merely serve as a momentary instrument to set one's affections on the eternals which rival God in their importance and outdo God in their authority as He is subject to them. But Fuller has more of this to offer. Still distinguishing eternal reason from the temporary revelation of God's voluntary will, he says:

> We can clearly perceive that it were inconsistent with the perfections of God not to have required us to love him and one another, or to have allowed of the contrary. Children also must needs be required to 'obey their parents; for this is right.' But it is not thus in positive institutions. Whatever wisdom there may be in them, and whatever discernment in us, we could not have known them had they not been expressly revealed; nor are they ever enforced as being *right* in themselves, but *merely as being of Divine appointment.*[86] Of them we may say, Had it pleased God, we might in various instances have enjoined the opposites; but of the other we are not allowed to suppose it possible, or consistent with righteousness, to require any thing different from that which is required.
>
> The design of moral obligation is to preserve order in creation; that of positive institutions, among other things, to prove us, whether, like Abraham in offering up his son, we will yield implicit to God's commandments, or whether we will hesitate till we perceive the reason of them. The obligation of man to love and obey his Creator was coeval with his existence; but it was not till God had planted a garden in Eden, and there put the man he had formed, and expressly prohibited the fruit of one of the trees under pain of death, that he came under a positive law. The former could approve itself to

his conscience as according with the nature of things; the latter as being commanded by his Creator.

Laws of *mere* Divine appointment
Here is Andrew Fuller's view of the inspiration of the Bible and the laws and precepts of God revealed in the Bible. All that fallen man's reason and conscience - Fuller has apparently never heard of a seared conscience - dictate to him, all that fallen man can 'clearly perceive', is what religion is made of. All God's precepts must be tested by this yardstick and if this yardstick reveals that the precepts are '*merely* as being of Divine appointment', then we can be safely assured that this revelation is completely arbitrary, is not 'right' in itself, and can be revoked at any time according to God's ever-changing voluntary will. Fullerites find in such statements of Fuller marks of genius but to claim that God's laws are merely of Divine appointment in contrast to the eternal laws of the fitness of things, and that God might just as easily have commanded the very opposite, is downright blasphemy and the height of Antinomianism. It is thus quite ominous that, when quoting Ephesians 6:1, Fuller leaves out those important words 'in the Lord' which, to him, would refer merely to a 'positive obligation' and merely quotes what he feels is the true moral law which is 'Children also must needs be required to "obey their parents; for *this is right*"'. Orthodox Christians would argue that what is absolutely right is that which is 'in the Lord' and if the Lord's will is left out, there is no guarantee of rightness.

Understanding the light by its shadow
Fuller's use of the story of Abraham and Isaac shows how far he is from gospel truths. Here we have a unique example of God testing a unique individual who plays a key part in the story of redemption which is completed and perfected in the New Testament. This moved the inspired author of the book of Hebrews to call the Old Testament concepts mere shadows and pointers of what is to come. Instead of using the light of the New Testament to illuminate the old, Fuller grovels around in its shadows, using the light of fallen reason to illuminate his path. A path which leads him to believe that shadows are the true revelation concerning Christ and Christ's New Testament precepts are only there to be illuminated by the shadows. When realising that the covenant of works was a mere 'positive', i.e. arbitrary, rule for Fuller, one can understand why he can dismiss its permanency. In doing so, he leaves out of account that it is Christ's work on the cross that fulfils the covenant of works on our behalf and on the Day of Judgement we shall only stand righteous before God because of

Christ's redemptive deed. Our eternal life is fully dependent on Christ's eternal keeping of the covenant of works in His own nature. Christ never changes in the way He fulfils and establishes the law. This means that the requirements of the law which Christ kept, reflect His own eternal character which is imputed to us. Never was there a greater substitution of 'the nature of things' for the will of God, natural revelation for Divine revelation, prophesy for its fulfilment, natural morals for the character of Christ and the law of reason for grace than in the system of Andrew Fuller. It is no wonder that modern Fullerites are anxious to label such men as Crisp, Gill, Romaine, Hervey, Toplady, Huntington, Hawker and Gadsby as Antinomians as they strove to show the folly of being ruled by reason and looked to the grace of God and His Divine eternal will for their unchanging rules of life. They fully believed, as Scripture testifies, that the path to true holiness was through faith in Christ and obedience to His precepts through the indwelling power of the Holy Spirit. Judged by the standards of such men which are the standards of both the Old Testament and the New, Fullerism is the gospel of Antinomianism which is no gospel at all.

To which Law was Christ obedient and which is our rule of life?

True to his own nature of redefining the lovingly-held Bible concepts of orthodox Christians, Fuller is not done with explaining away the laws and precepts of God. After telling his flock that positive laws are arbitrary, he goes on to explain that even moral laws are not what they seem to be. He now tells them that if they did 'everything according to the letter of moral precepts, we shall often overlook the true intent of them, and do that which is manifestly wrong.' Indeed, he argues that, 'It was not our Lord's design, in these precepts, to regulate external actions so much as motives.'

This view completely challenges the Reformed faith which maintains that it is Christ's obedience to the law which shows Him to be worthy of becoming the Captain of our salvation. We must now ask Fuller to which of his laws Christ was obedient. If Christ were obedient to a mere 'positive law', He was not obedient to the eternal nature of God but merely to a temporal, arbitrary law of God which was not *ipso facto* right therefore it was commanded but it was only arbitrary and temporally right because it was commanded for and applied to a particular situation at a particular time. Even in this particular situation and at this particular time, God, explained Fuller, never expected obedience to cover the letter but the principle and spirit only.

Here again, we see how Fuller takes normal words and radically changes their meaning. A 'positive' precept, especially when it is known as a precept of Christ's, would mean to a normal English-speaking person something good and permanent and worthy of following to the letter. Fuller, however, gives the word 'positive' a negative meaning by introducing 'positive obligations' as temporary obligations which are less than perfect. Fuller even speaks of Christ's obedience to His Father's Law, which traditional Christianity sees as being an obedience to every jot and tittle, as if such obedience were not at all necessary and the Law not worth the effort. One is reminded of the old pagan Roman sacrifices whereby the Christians were expected to give a token sign of acceptance of the Roman Laws by throwing a pinch of incense into a fire, even when it was obvious that they did not believe one jot or tittle of them. Fuller can thus argue concerning the Saviour who died for him, 'though he may not confine himself to a literal conformity to those rules of justice which he has marked out for us, yet he will certainly not depart from the spirit of them. Justice must be satisfied even in this way. An atonement made by a substitute, in any case, requires that the same end be answered by it, as if the guilty party had actually suffered. It is necessary that the displeasure of the offended should be expressed in as strong terms, or in a way adapted to make as strong an impression upon all concerned, as if the law had taken its course, otherwise atonement is not made, and mercy triumphs at the expense of righteousness.'

Here we have Fuller's Antinomianism unleashed again. Christ has one law for sinners and saints and another for Himself. It was not necessary for the Law to take its course in the vicarious atoning death of Christ. It is thus no wonder that Fuller does not believe in imputed righteousness as Christ went another way than the one intended for mankind. It is also no wonder that Fuller has no doctrine of Christian holiness and sanctification as absolute conformity to the will of God as reflected in His nature and expressed in His Law, though seen as a 'positive' law for the Jews, is in no way called for concerning Christians. Absolute conformity seems to be contrary to 'the nature and fitness of things'. As God commands, 'Be ye holy as I am holy,' we are only to presume, according to Fuller, that God does not demand absolute holiness even of Himself as such commands are merely 'positive'!

Parity of reasoning
Here we note several points that stand at enmity with both God's Law and His gospel. A literal conformity to the law is not required but to its spirit or, as Fuller says elsewhere, its principle. It is still not clear, however, whether Fuller is referring to his positive or his moral law. Is he thinking merely of revealed precepts or the law of the fitness of things? Though Fuller strives

to define what he means by 'spirit' and 'principle' in several essays,
especially in his *On Moral and Positive Obedience*, he presents such a
arbitrary meaning of the words that one is reminded of the 'situation ethics'
of later Liberalism. It would seem that what is the spirit of the law to one
person at one particular time could be differently interpreted by another
person at another time. Indeed, following Fuller's system, Christ Himself
would apply and fulfil the law, be it positive or moral, in one situation and
time-period differently to another. Christ, according to Fuller, certainly
fulfilled a less strenuous law than was required by the Mosaic Law of man.
Fuller seems to place his hope here on what he calls 'parity of reasoning'.
It is up to Christ, as it is up to believers to apply the correct reasoning to
the correct situation. Here again, we have nothing but situation ethics
which does away with all absolutes and sure and certain guidelines. Indeed,
Fuller spends far more time telling his readers that they are liable to
misunderstand moral precepts if they keep to their letter than he does in
teaching them what these moral precepts really mean and how one can live
a life in the Spirit. It would be interesting to know, for instance, how it
would be wrong in following the letter of the moral law which says, 'Thou
shalt not bear false witness against thy neighbour' and how one might
carry out its spirit without obeying the letter. Surely the point of God's
laws is that one should not merely follow their letter but also their spirit.
This is not an 'either or' matter but a 'both the one and the other'.

Ends without means

It is very noticeable in all Fuller's pronouncements regarding Christ's
redemptive work that the exact role of Christ in His obedience to the law is
blurred and at times explained away. The end is always put forward in a
way which makes the means almost superfluous. The end, too, is highly
questionable. Thus the goal of the atonement, for Fuller, is merely 'to make
as strong an impression on all concerned' through the sufferings of the
moral substitute. This again, is pure Grotianism. Grotius sees the atonement
as a mere moral deterrent to make an impression on men so that they will be
frightened off sinning. In emphasising that this 'strong impression' was
just 'as if the law had taken its course', Fuller is highlighting that for him
the law did not take its course in the vicarious penal and capital punishment
of Christ. It was not necessary as God did not expect His Son to fulfil the
letter of the law but merely to give God the opportunity to demonstrate His
displeasure at law-breakers tokenwise.

Fuller is never more self-contradictory, however, as when he is dealing
with the moral law which he continually mistakes for the Gospel itself.
Though Fuller denies that the revealed law was ever meant to give life, he

does actually believe that fallen man can still find life in natural law. He also believes that through the moral law, which is his interpretation of natural law, man, encouraged by the promise of clemency and rewards in the gospel, can find Christ. The moral law therefore, does not condemn men directly but it points to Christ and in rejecting Christ the aim of the law is not met and damnation ensues. This is the theology of the old Latitudinarians who believed that faith came through obeying the duties of the moral law. This duty-faith was then a legal duty faith and not faith which is a gift of God through grace. The Latitudinarians believed they had surmounted this difficulty by arguing that the goal of the moral law was Christ, thus keeping the law was keeping in Christ, thus receiving all the graces of Christ. This is hardly Fullerism, however, as Fuller emphasises the actuality of living a life in harmony with the nature and fitness of things, but he rejects receiving anything whatsoever by way of transfer from Christ, let alone 'all the graces'. Fuller's often mentioned 'end' of which gospel revelation is a mere figurative 'means' is never actually revealed or fully reasoned out in Fuller's system. Thus there is no solid hope of salvation in Fuller's teaching. The Biblical way to heaven in his map of salvation is marked out in winding paths of symbols of signs of imagery and metaphor illustrated with pseudo-philosophic axioms which can only totally confuse and disorientate the Christian pilgrim.

The Gospel merely encourages man to see where he is better off
In his essay *Faith in Christ Being a Requirement of the Moral Law* [87] against Dan Taylor, Fuller takes up this Latitudinarian thought that one can still approach God in Christ through following one's duties to the Law. [88] Taylor sees the Law as the invariable rule of what is right or wrong, yet Fuller still accuses him of abrogating the law as he does not view following the Law as equivalent to following Christ. He also accuses Taylor of believing that the gospel brings in new injunctions as he does not believe that the moral law contains all the injunctions necessary for understanding and accepting the gospel. In his typical evasive and ambiguous language, Fuller claims, 'I suppose the gospel, strictly speaking, to contain no injunctions at all, but merely the good tidings of salvation by Jesus Christ; and that, whatever precepts or injunctions are to be found respecting its being embraced, they are the diversified language of the moral law, which obliges men, as P. (Taylor) himself allows, to 'embrace whatever God reveals,'

Again, Fuller is showing himself as less of a Bible theologian than Taylor as he completely abrogates the clear distinction between law and gospel. He argues that the only difference between the law and gospel is that the former *obliges* the sinner to turn to Christ but the latter *encourages* him to follow his obligations. Using the story of the Prodigal Son, Fuller argues that it was only right that the Prodigal should return to his father, but he was encouraged to do so knowing the clemency of his parent and that there was bread enough in his house. It was the pardon expected that encouraged him to follow his obligations. Thus, it is right and proper for man to turn to Christ through the law as this obligation, Fuller claims, is clearly defined, but the gospel gives him the encouragement needed to take the step. Rewards are given where duties are performed. This is Fuller's view of duty-faith which is still works-faith based on seeking rewards by the cool calculations of natural reason which, Fuller maintains, the gospel encourages. The Prodigal's salvation was due to his carefully calculating where he was better off. Typical here is Fuller's recognition that the Prodigal 'came to himself', that is, he saw the nature and fitness of things, or, as Fuller puts it here, he saw what was 'right and fit'. He obeyed the moral law which shows what is right because it is right in itself. Luke 15 tells us, however, that the Prodigal realised that he had sinned against heaven and in his father's sight and was not worthy to be his son. This is not mentioned at all by Fuller, probably because this would refer to his so-called 'positive law' which Fuller believes is only right because God says so. He thus tells Taylor in another letter on the same subject, that he confuses the positive law with moral law. The latter, Fuller tells Taylor, arises from 'the nature of things,' but the former 'from the mere will of the lawgiver'.[89] It seems thus that Taylor, the Arminian, believed that the will of the Father (positive law) was that which determined the 'nature and fitness of things'. Calvin would have agreed. Such a thought is folly to Fuller.

In his masterly analysis of the relation of law to gospel entitled *The Law Established in a Life of Faith*, William Huntington points out that the work of the Law is to discover sin and deliver man up as a condemned criminal. It furnishes the unjustified sinner with an accuser before God and thus the Law separates the sinner completely from his Maker. The Law, however, cannot subdue sin; it cannot give the sinner dominion over it; it cannot give man a second chance nor lift the sentence of death from him. The Law knows no pardon and can neither give life to the sinner or quicken him spiritually. The Law cannot justify a man nor even bring a man to the Saviour of itself without God's effectual call. Huntington thus concludes that it is scandalous to argue that the Law contains all the injunctions and powers of the gospel. It has its own work to do as also the Rule of Faith and the Rule of Christ. Those who confuse them, as he believed Fuller certainly did, confuse Law with gospel and thus have no true Law and no true gospel.

Carrots and lollipops

What Fuller is saying in his works against Taylor, is that in doing one's duty to the law[90] one is expressing one's love to God and thus faith in Christ. 'If love to God *include* faith in Christ wherever he is revealed by the gospel, then the moral law, which expressly requires the former, must also require the latter.' Here we see that both law and gospel in Fuller's theology provide a way for a sinner to trust in Christ. There are no new rules in the gospel, it is merely the good news to encourage a sinner to keep the moral law. It is the carrot to keep the donkey moving. But what human agency can keep up with Fuller's donkey and where is the donkey going? Returning to the Prodigal, i.e. to Fuller's example of a human donkey, we see that if there is any indication of a known 'end' of salvation in Fuller's system of metaphorical means, it is not union with Christ; it is not God's glory; it is not even obtaining Christ's righteousness. In confusing new covenant faith in Christ with old covenant legal duties, Fuller is metaphorising away Christ's Person, Work and Office. The 'end' is merely the happiness of being satisfied in reaching one's aims and knowing that one is pardoned into the bargain! God's purpose is thus revealed in his being an indulgent and benevolent father, giving his spoilt brat the lollipop that he basically desired. This is obviously why Fuller could not accept the teaching of the Marrow Men who taught that the Mosaic Law was established in the Law of Faith and the Law of Christ. These take one far away from the Hopkinsian doctrine of the law of personal happiness which is the natural law of Fuller. It is interesting that Fuller here refers his readers to pp. 351-353 and 377[91] of his work *The Gospel Worthy of All Acceptance* for proof that 'love to God includes love to Christ'. These pages, however, deal with Fuller's doctrine of natural theology on which he bases his system that it is the duty of all fallen men to believe in Christ savingly. Every man has his own natural gospel within him i.e. Natural Law.

Fulfilling the law is allegedly accepting the gospel

As a corollary of this, Fuller believes that the accusation which comes via the law is not that the law has been disobeyed as *law* but that in disobeying the law *Christ* has been disobeyed and judgement comes through denying Christ. As proof of this, Fuller gives John 5:45, 'Do not think that I will accuse you to the Father: there is one that accuses you, even Moses, in whom ye trust. For if ye would have believed Moses, ye would have believed me: for he wrote of me. But if ye believe not his writings, how shall ye believe my words?' Of this passage Fuller says, 'It is very plain, I think, from this passage, that the thing for which Moses would accuse them was a rejection of Christ and the way of salvation by him; which, according to

our Lord's reasoning, implied a rejection of the writings of Moses. From
hence, therefore, it is inferred that a compliance with the gospel is what the
law of Moses requires, and a non-compliance with it is a matter for which
that law will accuse and condemn.'[92]

A number of objections must be brought against such an interpretation.
First, the statement that Moses wrote of Christ refers to the promises not
the commanding and condemning aspects of the Mosaic Law. The Mosaic
Law points to the state and needs of man and the Promises point to the
grace that is to come with Christ to meet those needs and transform that
state. This is the grace which Abraham, also in covenant with God, looked
forward to, although he did not know the Mosaic Law. Second, Christ in
speaking of the accusations of Moses refers to the covenant of works but
the reference concerning Moses writing of Christ is to the covenant of
promise, leading to the New Testament covenant of grace. Both of these
covenants were rejected by the Jews in question. They had failed to live
according to the Law and failed to believe the One with whom they were
speaking. They had thus rejected both the Law and the Promises. Christ,
however, was not accusing them but the law which they had broken. Their
ensuing blindness had rendered them unable to see the revelation of Christ
of which Moses had spoken. The Scriptures make it plain that though all
have broken the Law, those who believe in Christ will be saved. The Jews
were law-breakers and grace-rejecters at the same time. They were thus
doubly and finally damned. Third, it does not follow from this that the Law
is identical with the Promises and thus the Law equally proscribes an
acceptation of the gospel. The Law condemns and slays when it is broken
and the gospel brings liberty and life when it is accepted. Confusing the
Law and the gospel in this way leads to Antinomianism as the very purpose
and function of the Law is denied. It also is a rejection of the gospel which
plainly teaches that there is no hope for fallen man in seeking righteousness
by performing the works of the Law. This is why God gave the Jews the
promises. The gospel teaches that the free gift of the righteousness of
Christ will be given to those who are granted repentance and believe, not
to those who are under the Law. 'By him all that believe are justified from
all things, from which ye could not be justified by the law of Moses.' (Acts
13:39)

Grace subservient to the Law
In concluding this section it is obvious that grace for Fuller is subservient
to the law but his view of the law is entirely different from the Biblical
conception i.e. as God's eternal standard accomplished and fulfilled in
Christ who stands in our stead. As to what law the believer, as indeed,

Christ, should follow, Fuller teaches that our natural reason and desires ought to make clear. Fuller's gospel is telling the spiritual blind that their reason can make them whole. This is not Christianity. It is certainly the most Antinomian of man-made religions ever designed as it teaches that man's agency triumphs and decides over God's purpose. It is with this thought in mind that we now consider Fuller's doctrines of the gospel in more detail.

---

[1] *Works*, vol. II. See especially pp. 686-687.

[2] *Works*, vol. II, pp. 686, 688, 690-91.

[3] P. 688.

[4] Ibid, p. 688.

[5] Ibid, p. 688, also vol. III, p. 694.

[6] Emphasis Fuller's.

[7] *Conversation on Imputation, Works*, vol. II, p. 683.

[8] *Works*, vol. II, p. 155 ff. Note that here, as so often, Fuller is speaking in terms of 'the nature and fitness of things' rather than in Biblical terminology and concepts.

[9] E. Clipsham, *Andrew Fuller and Fullerism*, 3, BQ, p. 222.

[10] *Works*, vol. II, p. 682.

[11] *Works*, vol. II, p. 689.

[12] Ibid, p. 375.

[13] Ibid, pp. 682-683.

[14] See this essay in *Works*, vol. II, pp. 680-687 and Fuller's Letter II against Booth, vol. II, pp. 702-706. Both these articles are typical of Fuller's method of both dodging and confusing the issue. In his attacks on Booth, Fuller is guilty of downright duplicity and self-contradiction.

[15] Vol. II, p. 682.

[16] *Works*, vol. IX, pp. 277-278.

[17] *Works*, vol. II, p. 705, note and passim.

[18] 1 Peter 1:16.

[19] See *Works*, vol. II p. 438, *Reply to Mr. Button.*

[20] Ibid, vol. II, p. 745. Modern Fullerite criticism is met in my Chapter 'A Saint is Slandered', *John Gill and the Cause of God and Truth.*

[21] *Memoir of Mr. Fuller, Works*, I, p. 38. A. G. Fuller's emphasis.

[22] *Apparent Contradictions, Works*, vol. I, p.668. Emphasis Fuller's

[23] See Arthur Kirkby's PhD thesis, *The Theology of Andrew Fuller and its relation to Calvinism*, Edin., 1956, p. 160.

[24] *Works*, vol. II, p. 667.

[25] *Works*, vol. III, p. 38. See also *i. The Image of God*, E. Clipsham, *Andrew Fuller and Fullerism*, 3, BQ, p. 218,

[26] *Works*, vol. III, *Moral and Positive Obedience*, p. 357.

[27] *Works*, vol. III, p. 452.

[28] *Works*, vol. I, pp. 124-125.

[29] *The Reality an Efficacy of Divine Grace, Works*, vol. II, pp. 546-547.

[30] *Works*, vol. II, p. 355.

[31] Particular Baptists who still hold the doctrines of grace in the U.S.A. refer to Calvinistic Baptists of the pre-Fullerite age as the Old School and those adopting Fullerite teachings as the New School.

[32] *Works*, vol. II, p. 367.

[33] *Works*, vol. II, p. 829 ff.

[34] *Works*, vol. II, p. 660 ff.

[35] Ibid, p. 762 ff.

[36] Ibid, p. 737 ff.

[37] See Fuller's *Reply to Philanthropos, Works*, vol. II, p. 459 ff.

[38] See *Reply to Philanthropos, Works*, vol. II, 459 ff.

[39] Ibid, p. 505.

[40] Fuller's emphasis.

[41] *Works*, vol. II, pp. 701, 709.

[42] Collingridge, vol. III, *Every Divine Law in the Heart of Christ*, p. 530.

[43] *Works*, Posthumous Letters, Letter CXXIV (Dec. 28, 1807), vol. 8, Bensley, undated, p. 306.

[44] See Letter CXLVII, *Gleanings from the Vintage*, Collingridge, vol. V, p. 192.

[45] Fuller's emphasis.

[46] My emphasis.

[47] See Dr. J. Ryland's, *Memoir of Mr. Fuller*, London, 1818, p. 238.

[48] *Works*, vol. II, p. 762 ff.

[49] Angus Library Collection.

[50] As the church members came from several different denominations, plus the newly converted, the Serampore church practised open communion. Fuller protested that 'none but "real Christians" should be admitted to communion', meaning those who were baptised according to *his* understanding of the people of God, Church order and baptism. See E. Daniel Potts, *I Throw Away the Gun to Preserve the Ship: A Note on the Serampore Trio*, B.Q., xx, 1963-64. See also *Works*, vol. II, p. 503 ff.

[51] Bensley, vol. 8, *Posthumous Letters*, Letter CXXIV, pp. 307-309.

[52] Fuller distinguishes between the law considered as moral and the law considered as 'positive obligations'. The inadequacy of this distinction will be discussed later.

[53] Explanations mine.

[54] *I Throw Away the Gun to Preserve the Ship: A Note on the Serampore Trio*, vol. 2, Deuteronomy to Kings, The Baptist Standard Bearer, pp. 32, 38-39.

[55] Job 42:7 ff.

[56] Ibid, p. 756.

[57] A reference to the famous London market.

[58] See Fuller's review of the *Voice of Years*, *Works*, vol. II, p. 762 for another scurrilous, indeed, sordid attack on Huntington.

[59] Taken from Letter CCCCLXIV, Cricklewood, *Huntington's Posthumous Letters*, vol. 3, p.162.

[60] See Huntington's detailed analysis of Antinomianism in *Moses Unveiled in the Face of Christ*, Collingridge, vol. V, pp. 557-8. Apart from a thoroughly Scriptural view of the subject it is, at the same time, a masterly refutation of Fullerism.

[61] *Works*, vol. II, p. 418.

[62] Mr. Wesley's Letter, Hervey's *Works*, p. 477.

[63] Prefaced to Hervey's *Aspasio Vindicated.*

[64] *Letters to the Rev. Mr. Wesley, Works*, p. 539.

[65] See Berkof's *Systematic Theology*, BOT, IV., *Man in the Covenant of Works.*

[66] See *The Economy of the Covenants Between God and Man*, Chapter IX. *Covenant of Works.*

[67] Ibid, p. 152.

[68] *Works*, vol. II, p. 375.

[69] See also Ezekiel 20:11, 13,20; Luke 10:28 and Galatians 3:12.

[70] *Works*, vol. II, p. 375.

[71] See E. Clipsham's apology for this teaching in his *Andrew Fuller and Fullerism 3.* , BQ, p. 220.

[72] Some modern Fullerites would reject this Antinomian thought but how is one to give Fuller's words another interpretation? He says, 'God requires nothing of fallen creatures as a term of life. He requires them to love him with all their hearts, the same as if they had never apostatised.' *Works*, vol. II, pp. 375-376.

[73] *Works*, vol. II, p. 156, *The Promotion of Morality in General.*

[74] Taken from *Hastings Encyclopaedia of Religion and Ethics*, vol. III, entry under Cambridge Platonists, p. 167 ff.

[75] Ibid, p. 168.

[76] Psalm 51:5, Isaiah 48:8, Romans 8:7, Romans 3:12, 18, Genesis 6:10, Titus 3:3, Ephesians 2:3.

[77] *Works*, vol. III, p. 452.

[78] Fuller's emphasis. See John Gill's refutation of this philosophy in favour of 'the superior force and evidence of divine revelation' in his *The Moral Nature and Fitness of Things Considered, occasioned by some passages in the Rev. Mr. Samuel Chandler's Sermon, Lately preached to the Societies for the Reformation of Manners, Sermons and Tracts*, vol. 3, p. 463 ff.

[79] See *One Heart and One Soul*, EP, 1995, pp. 139 ff., 300 ff. Haykin teaches that Grotianism is of the very substance of Evangelical Calvinism. He surprisingly links John Sutcliff and David Brainerd with Grotianism through the New Divinity School. Here Haykin's evidence is weak in the case of Sutcliff and non-existent in the case of

Brainerd. The latter had great difficulty in preaching penal substitution to the Indians as they had no legal or commercial culture to provide forms of expression for it. Nevertheless, he stuck to the penal and commercial language of the Bible. If he had been a Grotian, this would have been the first phraseology he would have abandoned as Grotians do not believe in the idea of sin being a debt to the Law and Christ being a Ransom paid. See Sect. IV, *Second difficulty in converting the Indians, viz. To convey divine truths to their understanding, and to gain their assent to them as such.* Brainerd's Journal, Edwards *Works*, vol. ii, BOT, p. 425 ff. (esp. 427). On the other hand, Andrew Fuller rejects 'commercial' and penal language repeatedly in his works, thus showing that he is a true Grotian. See Hastings, Schaff-Herzog and Luis Berkof for entries on Grotius. For references in Haykin's book defending Grotianism see general remarks on pp. 53, 139, 209 and 226. For the main argument see pp. 300-302. For Haykin's defence of Grotianism against Hawkin's criticism, see pp. 348-351.

[80] See Benjamin Warfield's *Edwards and the New England Theology, Works*, Baker, 1981, vol. ix, p. 515 ff. for the differences between Edwards' theology and that of the 'New Divinity' of his students and successors.

[81] Fuller's italics.

[82] *Works*, vol. II, p. 345.

[83] Ibid, p. 351.

[84] Ibid, p. 352.

[85] *Works*, vol. III, *Moral Inability*, p. 768.

[86] My emphasis.

[87] I am aware that Fuller later rejected the position he held against Taylor for a more radical one but I am using this work to emphasise that even at this stage of development, seen as his most orthodox, Fuller's system was still far from deserving that title.

[88] See also Letter VII, in *The Reality and Efficacy of Divine Grace*, vol, II, p. 539 f. where Fuller claims that the moral law may be opposed to the 'mere will of the lawgiver' in applying His 'positive laws'. See also *Faith required by the Moral Law*, vol. III, p. 781. Here Fuller, as usual, redefines Old Testament legal faith in Christ as 'fidelity' or 'veracity' to maintain his point, without explaining what the re-definition entails.

[89] Letter VIII, vol, II, p. 540.

[90] By now the reader will be wondering what on earth Fuller means by the law. After reading all his appropriate works on the subject, this writer has come to the conclusion that Fuller makes the word mean what it is to suit his particular purpose. It is to him a 'positive' thing, i.e. its meaning is not based on 'the nature and fitness of things' but merely on Fuller's will.

[91] Fuller's claims concerning his arguments from natural religion in the pages he lists, 'I do not recollect that anything like an answer to it is attempted by any one of my

opponents. If the reasoning is inconclusive, I should suppose its deficiency is capable of being detected.' *Works*, vol. II, p. 486. One would have thought Romans 1-2:1 would have been answer enough. No man can come to Christ through natural revelation as it is that — as the law — which tells us that we are without excuse. Natural religion just as the revealed law are there to condemn man. The gospel is there to bring him life.

[92] *Works*, vol. II, pp. 486-489.

Part III
The Universal Gospel and the Gospel which Saves

1. The Redemption that is in Christ Jesus

The atonement and Hyper-Calvinism

Modern evangelicals criticise what they call Hyper-Calvinism by arguing that, 'Because of the distorted view of unconditional election, preachers are unable to call people generally to repentance and faith, and assurance is based on an inner experience instead of the Word and work of Christ.'[1] This definition would make Andrew Full a Hyper-Calvinist on three counts. a. He has one of the most distorted views of unconditional election on record by a so-called Calvinist. God's plan of election is completely reversed. His doctrine of election is not grounded in the atonement but in the 'whosoever wills' who believe and have the merits of the atonement applied to them. Thus instead of the atonement objectively securing faith and reconciliation for the elect, it is the subjective believing of the sinner which makes the atonement, working backwards, effective. It is repenting and believing that gives the atonement its power, not the atonement that empowers the sinner to believe. Fuller's theory of unconditional election is thus riddled with conditions through and through. b. His call to repentance and faith is so divorced from Christ's vicarious, penal redemption on the cross that it can be summarised as a subjective acceptance of God's moral deterrent demonstrated by the sufferings of Christ which brings with it God's favour and acceptance in the Beloved. Indeed, it is quite obvious when reading the little Fuller has to say about repentance and how it comes about that the atonement is set in motion when repentance is made. Not only is assurance a mere 'inner experience' to Fuller which works backwards and makes the atonement efficacious, this can be said of belief, faith, reconciliation, righteousness and justification. c. In fact the whole Christian walk of the believer is isolated from the objective decrees of God and objective work of Christ and grounded in the initial step of belief which brings with it pardon, though guilt remains. Salvation is thus not resident in the mind of God but in the mind of man exercising his agency in salvation. Such belief is a grasping out to feast at the table God has prepared for sinners thus initiating actual reconciliation (Fuller's term to distinguish between that and the pseudo-reconciliation of the atonement), righteousness and justification.

The atonement is thus not unconditional for the elect but a conditional open matter until it is applied to the already-believer. Fuller emphasises repeatedly that the atonement could be applied to one or it could be applied to all. It was a universal not a limited atonement. Arguing against Abraham Booth's Scriptural views on the subject, Fuller says:

> If there were not a sufficiency in the atonement for the salvation of sinners, and yet they were invited to be reconciled to God, they must be invited to what is naturally impossible. The message of the gospel would in this case be as if the servants who went forth to bid the guests had said, 'Come', though, in fact, nothing was ready if many of them had come. If there be an objective fullness in the atonement of Christ sufficient for any number of sinners, were they to believe in him, there is no other impossibility in the way of any man's salvation to whom the gospel comes than what arises *from the state of his own mind*.[2]

Such a theorising cannot possibly be interpreted as unconditional election based on particular atonement. How Fuller can possibly argue that the atonement is *objectively* there for *all* yet, at the same time, *conditionally* there for *some* according to the state of their minds is one of the paradoxical mysteries of Fullerism. However Fuller might bridge the two sides of this paradox, neither reflects the Biblical truth that Christ died for His sheep and loses none of them.

An atonement in name only
Actually, Fuller's atonement is a mere abstract, neutral demonstration of Christ's suffering with no particular aims in view apart from serving as a moral deterrent. It is thus not an atonement at all as it was not carried out with a view to accomplishing the salvation of the elect but to open the way so that anybody in general but nobody in particular could benefit by it. This means that, though the atonement is sufficient for all, it is efficacious for none as it in no way secures anyone's salvation. It was no more an

atonement for Cain as it was for Abel, for Paul or for Judas. The atonement was not the payment of redemption money to buy the freedom of slaves unable to apply for freedom themselves. The atonement is a fund of unlimited riches which is available to anyone who asks for it. Thus it is quite surprising to find that Tom Nettles in his book *By His Grace and for His Glory* overlooks this factor and claims that, in spite of his Grotianism, inherited from the New England theologians, Fuller held to particular atonement. More surprising still is the proof Nettles offers for this from Fuller's *The Deity of Christ Essential to Atonement.* In this work, particular atonement is not even mentioned but merely Fuller's token theory of atonement which rules out 'what sin deserves' and maintains 'what God requires in order to exalt the dignity of his government,' so that 'the same end be answered by it, as if the guilty party had already suffered.'[3]

Seeking the best of two worlds

In stating his system of redemption and atonement Fuller is doing his best to be an original thinker, combining what he obviously feels is the best of the two different worlds of Calvinism and Arminianism or Particularism and Universalism. Faithful John Bunyan would have called this Mr. Facing-Bothways. Fuller never seemed to be aware of this himself and expressed his amazement that Calvinists such as his friend and publisher William Button and those Arminians who were more faithful to the Gospel such as Dan Taylor should both oppose him. His son feels he knows why Button and Taylor could not accept Fuller's syncretism. He tells us, 'If I am not greatly mistaken, they both particularly agree in denying faith in Christ to be a duty required by the moral law; and in excusing the sinner, unless grace is bestowed upon him, in his non-compliance with every thing spiritually good.'[4] Here, of course, the younger Fuller was greatly mistaken on two counts. First, he maintains that there is no difference between being under the Law and under grace and second, both Button and Taylor certainly argued for the responsibility of fallen man for his own predicament. This aside is especially harsh coming from Andrew Gunten Fuller as Button, though a convinced Calvinist of the Old School kind, supported Fuller's views on evangelism and world wide missionary work. Taylor's great energies in bringing salvation to fallen man cannot be questioned, indeed Taylor was perhaps the greatest evangelist and soundest theologian the General Baptists ever had.[5] Fuller, as is clear from what his son argues here, placed himself both outside of sound Calvinism and outside of the best of Arminianism. Indeed it was both Button's and Taylor's main point that Fuller did not teach reformed doctrines. It is also in replies to Button and Taylor that Fuller gives the clearest evidence that his accusers were correct.[6]

Much of Fuller's defence of his system is taken up with William Button's Biblical stance. Button, as many others, saw through the weakness of Fuller's system in promoting human agency to compete with God's purpose. In his work against Fuller's unworthy treatise on the gospel, Button writes:

> Mr Fuller's treatise appears to me to be opposite to Scripture and experience; and tends to overthrow the distinguishing and glorious doctrines of the gospel. Yet I wonder not at its prevailing, as it is exceedingly pleasing to human nature, and very gratifying to a proud man to be told he can believe *if he will*. But it is too humbling and too degrading to tell a sinner he has neither will nor power. So that those ministers who maintain the hypothesis of the creature's natural ability, will be sure to please the ear of men in general, and so gain what is much sought after in the present day—vain popularity.[7]

A redemption without paying the price

In rejecting the literal meaning of what he calls the 'commercial language' of Scripture, Fuller is, in reality rejecting redemption and limited or particular atonement. A redemption is the exact money paid to redeem an exact debt or release a prisoner on payment of a fixed price which is demanded. This is the very meaning which Fuller utterly denies. If he had only accepted that Christ's atonement was for His Bride and her alone, the artificial paradox he felt he must set up, flanking a universal atonement against a limited application, would be seen as the unbiblical and, indeed, illogical construction it is. In his arguments to discredit literal redemption in *On Particular Redemption*, Fuller caricatures the traditional Reformed doctrine of atoning redemption, saying:

> To ascertain the force of the objection, it is proper to inquire wherein the peculiarity of redemption consists. If the atonement of Christ were considered as the literal payment of a debt — if the measure of his sufferings were according to the number of those for whom he died, and to the degree of their guilt, in such a manner as that if more had been saved, or if those who are saved had been more guilty, his sorrows must have been proportionally increased— it might, for aught I know, be inconsistent with indefinite invitations. But it would be equally inconsistent with the free forgiveness of sin, and with sinners being directed to apply for mercy as supplicants, other than as claimants. I conclude, therefore, that an

hypothesis which in so many important points is manifestly inconsistent with the Scriptures cannot be true.

On the other hand, if the atonement of Christ proceed not on the principle of commercial, but of moral justice, or justice as it relates to crime—if its grand object were to express the Divine displeasure against sin, (Rom. viii. 3,) and so render the exercise of mercy, in all the ways wherein sovereign wisdom should determine to apply it, consistent with righteousness (Rom. iii. 25)—if it be in itself equal to the salvation of the whole world, were the whole world to embrace it—and if the peculiarity which attends it consists not in its insufficiency to save more than are saved, but in the sovereignty of its application—no such inconsistency can justly be ascribed to it.[8]

Fuller repeats these sentiments in *Conversation on Particular Redemption*, arguing:

If satisfaction was made on the principle of debtor and creditor, and that which was paid was just of sufficient value to cancel a given number of sins, and to redeem a given number of sinners, and no more; it should seem that it could not be the duty of any but the elect, nor theirs till it was revealed to them that they were of the elect, to rely upon it; for 'whereof should we set our eyes on that which is not?' But if there be such a fullness in the satisfaction of Christ as is sufficient for the salvation of the whole world, were the whole world to believe in him, and if the particularity of redemption lie only in the purpose or sovereign pleasure of God to render it effectual to some rather than to others, no such consequence will follow; or if it do, it will also follow that Divine predestination and human accountableness are utterly inconsistent, and therefore, that we must either relinquish the former in favour of Arminianism, or give up the latter to the Antinomians.[9]

Christ was afflicted without vicarious punishment

Here Fuller is building up an artificial argument which is not representative of any school of thought, whether it be Hyper-Calvinist, Calvinist, Fullerite, Baxterian, Arminian or Socinian. None of the Old School Calvinists whose teaching Fuller rejects argue that God required of Christ a suffering relative to the exact amount of individual sins committed by sinners so that if they had committed more or less, Christ's sufferings would have been heightened or lessened accordingly. Fuller's predecessors from Old

Testament days on, taught that the soul that sinned would die and that the
wages of sin is death.[10] This teaching implies that whether one sin is
committed or a thousand that sin must receive its just penalty in the death
of the sinner. Sin is not comparative, nor is the guilt which comes with it.
Death is not relative and there are no degrees of death. Fuller, however,
always backs away from regarding the death of Christ as the substitutionary
punishment in place of man's death. It is Christ's token suffering which
propitiates God's displeasure in Fuller's theology. Christ's death, to Fuller,
is merely the consequence of Christ's suffering. The Bible teaches that
Christ's suffering was the logical consequence of and crowning aim of His
voluntary redemptive death. It is the blood shed in the slaughter of the
Victim which atones. Fuller argues that Christ being made sin, i.e. being
made to bear sin in a figurative way, was preparatory to Christ's death, and
is not to be identified with that death itself.[11] Fuller's disinclination to
accept this doctrine makes his atonement theology smack at best of
Arthurian or Classical displays of bravery and at worst as the arbitrary
hazards of a soldier in battle. Indeed, in arguing that Christ was not punished
for the sinner's sake but merely suffered, Fuller's 'proof' cannot possibly
be accepted by anyone grounded in the Scriptures. After explaining that
he had changed his mind after writing against Dan Taylor and after saying
that he now opposed the views of Robert Hall of Arnesby, Fuller explains:

> I. Is there not an important difference between *punishment* and
> *suffering*? All punishment is suffering; but all suffering is not
> punishment. If a soldier have his hand cut off for lifting it up against
> his commander, it is punishment; but if it be shot off in battle, it is
> mere suffering.
> II. Though an innocent creature cannot be justly exposed to
> punishment, yet may it not be to suffering? If a commander-in-chief
> order a troop of his best soldiers to scale a wall in the mouth of
> danger, they are exposed to suffering; nor would they think of
> replying, as in case of his ordering them to receive each a hundred
> lashes, 'What have we done to deserve this treatment?' But if a
> human commander, for the accomplishment of a wise, just, and
> good object, may thus expose his innocent men to suffering, why
> may not the same be said of the great Master of the universe.[12]

Punishment for Adam, affliction for his offspring
The extraordinary point Fuller seems to be making here is that due to the
fall, man is not imputed with Adam's sin so that he is punished along with
Adam but must *innocently* suffer for what Adam has done. He can thus

ask provokingly the rhetorical question, 'Now what consequence would follow were I to suppose the sentence of death, and of its antecedent miseries, passed upon all mankind in consequence of Adam's sin, to be to him a punishment, but to them merely an affliction?' Fuller then goes on to argue that the sufferings of Christ must be understood according to the same principle. Christ's sufferings must be likened to the innocent soldier who happened to have his hand shot off in battle. Just as the innocent soldier would never think of challenging his officer's decision to give him a hundred lashes, so Christ did not challenge His Father's decision to have him suffer as though he were such an 'innocent creature'.

The whole metaphor is staggering in its presumption, false conclusions and application. It is as far from the Biblical account of sin and salvation as Fuller could possibly have made it. One cannot compare Adam's offspring with soldiers who suffer innocently for what their arbitrary officer does to them. Is Fuller comparing the officer who arbitrarily gave the innocent sufferer 100 lashes with God's treatment of man and Christ? This would make Fuller a thorough-going Grotian who taught that, apart from natural laws, other laws of God, including a number of moral laws, are arbitrary and have no eternal standard due to God's own eternal character. Furthermore, the officer obviously regarded the 100 lashes as some punishment or other but Fuller ignores the officer's point of view and deals solely with the 'innocent creatures' who suffered. This is seen throughout Fuller's entire system in which man's agency is given far more pre-eminence than God's purpose. One might ask what all this has to do with atonement and imputation?

God did not impute Adam's sin alone to Christ but Christ had the sin of the entire elect imputed to Him and placed upon Him. He was not made sin for Adam alone but for His Bride the Church. Nor did Christ believe He was to die for 'innocent creatures'. He suffered and died for His people because they were the very opposite and He loved them so much that He decided to save them. Moreover, Christ did not suffer and die because He felt that it was morally unjustifiable that God should have man suffer for Adam's sin. He suffered to fulfil the eternal law of God on their behalf and died to bear the punishment of their transgressions on their behalf. Nor did Christ suffer for His innocence's sake but for the sake of the sins of His people which he bore in His own person. Hero-like suffering in the course of duty was not enough for Christ. He did not come to lose a hand for us or receive 100 lashes for us but to make a perfect sacrifice for us, in order to redeem us from our killing debts of sin. Nor did He suffer in vain under an arbitrary Commander but accomplished that which he set out to do in joint and sovereign love with His Father.

Christ made a moralist and martyr but not a Saviour
Are we to believe that Christ merely *suffered* in a moral battle against
Adam's sin? This would make Him a moralist and a martyr but not a
Saviour.[13] Surely there is more to the atonement than this? If another officer
had volunteered to take the soldier's penalty for him in Fuller's illustration,
he would have been nearer the Biblical mark. It seems odd that though
there are so many stories in the Bible of the righteous dying for the
unrighteous (i.e. the Suffering Servant), Fuller should resort to illustrations
quite foreign to the subject. To Fuller, of course, such an illustration is not
foreign as he empties the doctrine of the atonement of its penal and
substitutionary 'proper' meaning and gives it the 'improper' meaning of a
victory merely in the realms of morals. This is why Fuller claims that the
moral law, standing alone without the promises, contains all that is required
of the sinner to believe the Gospel. His Gospel is not a theological matter
but a mere matter of morals.[14]

A Saviour who gets his hand shot off in battle might be seen as a hero
by some and a fool by others. If our salvation were in the hands of either,
we should be of all men most miserable. How different from Fuller's fables
are the words of Isaiah:

> Surely he hath borne our griefs, and carried our sorrows: yet we
> did esteem him stricken, smitten of God and afflicted. But he was
> wounded for our transgressions, he was bruised for our iniquities:
> the chastisement of our peace was upon him; and with his stripes
> we were healed. All we like sheep have gone astray; we have turned
> every one to his own way; and the Lord hath laid on him the iniquity
> of us all. He was oppressed, and he was afflicted, yet he opened
> not his mouth: he is brought as a lamb to the slaughter, and as a
> sheep before her shearers is dumb, so he opened not his mouth. He
> was taken from prison and from judgement: and who shall declare
> his generation? for he was cut off out of the land of the living: for
> the transgressions of my people was he stricken. And he made his
> grave with the wicked, and with the rich in his death; because he
> had done no violence, neither was any deceit in his mouth. Yet it
> pleased the Lord to bruise him; he hath put him to grief: when thou
> shalt make his soul an offering for sin, he shall see his seed, he shall
> prolong his days, and the pleasure of the Lord shall prosper in his
> hand. He shall see the travail of his soul and shall be satisfied: by
> his knowledge shall my righteous servant justify many; for he shall
> bear their iniquities. Therefore will I divide him a portion with the
> great, and he shall divide the spoil with the strong; because he

hath poured out his soul unto death: and he was numbered with the transgressors; and he bare the sins of many, and made intercession for the transgressors.

This is the Biblical doctrine of imputation. This is the gospel of truth on which our faith stands. This is the gospel that is worthy of all acceptation because it is the gospel of Christ who alone is worthy to receive glory and honour and power: for He alone has created all things, and for His pleasure they are and were created.[15]

Diversity of opinions are believed to indicate unity of thought
Yet Fuller is not finished with this revision of his system of imputation. Though he saw fit to re-publish his re-thinking on the topic, he neverthe-less added the claim that since writing his revised views, he had, once again, changed his opinions. He now believed, he said, that imputation was not a *treatment* but a *ground of treatment*, thus paving the way for yet further speculations based on playing with words. It is very odd that Fuller, who often changed his mind, did not reject his older views but allowed them to be published up to his death and professed to stand by them.[16] Indeed, three completely different attitudes towards the atonement can be traced, all of which Fuller professed to accept until the end of his days. This attitude is like the church of Rome who continually proposes new things to broaden her system but never gives up any of her old beliefs no matter how paradoxical they are. Diversity of opinions to them, as to Fuller, indicating unity of thought.

The essential conjectural paradox
There is indeed much talk amongst Fullerites about the essential paradox of Christian doctrine which has led to apparently sound theological insti-tutions such as the Westminster Seminary refusing to recommend candi-dates for the ministry such as Dr. Gordon H. Clark. This Christian man refused to believe that he must hold to two contradictory gospels; one teaching a universal atonement and one teaching a particular application, both of which must be taught. Needless to say, he earnestly believed that the true gospel should be preached to all men. In March/April, 1987 the *Trinity Review* published an account of the persecution of Dr. Clark for finding no paradoxical contradictions in the gospel.[17] The writer, Garrett P. Johnson, a member of the board of the Trinity Foundation, brought John Owen forward to defend Clark. This great Puritan had said, 'They (the Remonstrants, i.e. Arminians) affirm that God is said properly to expect and desire divers things which yet never come to pass. "We grant," saith

Corvinus, "that there are desires in God that never are fulfilled" now, surely, to desire what one is sure will never come to pass is not an act regulated by wisdom or counsel; and, therefore, they must grant that before he did not know but perhaps so it might be. "God wisheth and desireth some good things, which yet come not to pass," say they, in their Confession; whence one of these two things must need follow—either first, that there is a great deal of imperfection in his nature, to desire and expect what he knows will never come to pass; or else he did not know but it might, which over-throws his prescience.'[18] This led Johnson to admit that if Owen had been a colleague of Clark's and had spoken not in the 1640s but in 1944, Owen would have been drummed out of the Orthodox Presbyterian Church. Of course, this feature of striving to set up a synthesis of Biblical argument based on a presumed Biblical thesis and anti-thesis may suit the dialectics of Hegel or even Van Til but it is a far cry from the One Gospel. In *The Modern Predicament*, Prof. H. J. Paton says aptly:

> There are some who maintain that these problems can be solved by a kind of dialectic which enables us to say both 'Yes' and 'No', and to reconcile these in a higher synthesis. The dialectic of Hegel is certainly to be treated by those who are not its votaries with a respect not wholly void of suspicion. But there is a danger that lesser men may use these devices mechanically as a kind of gadget to make the commonplace profound and the ridiculous intelligible. The danger is increased when the system of the master is twisted or corrected into something quite different, as it is by later thinkers who reject the thought but cling to the terminology.[19]

These words, though originally intended for the ears of followers of Hegel, Marx and Kierkegaard are a useful comment on the Hegel of dialectical theology Andrew Fuller and the modern Marxes and Kierkegaards of com-monplace theology who have produced the present day Hyper-Fullerism which is storming the evangelical 'Establishment'. A case in point is Kenneth Good's recommendation of Erroll Hulse's evaluation of Fuller as one who 'held the antinomy of Predestination and Responsibility with an iron grasp'.[20] The word 'antinomy' is from the same root as the word 'antinomian' and means contrary to the law. Hulse uses the term in the sense of a 'self-contradiction'. How the fact that God predestinates the elect to responsibility must be seen as a self-contradiction, neither Good nor Hulse explain. But this is the Fullerite dogma and it must be believed. The Fullerites are little aware that their teaching on antinomies is Antinomian.

Redemption not accomplished but applied

Redemption in Fullerism never took place. It was not even necessary. The word redemption is 'commercial language' for Fuller and therefore not applicable to God's saving work which, he believes, is a moral work only. The fact that the Bible uses such a word does not trouble Fuller as his metaphorical interpretation of the Scriptures enables him to give a word whatever meaning he wants. We must thus interpret the word 'redemption' morally not commercially; nor in terms of vicarious punishment. In other words, we must empty the word of its meaning and give it a new meaning in order to understand it. Concerning the old ransom meaning of redemption, Fuller tells us that 'In atonement, or satisfaction for crime, things do not proceed on this calculating principle.' Fuller's proof of this is that if we are to take redemption literally, Christ's sufferings 'would require to be exactly to the nature and number of the sins which are laid upon him; and if more sinners had been saved, or those who are saved had been greater sinners than they are, he must have borne a proportionable increase of suffering.'[21] Fuller is forgetting that the wages of sin is death, whatever the number of sins committed and Christ took on Himself these wages that we might live. But this is no argument to Fuller who rejects the Biblical conception of sin just as much as he rejects the Biblical conception of redemption. Again, to get over the embarrassment of not being able to explain how Christ *really* redeemed His people, Fuller merely tells us that the important thing is that the saved believe that 'to *them* his substitution was the same *in effect* as if their sins had by number and measure been literally imparted to him.'[22] It is all in the mind! Fuller is also telling his readers that the proof of the pudding is in the eating. The believer is redeemed—however this may have come about and whatever this may mean—and he should be satisfied with this outcome. It is an 'in effect' and an 'as if' salvation but the means are not important; it is the end that counts. Hardly comforting words for a sinner whose sins are ever before him and he wants them truly blotted out. The Bible makes it clear that such a redemption actually took place. Only a sinner who knows that he has been bought with a price can truly glorify God in his body and in his spirit (1 Corinthians 6:20). Such a man will not deny the Lord who bought him (2 Peter 2:1).

Fullerism is a gospel of speculation

Fuller's gospel of atoning redemption which he claims is worthy of all acceptation is, in its greater part, not only based on a figurative understanding, or rather misunderstanding, of the Scriptures but it is also the outcome of a sheer speculative supposition. He campaigns for a figurative atonement that saves no one as a sovereign work of God in itself

but which may be applied savingly to anyone, should they return to God
and claim it. Fuller, to give his theory a resemblance of respectability,
argues that he finds it reflected in the works of Herman Witsius (1636-
1708) who wrote, 'The obedience and sufferings of Christ *considered in
themselves*, are, on account of the dignity of the person, of such value as
to have been sufficient for redeeming not only all and every man in particular,
but many myriads besides, *had it so pleased God and Christ* [23] that he
should have undertaken and satisfied for them.'[24]

Herman Witsius misunderstood

Fuller has obviously either misunderstood Witsius here or merely spotted
this special passage out of context and immediately grasped it, believing
that it supported his own theory of an atonement efficacious for none in
itself but sufficient for all on application. He thus removes the passage
from a context in which Witsius is actually denying what Fuller maintains,
as is clear from the very title which Witsius uses. Witsius prefaces his
argument concerning *Of the Persons for whom Christ engaged and satisfied*
with the words Fuller quotes to emphasise that *had it so pleased God*, He
could have worked out a plan of salvation on the terms of Arminius, whose
views he is discussing, but *He was not pleased to do so* [25]. Witsius is
stressing that atonement has nothing to do with a general intrinsic power
and capability of God to do what He wants when He wants. His almighty
power is taken for granted.

In the atonement, Witsius points out, we are dealing with God's specific
will in Christ to separate a people for Himself. This is made quite clear in
the words both preceding and following those which Fuller quotes. Witsius
introduces the point in which he differs from Arminius by saying, 'We
should have no certainty of all those things, which it is proper for us to
know, for the glory of our Lord Christ, and our own consolation, concerning
this suretyship and satisfaction, did it not also appear, for whom he satisfied
according to his covenant-engagement. The solution of this question is
indeed of very great moment, but it does not appear so very difficult, if we
only carefully attend to the nature of Christ's suretyship and satisfaction,
which we have already explained, proved and defended. For since Christ
did, by his engagement, undertake to cancel all the debts of those persons
for whom he engaged, as if it was his own, by suffering what was meet, and
to fulfil all righteousness in their room; and since he has most fully performed
this by his satisfaction, as much as if the sinners themselves had endured
all the punishments due to their sins, and had accomplished all
righteousness: the consequence is, that he has engaged and satisfied for
those, and those only, who are actually saved from their sins; as is evident

to reason. For Christ neither engaged, nor satisfied, but for those whose person he sustained. Which Arminius himself, Adversus Perkinsum, p. 72. frankly owns. Moreover, that any of those whose person Christ sustained, and for whom he satisfied as their Surety, should be obliged to satisfy for the same debt, by eternal death, is most inconsistent with, and contrary to the faithfulness and justice of God. Nor can we, on any account, think it possible, that anyone should in earnest plead, that Christ died for all and every one in particular, till he has weakened the force of that expression, to die for any one, by which, as we lately made appear against the Socinians, is denoted a substitution in the place of another. But it is worthwhile distinctly to set forth the true doctrine in these following positions.'

Witsius then uses the words Fuller quotes and goes on to show how mankind in general profits from Christ's love and how the obedience and suffering of Christ are of such worth to save all who come to Him, nevertheless, 'Christ, according to the will of God the Father, and his own purpose, did neither engage nor satisfy, and consequently in no manner die, but only for all those whom the Father gave him, and who actually saved. This is the truth which is controverted, and which we are now to confirm, in a concise and solid manner, from the sacred writings.' This is the very truth that Fuller controverts and it is highly unfair of him to twist Witsius as if he were approving of Fuller's view of the atonement rather than severely contradicting it. This is especially so as Witsius is arguing for what Fuller calls the 'commercial' doctrine of the atonement, a doctrine Fuller radically rejects!

Witsius' points of difference with Fuller

It is clear from Witsius' account that he believes the Scriptures teach the following points which Fuller refuses to accept: a. The suretyship, satisfaction and covenant-engagement of Christ was wrought out in the atonement for such as God chose to save and for none other. b. The debts of the elect, incurred through their sins were fully and actually paid by Christ in the atonement and not the debts of anyone else. Thus the atonement was particular and limited. c. Though, in the matter of paying the elects' debts, man is now viewed *as if* he had paid them himself, in fact they are *actually paid* by Christ in full and thus the elect are debt-free and therefore *actually righteous* in God's sight.

Fuller's theory of the atonement is formed irrespective of the purpose of God in Christ

Fuller, however, does not take into account the context of the words he so carelessly culls from Witsius. We thus find him arguing against Abraham

Booth that, 'Concerning the death of Christ, if I speak of it irrespective of the purpose of the Father and the Son as to the objects who should be saved by it, referring merely to what it is in itself sufficient for, and declared in the gospel to be adapted to, I should think I answered the question in a scriptural way in saying, It was for sinners as sinners. But if I have respect to the purpose of the Father in giving His Son to die, and to the design of Christ in laying down His life, I should answer, It was for His elect only.'[26]

The weakness here in Fuller's argument is that he is thinking, as he freely acknowledges, 'irrespective of the purpose of the Father and the Son'. Such thoughts are completely superfluous to a Christian and detract from his own purpose and calling which is to do God's will in Christ. Fuller knows that he is merely speculating about what the atonement might or might not have been able to accomplish were it not specifically shown in Scripture what it was meant to accomplish. Yet, the amazing, indeed alarming, factor of Fuller's system is that he makes that which is irrespective of Scripture the very ground of being of his gospel to all men which is that Christ died for sinners as sinners. 'If we were to suppose, for arguments sake,' he tells his readers, 'that all the inhabitants of the globe should thus return, it is supposed not one soul need be sent away for want of a sufficiency in Christ's death to render his pardon and acceptance consistent with the rights of justice.'[27]

What is the purpose, one might ask, of this wishful thinking? Furthermore, when speaking of particular redemption, Peter asks James, alias Fuller, 'Is there anything in the atonement, or promised to it, which infallibly ascertains its application to all those for whom it was made?' James answers, 'If by this you mean all for whose salvation it was sufficient, I answer, There is not. But if you mean all for whose salvation it was intended, I answer, There is.' It seems here that we have the Amyraldian and Baxterian system whereby it is stated that Christ died for all men but as all men would not believe God as a second thought, appointed some to be saved.' If Fuller did not believe this, and he claims indirectly that he does not in his essay on Baxter,[28] why does he put forward his sufficient for all but only applicable to some philosophy as the gospel worthy of all acceptation? Fuller's answer to this question seems to be that it encourages evangelism because the preacher feels he is sent to preach to all that all might be saved. Again, paradoxically, in aiming for right ends, he uses wrong means.

Fuller's claim that John Owen backs him up on redemption
Fuller maintains that another great Puritan, this time John Owen, 'as well as many others',[29] makes exactly the same distinction that Fuller makes in

his speculative gospel of paradoxes. He gives the *Death of Death*, Book iv, chapter I as his source. In this chapter Owen does indeed argue for the infinite value and dignity of Christ's sacrifice. His differences with Fuller's view of the atonement are, however, enormous.

1. Owen is solely arguing for the distinction between particular redemption and universal redemption. Fuller's distinction has nothing to do with this as he is arguing for the conditional redemption of a few according to the application of an atonement which is open to all.

2. Owen argues that the atonement cannot be viewed apart from its redemptive purpose, which is to redeem the elect. This is unconditional election. Fuller views the atonement first in a universal capacity - everyone could partake of it if he would, and then as being applied particularly to those who do partake of it. This is conditional election.

3. Owen warns against concluding that the atonement is sufficient for all regarding its purpose in redemption. Fuller stresses that the atonement is sufficient for all in a redemptive sense.

4. Owen, however, believes in a literal redemption from sin accomplished in the atonement. Fuller believes that redemption is figurative and comes into being only when it is applied to the sinner in salvation.

5. Owen's atonement is factual and absolute. It secures the redemption of those for whom it is intended. Fuller's atonement is hypothetical, being available to any or none as the case might be.

Jim Packer sums up these distinction succinctly in his *Preface* to the *Banner of Truth Trust* reprint of Owen's book, 'Christ did not win a hypothetical salvation for hypothetical believers, a mere possibility of salvation for any who might possibly believe, but a real salvation for His own chosen people.' Fuller, however, continually quotes Owen to back up his own entirely different view of redemption and the atonement as if Owen supported him.

Booth accuses Fuller of departing from Scripture
Again, when Booth rightly accused Fuller of changing his Calvinistic sentiments and leaving the Reformed path, Fuller did not reply to him saying either 'Yea' or 'Nay' but gave his friend a sophistic piece of speculation based on his controversy with Arminian Dan Taylor which had caused Fuller to change his views on particular redemption. He thus argued:

> I conceded to my opponent that the death of Christ *in itself* considered, i.e. irrespective of the *design* of the Father and Son as to its application, was sufficient for all mankind; but a way was

opened by which God consistently with his justice could forgive
any sinner whatever that returns to him by Jesus Christ; that if the
whole world were to believe in him, none need be sent away for
want of a sufficiency in his death to render his pardon and acceptance
consistent with the rights of justice.'[30]

A sufficient atonement with no object for its sufficiency

Fuller, who takes up Booth's accusations concerning imputation,
substitution and Christ's vicarious sacrifice[31] expects Booth, for the sake
of the argument, to imagine a sufficient atonement in isolation from what it
was sufficient for. He then uses this as *a priori* evidence that such an
atonement really exists and then goes on to argue that an atonement which
is sufficient for all is sufficient for anybody who avails themselves of it.
The whole idea, however, of philosophising about God's actions
irrespective of God's will or design belongs to metaphysics and not to the
gospel which maintains that Christ has died for His sheep who are enabled
to hear His voice and come when they are called.

In *Conversation on Substitution* Fuller applies his speculative principle
to foreign missionary work by arguing 'Were I asked concerning the gospel,
when it is introduced into a country, for whom was it sent? if I had respect
only to the revealed will of God, I should answer, It is sent for men, not as
elect or non-elect, but as sinners.' This may seem, on the surface, like
sound evangelism. Was this not the view of John Gill who taught that the
gospel must be preached to all sinners, as the Spirit leads, because it has
a function for all? It comes as a savour of life unto life to some and a savour
of death unto death to others. But this is only half of the paradox of
Fuller's view of evangelism. He immediately goes on to take back what he
has said about bringing the revealed will of God to both the elect and non-
elect as sinners and says, 'But if I had respect to the appointment of God
with regard to its application, I should say, He hath visited that country to
'take out of them a people for His name.'[32]

The God of the two amens

Here we have a number of sheer suppositions concerning for whom Christ
might have died, with no concrete answer given. Fuller is confusing the
issue by telling his readers:

1. According to God's *revealed* will Christ *could have* died for all mankind.
2. *If* we reason according to God's *secret* will, two alternatives are open to
us.

a. *If* God acts according to our experience of Him, Christ died 'to take out a people for his name'.

b. But what if 'the Divine conduct in this instance' does not 'accord with what it has been in other instances'? This cannot be answered conclusively. The answer could be either

i. Christ died for all mankind, or

ii. He died to take out a people for Himself, or

iii. He did something quite different.

Here, of course, Fuller is applying his Grotian *a posteriori* test which allows him to judge the nature and fitness of things correctly. It would seem that the test, when discerning the will of God, fails for Fuller.

With arguments like this it is no wonder that Booth understood Fuller, 'to deny that Christ obeyed and died as a substitute, and to disown a real and proper imputation.' What Fuller is doing is dodging the issue of for whom Christ died completely and teaching absolute scepticism! His whole idea of preaching the gospel seems to be to exhort man to do what he knows man cannot do. Though this may (and equally may not) make man aware of his responsibility, it would be, in effect, making him aware of a pseudo-responsibility. Man's duties to natural theology and the law and the spiritual life of faith of the elect are completely distinct entities which cannot be engendered by exhorting fallen once-born man to reach out and grasp second birth privileges by means of performing such law-bound duties. Here obviously Fuller's Grotian view of the law is behind his thoughts. God's revealed will is only right because God wants it to be right at that moment. The eternal, natural law, shows what is right because it is *ipso facto* right. The validity of the former can only be tested by the rationality of the latter. Thus the believer must ask himself if there is an *a posteriori* case. It is thus no wonder that when John Stevens summed up Fullerism some 25 years after Fuller's death, he found it 'contrary to absolute election; real and particular redemption; (and) the sure and effectual conversion of all the redeemed.' Stevens goes on to outline the enormous negative influence Fullerism scepticism had on the churches during the first half of the 19th century.[33]

God's 'yea' may really mean 'nay'

Fuller argues that the revealed will of God i.e. that will which God displays in addressing sinners through the preached word, is a different will to that expressed in its application of that message on the lives of the hearers. He is again building on the idea that God has two minds in salvation and reveals Himself in two different modes. One is theoretically addressed to all men for whom the atonement is sufficient and the other addressed practically to the number of men to whom the all sufficient atonement will be limited and applied. This view of God's two wills is again emphasised in Fuller's third letter to Dr. Ryland concerning his controversy with Abraham Booth on imputation and substitution. Fuller claims that Booth is wrong to believe in a literal substitution. In answer to the question for whom did Christ die, i.e. for whom was He a substitute, Fuller, as *in Conversations on Substitution*, concerns himself with the revealed will of God to mankind in general, and argues that His will to take out a people for Himself is not His *revealed* will but His *secret* will. It would seem then, that the true gospel to Fuller is different to the revealed gospel. This is all in keeping with his idea of moral laws and positive laws, eternal laws and temporary laws. Fuller's revealed gospel obviously belongs to the 'positive' type which is merely a letter whose spirit needs to be both looked for and found. Presumably Fuller finds his spiritual interpretation in the secret will of God, a secret which he finds out through his proficiency in prying into the 'nature and fitness of things'.

It seems that the truth of the Scriptures that God changes not and that the atonement is sufficient for whom it was intended and is therefore applicable to those alone seems to have escaped Fuller completely. What makes Fuller's view of preaching the gospel quite radical is that he proclaims the idea of a God who actually offers a finished salvation to every man, explaining that their full acceptance with God is warranted and guaranteed, only to believe secretly that God will most definitely not give such a salvation to them all and perhaps to none of them. Fuller thus uses his speculative gospel of the objective, universal sufficiency of the atonement to draw men to the true gospel for the lost sheep of the House of Israel. As he would say himself, it is the end that is important, not the means.

Working *a posteriori* from particular faith to universal salvation
Fuller was apparently aware of the fact that his position was not literally Scriptural but merely suppositional but he had become a slave of his own logic in interpreting Scripture according to the spirit of 'the nature and fitness of things.' It would thus seem quite logical for Fuller to work backwards in his reasoning, i.e. *a posteriori*, and conclude that because anyone who applies to God for salvation will be saved, then there is sufficient salvation for all—providing they should apply for it. He never seems to conclude that as a certain number have the atonement applied to them and not others, that atonement was thus only intended for those who eventually apply. Fuller rejects the latter view, believing that it smacks too much of the commercial view that a fixed price is paid for a fixed commodity. He thus says concerning his conditional view of atonement:

Whether I can perfectly reconcile these statements with each other or not, I embrace them as being both plainly taught in the Scriptures. I confess, however, I do not at present perceive their inconsistency. If I be not greatly mistaken, what apparent contradiction may attend them arises chiefly from that which has already been mentioned; namely, the considering of Christ's substitution as an affair between *a creditor* and *debtor,*[34] or carrying the *metaphor*[35] to an extreme. In that view the sufferings of Christ would require to be exactly proportioned to the nature and number of the sins which were laid upon him; and if more sinners had been saved, or those who are saved had been greater sinners than they are, he must have borne a proportional increase in suffering. To correspond with pecuniary satisfaction, this must undoubtedly be the case. I do not know that any writer has so stated things; but am persuaded that such ideas are at the foundation of a large part of the reasonings on that side of the subject.[36]

Fuller's extraordinary logic for assuming this speculative freedom to depart from the penal substitution and vicarious sacrifice of Scripture is by claiming that if Christ merely died for the elect and not for all sinners as sinners, then it would be no use preaching to sinners, one should only preach to those already saved. He does not seem to give any due regard to the fact that God's method of selecting the sheep from the goats is through the agency of preaching. Fuller is more interested in another kind of agency. In his essay on substitution, he presents another of his false antitheses:

I do not deny that there is difficulty in these statements; but it belongs to the general subject of reconciling the purposes of God with the agency of man; whereas, in the other case, God is represented as inviting sinners to partake of what has no existence, and which therefore is physically impossible.

He concludes, 'We must either acknowledge an objective fullness in Christ's atonement, sufficient for the salvation of the whole world, were the whole world to believe in him; or, in opposition to Scripture and common sense, confine our invitations to believe to such persons as have believed already.'[37]

Preaching salvation to the already saved
This is what actually Fuller believed the Old School Calvinists did, i.e.

preach the gospel of salvation to the already saved. He must have thought it a great wonder to find that such men as Richard Davis, John Gill, William Anderson, and William Huntington could be the means of rescuing hundreds of sinners from hell though they were supposed to believe that they should preach to believers only. Actually, as always, Fuller is in conflict with himself. In giving a warrant to all men that the atonement is sufficient for them, he is, in fact, guaranteeing what is impossible as the atonement is, even in his theology, applicable only to the elect. Though it would be difficult for him to quote passages in his predecessors' works which show that they did not preach to the unconverted, in his *Reply to Philanthropos* he clearly indicates that the full gospel for him is, indeed, for believers only. Leaning on his faulty belief that the atonement has no efficacy apart from that which it gains through application, he argues here openly that Christ's propitiation extends to believers only.[38] In the same work he also argues that 'Hence it is that the chief of those scriptures which we conceive to hold forth a limitation of design in the death of Christ, or any other doctrine of discriminating grace, are such as were addressed to believers.'[39] This is why Fuller cautions his fellow ministers about indiscriminately preaching what Cotton Mather and Zanchius call the comforts of predestination as these are the secrets of the Church i.e. a gospel for believers only. It is in this work, too, that Fuller, always anxious to plead for an atonement on the grounds that God loves all and the atonement could be applied universally to all men, should they will, he yet explains that God does not love all men alike.[40] Though we find a man such as John Gill, whom Fuller suspects of only preaching to the already saved, speaking of Christ knocking at the doors of sinners' hearts,[41] Fuller's ultimate teaching regarding the acceptance of the gospel is solely based on those who stretch out and grasp in faith all that the gospel has to offer. Fuller's elect believers always take the gift of salvation. Gill's elect sinners are always given the gift of salvation. This is the difference between Fullerism and the Reformed Faith.

Fuller's two gospels

Fuller has, in reality, two gospels; the gospel of the universal sufficiency of the atonement and the gospel of the particular application. As Fuller admits that the first 'gospel' is not the ultimate will of God in choosing a people for Himself, it is a mock gospel and ought not to be put forward as a gospel worthy of all acceptation. It is merely a speculative piece of metaphysics which confuses the plain and crystal clear message of the true gospel. Fuller argues continually that one must throw away what he calls the 'carnal ordinances' of the Bible to get at its spirit. It is a tragedy that he cluttered up his own testimony with such a large amount of dross, making it almost impossible for any reader to find spiritual value in his works.

In arguing against Dan Taylor, alias Philanthropos, Fuller, at times, jumps over his own shadow and comes very near a Calvinist position regarding the atonement, imputation and justification. The chief difference being that he continually views the matter from man's side rather than from God's revealed will. As he buried himself more in the rational moral government theory, he departed further and further from Calvinistic tendencies and sadly changed his views expressed to Taylor concerning the fall, imputation of Adam's sin and Christ's vicarious suffering until there was no semblance to Biblical truths.[42]

2. The Gospel of Reconciliation

Fuller's two views of reconciliation
Fuller, taking on the role of James, hardly surprises us when he begins his discourse on reconciliation by stating that the term can mean two quite different things in the same context.[43] Reconciliation could be, for instance, a synonym for the atonement and mean 'the satisfaction of justice only, or the opening of a way by which mercy may be exercised consistently with righteousness.' The second meaning of the term is, according to Fuller, 'being actually in friendship with God, through faith in the blood of Christ'. Neither of Fuller's definitions point to a work of God on Calvary in which God took the initiative and reconciliation was really made. As an example of both these meanings, he gives Romans 5:10, 'For if when we were enemies we *were reconciled* to God by the death of his Son, much more, *being reconciled*, we shall be saved with his life.' Here it is clear that in Fuller's opinion Romans 5:10 teaches that there is no true reconciliation accomplished through the atonement as such. Christ's death merely opens the way for an atonement to be performed. It serves no purpose in actually and immediately working out reconciliation through atoning for the personal sins of the elect. Indeed, Fuller denies an immediate connection between the atonement and sinners at all. Christ did not die to atone for His Church as a Church but in a manner compatible to God's arbitrary moral government of the world, showed God's 'displeasure' of *sin as sin.* This moral demonstration is used as a token of good will on God's part for anyone responding to it and thus having its merits (whatever they may be) applied to their own cases. This means that the atonement was not a once

and for all action whereby Christ redeemed His Church. It has no function
at all until it is applied to the believer on his demonstrating faith, through
believing. Actually, Fuller confuses atonement with the believer's electing
himself into God's grace through reception of the gospel.

Even then, one wonders what the function of the atonement really is in
Fuller's view, especially as he denies that Jesus atoned for the particular
sins of particular men. More radically still, Fuller emphasises that the
atonement is a mere token satisfaction of justice. There is no mercy in the
atonement itself as it merely makes a future display of mercy on God's part
possible. There is only mercy in God's utilising it by applying its justice i.e.
its demonstration of God's displeasure against sin in the abstract, to
believers. In this way Fuller de-objectifies and de-theologises the atonement
and limits its efficacy to the subjective reception of the so-called free-offer
of the Gospel which leads to the moral improvement of the believer. The
atonement is, at best, a parcel without contents until God fuses his Divine
purpose with the moral agency of man, so that the latter realises that sin
only brings suffering and fits himself in with God's moral government of
the world. At worst, the atonement is a mere catalyst in God's work of
salvation and the more one reads Fuller, the more one realises that God
could have used any other means to serve the same purpose.

Fuller separates the work of reconciliation from the cross
Traditionally Christians have spoken of redemption as being accomplished
in the atonement and applied in the work of the Spirit in the New Birth. It
was accomplished on the cross and then applied to those for whom it was
accomplished. This is reversed by Fuller who teaches that the atonement
is applied and thus accomplished. The words 'were reconciled' in Romans
5:10, Fuller argues, quoting Dr. Guyse, refer to 'a way of merit by his death
that was necessary to appease the wrath of God, and make way for the
riches of his grace to be communicated to us in full consistency with the
honour of all his perfections, and of his law and government.' The words
'being reconciled' in the last clause, Fuller, still quoting Dr. Guyse, argues,
'relate to the reconciliation taking effect upon us, or to our being brought
into a state of actual reconciliation and peace with God, through faith in
Christ's blood.' The first meaning thus does not refer to true reconciliation
at all but merely to the making of such a reconciliation possible. Fuller is
aware that this definition will cause his readers difficulty and has Peter
express what many must think, 'To view the atonement as merely a
satisfaction to divine justice, or as a *medium* by which mercy may be
exercised consistently with the Divine perfections, without considering
sinners as *actually reconciled to God* by it, is to retain little if any thing

more than the *name* of atonement.' Fuller replies, 'I see no grounds for calling that which was wrought for us while we were yet enemies *actual* reconciliation.' Here it is obvious that Fuller is not taking his stand on a contextualised interpretation of Romans 5:10 but from his background of refusing to believe that any justification, righteousness or reconciliation is possible without the prior agency of man agreeing to the purpose of God. This is how Fuller describes 'actual reconciliation' which is, for him, '*accomplished*[44] through faith'.

Reconciliation is not vouchsafed and effected in the atonement according to Fuller

Now Fuller is clearly wrong with his interpretation of Romans 5:10 as Paul is explaining in the whole context that justification, salvation and reconciliation are grounded in the atonement itself and it is stressed that 'God commendeth his love to us, in that, while we were yet sinners, Christ died for us' (v. 8). Fuller argues that reconciliation lies dormant, conditionally applicable to all men until God in his love applies it conditionally to the elect when they accomplish God's demands on them through their active human agency in salvation by exercising faith. Paul makes it quite clear, however, that the love of God exercised in reconciling elect sinners to himself was vouchsafed and effected in the atonement. Fuller would have us believe that this effectual reconciliation occurs merely on being applied to the believer after faith has been exercised. God, however, as Romans 5:8 clearly teaches, commended his love to the elect *whilst they were still in their sins*. Fuller says this is impossible. When John asks him, 'What are your ideas brother James, of that reconciliation which was affected while we were yet enemies', Fuller answers in his customary non-scriptural diction, 'I conceive it to be that *satisfaction to the Divine justice* by virtue of which nothing pertaining to the moral government of God hinders any sinner from returning to him; and that is upon the ground that sinners are indefinitely invited so to do.'

Thus the atonement, in Fuller's theology has only an indefinite relationship to reconciliation and though Fuller would have us believe that this is entirely in keeping with the Biblical meaning of reconciliation in regards to the atonement, it has certainly nothing to do with that reconciliation that Paul is talking about in Romans 5. When Paul says that 'being reconciled, we shall be saved by his life,' he is referring to the benefits received due to the one and only reconciliation mentioned in the first clause. This was reconciliation wrought through the death of Christ. One could paraphrase the sentence: 'We are reconciled by the death of His Son, and being thus reconciled, we shall be saved by his life.' It is obvious that the aorist participle καταλλαγεντεσ (from καταλλασσω, to change, exchange or restore to favour) in the second clause, retains the meaning of the first person plural Aorist indicative passive word κατηλλαγημεν in the first. The fact that the second occurrence of the word is a participle makes its dependence on the meaning of the first occurrence, a verb, even more certain. The context holds up this interpretation as, immediately after speaking of the reconciliation which took place at the death of Christ, Paul continues to speak of the atonement and its benefits to the elect. Death has reigned since Adam but the atonement has released Christ's righteousness to reign in those who have received His abundance of grace, though they were sinners and enemies of God before the atonement which was ordained for them was received by them. In other words, Christ died for those for whom his atonement was applicable.

2 Corinthians 5:18-21 refers to reconciliation no less than five times and in each case it is based on the atonement. a. 'And all things are of God, who hath reconciled us to Himself by Jesus Christ.' This is an obvious reference in the context to Christ's sufferings and death. b. 'And given us the ministry of reconciliation.' Here the reference is to the fact that believers are chosen of God to proclaim the reconciling work of Christ abroad. c. The contents of this message are plain, 'To wit, that God was in Christ, reconciling the world unto himself, not imputing their trespasses unto them.' Again this is an unmistakable reference to the atonement where Christ reconciled us to God and our sins were not imputed to us but imputed to Christ who bore them for us. The believer must witness to that reconciliation that was worked out on the cross. d. 'And hath committed unto us the word of reconciliation.' Again, it is obvious from the context that the preaching of the atonement is meant so that Christ may apply what is already accomplished. This is explained in e. 'Now then we are ambassadors for Christ, as though God did beseech you by us: we pray you in Christ's stead, be ye reconciled to God.' Even here, where the application of the atonement is being preached, it nevertheless keeps Christ's finished work on the cross central to its message as God's ambassador's preach 'in Christ's stead'. Christ is applying through them, what He has achieved for them on the cross. What actually happened when this actual reconciliation took place? Paul closes this mighty chapter with those words which Fuller would so eagerly diffuse into the mists of metaphor: 'For he hath made him to be sin for us, who knew no sin; that we might be made the righteousness of God in him.' The cross was the place where reconciliation was accomplished and the cross is the place where Christ's ambassadors have found it applied and it is the only place where anyone can find it. It was there that Christ exchanged His righteousness

for our sins, which is the 'proper' Biblical meaning of imputation, and in doing so, He reconciled us to God.

Reconciliation by means of imputed righteousness questioned

In his *Conversation on Imputation* and letter against Booth on imputation, Fuller believes he can best explain the Biblical doctrine of imputation linguistically using his favourite 'proper' and 'improper' explanation of terms. There is a 'proper' meaning of the word, he tells us, such as when Eli imputed drunkardness to Hannah. This meaning indicates 'judging a person and things according to what they are or appear to be'.[45] The term is also being used 'properly', Fuller tells us when we read that God does not impute sin to the believer. It is presumed that Fuller thus means, here, that saved sinners are not dealt with 'as they are or appear to be'. This must all be very confusing to readers as Fuller's examples of his 'proper' meaning of the word 'imputation' appear to indicate what is by no means 'proper' or literally 'correct'. Hannah was as we can read in 1 Samuel chapter 1, most sober so that drunkardness could not have been imputed to her and Romans 4:8 refers to people who certainly were not dealt with 'according to what they are' but according to what they certainly are not!

Fuller wrongly claims Calvin as an ally

The 'improper' use of the word, Fuller suggests is 'charging, reckoning, or placing to the account of persons and things that which does not properly belong to them, as though it did.' Again, Fuller appears to contradict his own definition. As examples of the 'improper' meaning Fuller gives Romans 4:3 and 4:5, 'Abraham believed God, and it was counted unto him for righteousness.' and 'To him that worketh not, but believeth on him that justified the ungodly, his faith is counted (imputed) for righteousness.' Here Fuller takes Wesley's side and argues that Paul is not speaking about the righteousness of Christ which is imputed to those who believe but a righteousness which is imputed because the person's own faith has 'a respect to the promised Messiah, and so to his righteousness as the ground of acceptance.' What Fuller calls 'the believing' must come first, i.e. a belief directed to Christ and then Christ's imputed righteousness follows. In order to give this view authority, Fuller refers, without quoting Calvin's words, to Calvin's *Institutes*, Book II, Chap. XI. §7. But this section neither refers to Abraham's faith; nor does it rule out imputed righteousness in such a case. Romans 4 is not even mentioned. In fact Calvin has already denied Fuller's interpretation in Paragraph 1 in arguing that where faith is expressed, it is the outcome of a believer being clothed in Christ's righteousness and can have no other cause. In Paragraph 6, Calvin argues that if any righteousness is present at all, it must be in the form of Christ our Righteousness, i.e. the imputed righteousness of Christ, and this argument is continued in Chap. XII where Calvin refers specifically to Abraham's case outlined in Romans 4. Furthermore Calvin explains how there is no such thing as a partial righteousness which serves as a preparation to receiving the imputed righteousness of Christ. In Chap. XI, §23 Calvin again stresses that there is no righteousness imputed but the righteousness of Christ which justifies us, and that 'the righteousness of Christ is communicated to him by imputation, while he is strictly deserving punishment.' In contrast to this, and in the passage Fuller mistakenly refers to, Calvin is criticising Osiander for *not accepting this doctrine* and putting forward his *essential imputation* theory which argues that the essence of Christ's divine nature is so diffused into us that we do not become righteous because of the free imputation of Christ's righteousness but because of the 'holiness and integrity which the divine essence dwelling in us inspires.'

Calvin emphasises *passive* faith, Fuller *active* in salvation

A further point worthy of note is that Fuller is here emphasising the *active* nature of faith in grasping out and taking the offer of the gospel which subsequently brings with it imputed righteousness. In Book III, Chap. XIV Calvin explains that 'in regard to justification, faith is merely *passive*, bringing nothing of our own to procure the favour of God.' Rather than teach active belief before justification and righteousness, the Bible pattern is that the gift of faith brings with it justification and righteousness in the form of Christ's imputed righteousness. Christ becomes 'our Righteousness' and thus faith and justification are sealed in us. Otherwise belief and justification would be there before a man was made righteous and Christ's righteousness would come to the already godly rather than the ungodly and there would thus be two kinds of righteousness; that which enables a man to stretch out and take God's offer and his being clothed subsequently with Christ's righteousness. It is thus 'proper' to conclude that where righteousness is imputed to Abraham, according to Fuller, it was because God was 'judging a person and things according to what they are or appear to be.' Yet Fuller cites Abraham's acceptance with God because of his belief as an 'improper' meaning of the word.

Linguistic juggling

Fuller's linguistic juggling of the word 'imputation' is again based on his own distaste of using what he calls 'commercial language' in expressing spiritual realities; a language which the Bible delights in using. The root meaning of 'to impute' in English comes from a Latin term meaning 'to enter into an account' or 'to put something to one's account'. This is a faithful rendering of the Greek word ελλογεω used in Romans 4:3. Its usage is illustrated in Philemon 18 where Paul says, 'If I have wronged thee, or owed thee ought, put that on mine account . . . I will repay it.' In clearing our accounts of debt through His own payment, Christ balanced our books so that we are no longer in the red in God's eyes. All our debts have been paid. All talk of 'proper' and 'improper' meanings of imputation is at best mere 'folk etymology', i.e. a most unscholarly approach to the subject, or at worst linguistic camouflage to rob a word of its true theological impact. It is interesting to note that even a secular work such as the *Concise Oxford Dictionary*, when dealing with the theological implications of 'to impute', states, 'ascribe (righteousness, guilt, to person) by vicarious substitution.' This is Christ's work of imputation in a nutshell. The definitive dictionary does not baffle its readers with 'proper' and 'improper' uses.

Fuller seeks the mock rather than the real thing
Why Fuller is so adamant in arguing that Paul used the word impute in an improper and therefore metaphorical sense is because he cannot believe that our guilt actually became Christ's guilt and Christ's righteous life actually becomes ours. He pays lip service to Scripture which says that Christ bore our sins, but argues that same Scripture away by saying that Christ bore them without having them. Fuller cannot admit what Scripture makes quite plain, i.e. that there is a partaking of man's likeness in Christ and a partaking of Christ's likeness in man. Paul says in Romans 8:3, 'For what the law could not do, in that it was weak through the flesh, God sending his own Son in the likeness of sinful flesh, and for sin, condemned sin in the flesh: That the righteousness of the law might be fulfilled in us, who walk not after the flesh but after the Spirit.' This is not a matter of metaphor but a reference to a historical event. The very fact that Christ was born of a woman and suffered, bled and died as a man showed that he partook of our frailties, which we bear as a punishment for sin. Fuller, however, bans physical infirmities from the concrete realms of the fall which has only taken place, in his opinion, in the nebulous, arbitrary, moral nature of things. Paul's argument has thus no hold on Fuller's logic. More difficult for Fuller must be the whole chapter of Isaiah 53 which stresses that Christ bore our griefs; carried our sorrows; was smitten and afflicted of God. We even read 'it pleased the Lord to bruise him;' and that, 'the Lord hath laid on him the iniquity of us all.' This does not sound at all like a token, metaphorical imputation without partaking of transferred iniquities and punishment. It sounds very much like what it is - the real thing!

Reconciliation through substitution and satisfaction re-interpreted
Matthew 5:17, 20 is most clear in its message that Christ came to fulfil the
Law and it is a central teaching of Christianity that Christ fulfilled the Law
on behalf of his Bride the Church, past, present and future. It is also a
central doctrine of the Christian faith that Christ was made liable for the
sins of His Bride and though just, he took upon himself the guilt, the
penalties and the punishment of His unjust loved ones that the claims of
God's broken law against them might be lifted. Galatians 3:13 even goes so
far as to say 'Christ hath redeemed us from the curse of the law, being
made a curse for us: for it is written, Cursed is every one that hangeth on
a tree.' So great was Christ's determination to save us that he became
accursed for our sake. This, the doctrine of penal and vicarious substitution
is the very heart-beat of Christianity and if that is taken away, we are still in
our sins and our faith is in vain.

All this talk of punishment, guilt and being accursed is terrible to Fuller's
ears who goes to great lengths to explain that these penal terms must be
re-interpreted because they cannot possibly mean that an innocent Person
was treated by God as guilty. Indeed, Fuller denies that there is any
provision for substitution in matters concerning the Law. Quoting faithful
Milton who claimed that man must die unless:

> Some other able, and as willing, pay
> The rigid satisfaction, death for death,

unfaithful Fuller begs to differ and says:

> The law made no such condition or provision; nor was it
> indifferent to the Lawgiver who should suffer, the sinner or another
> on his behalf. The language of the law to the transgressor was not,
> *Thou shalt die, or some one on thy behalf*, but simply, *Thou shalt
> die*: and had it literally taken its course, every child of man must
> have perished. The sufferings of Christ in our stead, therefore, are
> not a punishment inflicted in the ordinary course of distributive
> justice, but an extraordinary interposition of infinite wisdom and
> love; not contrary to, but rather above the law, deviating from the
> letter, but more than preserving the spirit of it. Such, brethren, as
> well as I am able to explain them, are my views of the substitution of
> Christ.[46]

Fuller is forgetting that the law did make provision for a whole row of
substitutionary sacrifices, all of which pointed to Christ as their true

fulfilment. Up to the time of Fuller for the simple, ordinary child of God, it was sufficient to know that Christ's substitutionary death showed that he was 'the Lamb of God which taketh away the sin of the world.' He was also seen as the One 'once offered to bear the sins of many' and was the One 'who his own self bare our sins in his own body on the tree, that we, being dead to sins, should live unto righteousness: by whose stripes ye were healed.'[47] Now Fuller maintains that substitution has nothing to do with the claims of the law on the sinner which Christ experienced in His own body. He tells us substitution is to be defined as 'an extraordinary interposition of infinite wisdom and love; not contrary to, but rather above the law, deviating from the letter, but more than preserving the spirit of it.'

The great benefit of the Biblical wording is that, deeply theological as it is, it is simple to understand and displays the love of Christ in a way which draws souls to Him. It is the gospel. Fuller's definition has no basis in Scripture which looks upon Christ's sacrifice as having a primary relation to the killing letter of the Law, although who would deny that Christ did not fulfil the spirit of the Law in His perfect obedience to it? Fuller's substitution theory is obviously contrary to the Mosaic Law because it is not centred in it. Fuller says that it is 'above the law'. This is Antinomianism at its most obtrusive as the Law reflects the very mind and character of God Himself and nothing can be above it as it is God's almighty will. Furthermore, Fuller's definition is quite meaningless as it does not in any way say wherein Christ's substitutionary work lay. It neither alludes to the lost state of the sinner nor to the divine method of lifting the death sentence from him. Nor does it refer to the nature and purpose of Christ's vicarious death. It is substitution without atonement and therefore a mock-gospel.

3. How Then Can Man Be Justified With God?

Job's question aired in Job 25:4 is the very question that the gospel preacher seeks to answer. His message is found in Acts 13:39, 'And by him (Christ) all that believe are justified from all things, from which ye could not be justified by the law of Moses.' It was in acting as Abraham and seeing Christ afar off as the One who could justify him before God that Job was able to utter those stirring words in Job 19:25, 'For I know that my redeemer liveth, and that he shall stand at the latter day upon the earth: And though after my skin worms destroy this body, yet in my flesh shall I see God.'

Justification as a purpose in the Divine mind denied
Fuller's doctrine of justification has not this clarity of sight, indeed, it

could not be more confused and confusing. When expounding Romans 3:24, Fuller departs from the view of traditional Calvinism expressed by John Gill who taught that justification is an act of God, determined before all time, yet terminating in the conscience of a believer when faith is given. Fuller denies that justification is an eternal decree of God as this would limit it, for him, to the secret will of God and not to the revealed will of God which, he believes, is the justifying factor. Thus justification is not 'a purpose in the Divine mind' but 'consists of the voice of God, in the gospel, declaring that whosoever believeth shall be saved'.[48] Though in his essay entitled *Justification*, Fuller is careful to stress that good works are the result of faith rather than the ground of faith, he yet leaves the onus of justification on man. He who seeks justification must sit down at the gospel feast spread and take and eat. Justification is thus not seen as a direct gift according to God's sovereign will, but a grasping out for an indiscriminately given 'free offer'.

Gill's position clarified
Here, as so often, Fuller has misunderstood Gill. When writing against the rationalistic view of the perfect nature and fitness of things being recognisable to fallen man, which became one of Fuller's favourite doctrines, Gill compared this with the Biblical doctrine of justification without which man was unfit to recognise anything which was perfect. He then shows how the doctrine so loved by Fuller leads directly to Antinomianism. Defending the doctrine of justification which Fuller rejects, he says:

> For if the moral nature and fitness of things is the supreme, original, universal, and most perfect rule of action to all reasonable beings whatsoever, prior to, and independent of the will of God, then what need is there of the law of God? or, what regard should be paid, to it? Since it is said, 'It is impossible that there can be a rule of action more excellent in itself, or more worthy the regard of reasonable beings.' Now, to set aside, and disregard the law of God, as a rule of life and conversation or action, is strictly and properly Antinomianism. For my part, I have been traduced as an Antinomian, for innocently asserting, that the essence of justification lies in the eternal will of God; my meaning is, that God in his all-perfect and comprehensive mind, had from all eternity, at once, a full view of all his elect; of all their sins and transgressions; of his holy and righteous law, as broken by them, and of the complete and perfect righteousness of his Son, who had engaged to be surety for them; and in this view of things he willed them to be

righteous, through the suretyship-righteousness of his Son, and accordingly esteemed, and accounted them so in him; in which will, esteem, and account their justification lies, as it is an immanent act in God. By this way of thinking and speaking I no ways set aside, nor in the least oppose the doctrine of justification by faith; I assert, that there is no knowledge of justification, no comfort from it, nor any claim of interest in it, until a man believes.[49]

Witsius' position is, in effect, the same
Fuller held Hugo Witsius in high respect but this great Christian scholar was one of Gill's greatest mentors. Indeed, it was Gill along with Brine and a few other gospel ministers that had Witsius re-introduced to Britain. It is thus no surprise to find that Gill is only echoing the thoughts of Witsius who gives good Biblical evidence for them. Witsius does not separate his doctrine of justification from election and says:

> Election is the eternal, free, and immutable counsel of God, about revealing the glory of his grace, in the eternal salvation of some certain persons. Most of the parts of this description are in the words of the apostle, Ephesians 1:4-6, 'according as he hath chosen us in him, before the foundation of the world, that we should be holy, and without blame before him in love: having predestinated us unto the adoption of children, by Jesus Christ to himself, to the praise of the glory of his grace, wherein he hath made us acceptable in the beloved.'[50]

Witsius argues how this election from eternity which was an election to the benefits and privileges of God's grace, includes effectual calling, adoption, sanctification, conservation, glorification and, of course, justification. All these are according to God's *purpose*, which is the same word as God's *decree* in the Greek. Witsius emphasises that no outside influence or any other factor has any co-function in working out this purpose. Thus Fuller's dualism in salvation composed of God's purpose partnered with man's agency finds no place in Witsius theology. Worthy of note here is that Witsius condemns the Socinian doctrine which speaks of a general predestination in eternity of all who obey Christ but a particular election when a person actually performs the conditions of the general predestination. This view, as we shall see, comes very near that of Fuller. Witsius looks upon saving faith as synonymous with justifying faith. If this is so, and Witsius' detailed expositions indicate that it must be so, then Fuller in teaching the duty of fallen man to exercise saving faith, is actually saying that fallen man has a duty to justify himself. This, to Witsius, would mean fallen man has a duty to place himself in the ranks of the elect. Needless to say, Witsius taught such a ridiculous notion as little as it is found in Scripture. To Witsius, just as the elect are declared saved, so they are declared justified. Justification is God's declaration of righteousness. This was sealed, not in time, though its outworking was in time, but in Christ's atoning death. Witsius takes up the argument that this would mean that full salvation was not worked out in the mind of God before time began but rejects it by pointing out that Christ was subject to God's decrees just as the elect. Christ, according to God's decree was 'slain before the foundation of the world.' Man's salvation with its accompanying justification are timeless entities in the mind of God.[51] Thus Witsius can argue that the oneness in Christ the elect have with Him is prior to the imputation of His righteousness for justification in time.

Fuller sees particular justification in the acceptance of a general invitation
Fuller criticises those who speak of justification as an appropriation of faith which is a gift of God as he believes it smacks to much of the decree 'in God's mind' which he cannot accept. He says rather, 'The gospel is a *feast freely provided*, and sinners of mankind are *freely invited* to partake of it. There is no mention of any gift, or grant distinct from this, but this itself is ground sufficient.' If, however, my justification starts when I reach out and grasp the gospel feast offered, what faith is exercised here to gain my justification apart from my own works? Obviously sensitive of giving the impression that faith is a product of works, Fuller argues that justification does not merely belong to the one who grasps out for it but is *ipso facto* a gift of God to all men. Thus he can affirm 'justification and eternal life are absolutely given, granted, and promised, to all who hear the gospel'.[52] This does not, however, explain why one grasps this 'gift' and the other refuses it. If God has given all men this gift, one wonders why all men do not exercise it, particularly as Fuller always insists that fallen man always desires the highest good which is the pursuit of happiness.

If justification does not proceed from God's mind, where does it come from?
Surely Fuller's problem is solved if he accepts the gospel revelation that God has loved His elect with an everlasting love and chosen them in Christ before the foundation of the world to be restored, forgiven, justified, sanctified and glorified in their Lord? It is also part of the gospel revelation that Christ does not lose even one of His sheep and all that He died for are justified, this being arranged before the foundation of the world. If this is

not 'conceived in the Divine mind', where was it conceived? It is certain that no sinner could conceive such a plan and even if he could, it would be a pointless conception for him. Fuller's idea of justification is as vague as his idea of redemption. Though he believes in justification as much as redemption, what he understands by these terms is something quite different to traditional usage and is explained in such a nebulous and unclear way that anyone hearing his 'gospel' must be forgiven for finding it a message of confusion and quite unworthy to be accepted.

The supposed 'holy disposition' prior to justification
Fuller, however, referring to Romans 4:5, does not accept 'that when a sinner is justified he is actually an enemy of God: for in the same text he is supposed to be a believer, which character is inconsistent with such a state of mind.' The well-known Baptist pastor Dr. Joseph Jenkins (1743-1819) of Walford, in true Calvinist manner, had argued that the text means that the Christian stops being an enemy of God on being justified. He is at enmity with God *until* justification. This does not satisfy Fuller by any means. He wants to know what state of mind a man is in 'with regard to enmity and friendship, *antecedent* to his justification.' He feels that prior to being justified, man cannot possibly be at enmity with God as he must have some 'holy disposition of heart' to reach out and grasp what God gives him. Fuller thus asks the question, 'Do the Holy Scriptures, which form the statute book of heaven, and fully express the mind of God, pronounce any man pardoned or justified in his sight, while his heart is in a state of enmity against him?'[53] 'Yes,' says Dr Jenkins. 'No,' says Andrew Fuller.

Fuller believes he can get round this problem by a neat piece of theological issue-dodging in his usual word-juggling manner. In his *Remarks on God's Justifying the Ungodly*,[54] He explains that such a verse as Romans 4:5, 'But to him that worketh not, but believeth on him that justifieth the ungodly, his faith is counted for righteousness.' is a unique passage in Scripture. We must then compare it with other clear passages on the subject in order to discover its true meaning. Fuller does not, however, come up with such passages but argues stubbornly on in the same course. The words cannot mean, he argues, that God justifies anterior to belief, i.e. while we were yet in our unforgiven sins, so it must refer to something else. As the Bible only speaks of believers being justified, this cannot mean that unbelievers are justified. Therefore, the word 'ungodly' does not refer to our state prior to belief at all but to the simple fact that believers remain ungodly until death. The saints are always ungodly! Fuller thus actually interprets Romans 4:5 to mean that Christ justifies *believers* who are *ungodly* and that 'ungodly' does not refer to a pre-faith state but the permanent state of sinners and saints alike. Realising that such a radical interpretation needs strong evidence, Fuller gives five reasons for his point of view:

1. There is no forgiveness without repentance.

Where there is no pardon, there can thus be no justification. Fuller mentions as 'evidence' such references as Psalm 32:5, Proverbs 28:13 and Mark 1:4 which he believes show that repentance must proceed justification so that one cannot say that a person is at enmity with God until he is justified. The 'ungodly' who are justified must thus be believers. The Scripture references which Fuller lists, but neither quotes nor expounds, are either irrelevant or contradict his theory full on. For instance he lists Acts 5:31 'Him hath God exalted with his right hand to be a Prince and Saviour, for to give repentance to Israel, and forgiveness of sins.' This is obviously a reference to God acting on an unbeliever in giving him repentance and faith before any previous belief is shown. It is God exercising grace on His enemies. Fuller might also have added Acts 11:18, Romans 2:4, and 2 Timothy 2:25 which all stress that it is God who *leads to* repentance; God who *grants* repentance and God who 'peradventure' i.e. according to his will, *gives* repentance. Rather than being a unique reference to God justifying His enemies, the texts Fuller quotes to explain away Romans 4:5 merely back it up. The whole purport of the Bible is that God grants forgiveness of sins, He grants faith and He grants justification—all to sinners. He does so from the point of view of His own decrees before the beginning of time and His own loving control of His world, motivated not by man's agency but by His Divine purpose. Fuller argues that in all God's gifts there is a cause and effect relationship with man's agency as the initial cause and not any factor in God's mind. But this is quite contrary to the texts Fuller himself quotes. They show that repentance, faith and justification are indeed 'in God's mind' and are not merely lying around to be grasped by 'whosoever will' leading to a justification in stages.

2. God only justifies already-believers.

Faith, Fuller argues, works by love and those who love God cannot be at enmity with him. Here Fuller quotes such verses as John 3:18, 36, Acts 13:39 and Romans 3:26, 28 to support his argument. Again, Fuller's argument reminds one of the conundrum concerning which came first, the hen or the egg. Creationists would say the hen but Fuller sees justification starting as a germinal step in faith (the egg) which develops into a mature justification (the hen). He never seems to consider the fact that the atonement brings the elect an all-in-one salvation because he does not believe that the atonement has this kind of efficacy. It has not bought man free in one redeeming act but is there as a mere moral deterrent, showing God's displeasure at sin which has to be applied in stages according to man's natural capacities and spiritual awareness in accepting it. Justification, he would remind us, is spread out before the wills of the whosoever to be taken by those who have the spark of faith to see their need for it.

Romans 5:10 quite contradicts Fuller and shows that Romans 4:5 is no unique dark passage. Indeed Paul often says the same thing as it is an essential part of the Gospel. Here, for instance, he says: 'For if, when we were *enemies*, we were reconciled to God by the death of his Son, much more, being reconciled, we shall be saved by his life.' No Scripture could more clearly show that God performed the work of reconciliation on unbelievers who were His personal enemies. They thus became justified believers which is what Fuller's proof texts all show in spite of his contrary interpretation. This was attained as a once-and-for-all-time act by Christ's vicarious death which, as Paul further explains, procured life-giving atonement. Paul then goes on to argue in v. 15. 'But not as the offence, so also is the free gift. For if through the offence of one many be dead, much more the grace of God, and the gift by grace, which is by one man, Jesus Christ, hath abounded unto many. And not as it was by one that sinned, so is the gift: for the judgment was by one to condemnation, but the free gift is of many offences unto justification.' The whole context here shows that God allows His abundance of saving grace to give full salvation, including justification, freely to those who were in rebellion against Him. Otherwise salvation, including justification, would not be of grace. It would be sending for the divine Physician to heal the already-healed. It is interesting to note that Fuller's major, and quite unfounded, criticism of his orthodox fathers was that they only had a gospel for believers. Fuller's gospel that justifies, he insists, is most definitely for believers only. This is not the gospel that God commands to be preached to all men.

Fuller's point that the sinner must feel love for God otherwise he would not reach out to Him is typical for the man who repeatedly stresses that God embraces the heart which is turned to Him. This is quite contrary to Scripture which firmly states, 'We love him, because he first loved us' (1 John 4:19). It is when God embraces us that our heart turns to Him.

3. Justification is preceded by vocation or calling.
As this calling is a 'holy calling'(2 Timothy 1:9) the hallowed called cannot be at enmity with God. Here Fuller gives Romans 8:29,30 and 2 Timothy 1:9 as his proof texts, albeit the former in a highly truncated version. He omits

124 124   *Law and Gospel*

the words 'to be conformed to the image of his son'. One cannot help thinking this is because this Biblical emphasis hardly fit into Fuller's general pattern of a mere symbolic or figurative imputation. In quoting Romans 8:29ff., which actually reads, 'Whom he did foreknow, he also did predestinate *to be conformed to the image of his son,*[55] . . . them he also called: and whom he called, them he also justified: and whom he justified, them he also glorified,' Fuller is contradicting his thesis that justification was not in the mind of God as a decree but merely a feast spread for the whosoevers to reach out and take. Here we see that the full and final conversion of the elect was decreed by God before time to be appropriated in time. Fuller, however, stresses both that there is a time sequence in man's experience of God's decree and that there is a procedure of events in keeping with *the order of nature*; vocation, for instance, comes before justification. This vocation, Fuller explains, 'is a holy one, the same with that mentioned in 2 Timothy 1:9 'He hath saved us, and called us with a holy calling;' which must therefore be inconsistent with enmity to God.' One would think here, Fuller is arguing that the holy call goes out from man to God rather than the reverse. The fact that God's call is holy in no way indicates that those who were called were holy before that calling. Obviously the opposite is meant. That holy call, as the texts say, was the fact of being saved which puts one who had no righteousness of His own, under the righteousness of Christ. This is all quite consistent with the fact that man was at enmity with God before salvation. Indeed this was the way God chose because man was at enmity with Him that man might be reconciled to Him. Romans 5:8 always shows up the follies of Fuller's argument with its clear and distinct message, 'But God commendeth His love towards us, in that, *while we were yet sinners*, Christ died for us.'

4. Faith must precede justification
In this section Fuller comes very near to saying that justification is not part of the Christian faith but something which comes as a bonus after faith is born, appropriated and used. In his doctrine of righteousness and justification by stages, he argues that 'justification by faith in Jesus Christ' shows that 'a holy disposition' must precede justification. Fuller is again resting on his Arminian interpretation of Abraham's faith which was counted as righteousness. His view, however, is that the righteousness that Abraham's faith wrought was other than the righteousness of Christ. It was that righteousness which looked ahead to the work of the Messiah and reception of Christ's righteousness. It does appear that Fuller, who wrongly accused Gill of having two doctrines of holiness, has two doctrines of righteousness himself.

When James Hervey, dealing with Romans 4, on Abraham's righteousness, asked Wesley 'What can this be, but the righteousness of Christ?', Wesley denied that there was any reference to Christ's righteousness in the example and replied, 'Paul tells us quite plainly in Rom. iv. "To him that believeth on him that justifieth the ungodly, faith is imputed for righteousness,"' and argued that it was Abraham's active faith that secured righteousness for him.[56] This strange exegesis is also Fuller's. It is clear from the context and from our Lord's own commentary on what constituted Abraham's faith, that Abraham looked forward to the coming of One who could give him that which he could not achieve himself. Paul says in the same context, 'He staggered not at the promise of God through unbelief, but was strong in faith, giving glory to God; And being fully persuaded that, what he had promised he was able to perform.' Paul then adds, '*Therefore*, it was imputed to him for righteousness'. Here it is obvious that Abraham is trusting in something that God is to perform, giving God the glory for it. When we turn to Christ's words to the Jews in John 8:56, 'Your father Abraham rejoiced to see my day: and he saw it, and was glad' we see that it was truly the promise of Christ that spurred Abraham on to believe. This is why Paul in Romans 4 ends the passage on imputed righteousness with the teaching that Christ 'was delivered for our offences, and was raised again for our justification' and it is through Christ that we have 'access by faith into this grace wherein we stand'. Realising that Christ died in our stead, the just for the unjust, it is surely not a long step away then to realise that we are only counted righteous because God in Christ would have it that way. We are accounted righteous in Christ because we have had Christ's righteousness put on us. This is why Paul can write, 'For if by one man's offence death reigned by one; much more they which receive abundance of grace and of the gift of righteousness shall reign in life by one, Jesus Christ.' Thus the righteousness which Abraham possessed was the righteousness with which Christ had clothed him and the justification given to Abraham stemmed, not from any 'holy disposition' separate from Christ's imputed righteousness and justification but because Christ's atonement covered Abraham's offences and guaranteed him justification. God does not apply these piecemeal to His elect, according to any 'order of nature' or 'order of time' but it was all accomplished at Calvary and it is all applied to the sinners for whom Christ died.

5. A righteousness by the renunciation of works

Keeping to Romans 4:5, Fuller now argues that it was not works which saved Abraham but his *renunciation* of works was the grounds of his acceptance with God. The renunciation came first, then the acceptance. Again, Fuller contradicts himself with his quotes. He lists Ephesians 1 to back up his theory that justification and Christ's imputed righteousness are posterior to the righteousness that comes with belief. However, this passage outlines our being made 'acceptable in the beloved' (v. 6), which is all part of our being chosen in Christ to be holy and without blame before the foundation of the world (v.4). Being made acceptable is not consecutive to any *renunciation* on man's part but purely out of grace. Acceptability with God brings with it all that is necessary to pronounce us 'holy and without blame', which can only mean that with God's acceptance of us in Christ, our Lord's righteousness is imputed to us and God's justification is ours, otherwise God would not have given us His gifts of acceptability and we would not be thus accepted. Ephesians 1 does not speak of acceptability in stages, nor does it speak of man's agency being at the forefront in salvation with man having to take the first step. Renunciation of works can only mean one of two things. Either the person involved looks upon such an action as his crowning work, and thus strives to be saved by showing great discipline in exercising such a strong will *or* He has already received the righteousness of Christ which makes him see the futility of works-righteousness. Obviously the latter meaning is the meaning of the Bible as Abraham, with this righteous act, became the father of believers in Christ.

However Fuller strives to explain that God embraced Abraham because Abraham turned his heart to Him, Fuller can never claim that it was Abraham's own faith, irrespective of Christ's faith that justified him. Paul tells Fuller in Galatians 2:16, 'Knowing that a man is not justified by the works of the law, but by the faith of Jesus Christ.'

Fuller's confusion in speaking of a time lag between faith, belief, righteousness and justification, caused elderly Abraham Booth to take up his pen against Fuller. He argued that Fuller did not so much teach a doctrine of ungodly believers, as he professed to do, but, in reality, he held to the absurd doctrine of a godly unbeliever; one who had virtually exercised faith before proper belief occurred. Booth denied absolutely that there was anything holy in a sinner even at the moment he believes. Belief is a gift of God. Seeing some validity in Booth's argument, but not considering it of any theological importance, E. F. Clipsham,[57] Fuller's modern defender and populariser, says: 'He (Fuller) was pleading for a priority in the order of nature rather than of time.' Clipsham explains what he means by saying 'an effect must immediately follow a cause.' But this would not be in the order of nature if it were not also in the order of time. Clipsham, in defending Fuller is reaffirming that Fuller taught the need for a man to turn his heart to God before God can embrace him. Up to the rise of Fullerism, it had been the accepted view amongst Particular Baptists that the believer loved God because God first loved him. It was God's embrace that changed the believer's heart. Hosea tells us in Chapter 11 of his prophecy, 'I drew them with cords of a man, with bands of love.' and Berridge says of the 'friend that sticketh closer than a brother':

> A method strange this Friend has shown,
> Of making love divinely known
> To rebels doomed to die;
> *Unasked*, he takes our humblest form,
> And condescends to be a worm,
> To lift us up on high.

In Fuller's five points to prove that God justifies believer's only, arguing that faith and belief precede righteousness and justification, it is obvious that in each argument, Fuller sees the onus in initiative to be on man's agency. Indeed one of Fuller's favourite phrases in summing up the work of the gospel is 'reconciling the purpose of God and the agency of man' The agency of man must be put to work before God's purpose can be carried out. Where is human agency in Hebrews 10:14, 'For by one offering he hath perfected for ever them that are sanctified?'

Fuller's is typical Arminian theology which brought Wesley's anger upon James Hervey's book *Theron and Aspasio* where Hervey outlines the Biblical doctrines of imputed righteousness and justification, 'That we might be made the righteousness of God in him, not intrinsically, but imputatively.' Wesley, in contrast, maintained like Fuller, that salvation is teamwork between God's purpose and man's agency with man displaying inherent righteousness, grasping out and receiving Christ's righteousness as a reward. For Hervey this took away the complete reliance on the righteousness of Christ without which the sinner was still lost. Any talk of two righteousnesses being merged in man so that he possesses half imputed righteousness and half of his own, Hervey tells Wesley, 'is like interweaving linen and woollen: the motley mixture forbidden to the Israelites. Or rather like weaving a thread of the finest gold with a hempen cord, or a spider's web. The righteousness which is of God, is perfect, consummate, everlasting. Not so inherent righteousness, your own self being judge, your own pen being witness.'[58]

Hervey then goes on to show how the Apostle counts his own righteousness as but dung but the transforming righteousness of God is revealed from Heaven. Hervey tells his former tutor, 'The righteousness of

God is always imputed; but, being imputed, it produces the righteousness inherent. Being justified by the former, saved from hell, and rendered meet for heaven; we are sanctified also, and disposed to love the Lord, who has dealt so bountifully with us. And if to love, then to worship him, to serve him, to imitate him.' This was all, for Hervey, part and parcel of being in union with Christ.

4. Partakers of the Divine Nature

Union with Christ

The doctrine of the believer's union with Christ is one of the sweetest and most comforting parts of the gospel. Speaking of Paul's words in Galatians 2:20, 'I live, yet not I, but Christ liveth in me,' Cotton Mather says:

> O the astonishing Felicity which we are now *advised* of! yea, now *invited* to! But, *will God indeed come to dwell on the Earth*! Yea, will he come to *dwell* in the Children of Men, who by Sin have become such *defiled Earth*! The Son of God come to *dwell* in them, and *live* in them, and keep them *alive* unto God! O the *Wonders*, O the *Triumphs*, of the *Free Grace*, which allows us this Expectation!

> We have here a Servant of God *writing his own Life*: And the sum of it is, That he hath *no Life of his own*. Tho' he were yet *living in the Flesh*, his *Life* was of a very *Spiritual* Character. It was a *Life* carry'd on with and by the Exercise of a *lively Faith* in the Son of God. Such a Faith duly exercised has this for the blessed *Concomitant*, and indeed the blessed *Original* of it, a *Christ living* in the Believer. The Believer now *lives* unto God; but it is a glorious *Christ* who makes him and keeps him *alive*, and by his good Spirit so *quickens* him in every *Motion* of his *Life*; and he so *lives and moves* in Him, that he may truly say, *''Tis not I that live, but Christ liveth in me.'* [59]

Mather expresses the joy all Christians experience when faced with the filth of their sins but with trust in the promises of God that He will make us new creatures in Christ Jesus and finish the work He has started in us from within us. Though Fuller uses the term 'union' with relation to the believer's standing in Christ, it soon becomes obvious that this expression does not mean to him what it has always meant in orthodox Christianity i.e. actual union with Christ. True, he uses the term to describe receiving 'the benefits or the effects of Christ's righteousness in justification,' but qualifies this by affirming 'I never met with a person who held the absurd notion of imputed benefits, or imputed punishments; and am inclined to think there never was such a person'.⁶⁰ Thus, whatever benefits the believer has from Christ, they are not due to imputation, they were not part of Christ and have now, by grace, become part of the believer.

Fuller cannot imagine Christ's actions becoming ours
What Fuller is objecting to, is the belief that union with Christ entails literally 'the actions of either becoming those of the other'. Thus any idea of Christ suffering the wrath of God at Calvary when paying the penalties of our sins or any idea of believer's becoming Christ-like through the indwelling Christ and through the power of the Holy Spirit, is denied completely by Fuller. Using Tobias Crisp as his example of Christians who believe this possible, pontifical James, alias Fuller, tells Peter and John, 'We have been told of an old protestant writer who says, that "In Christ, and by him, every true Christian may be called *a fulfiller of the law*;" but I see not why he might not as well have added, Every true Christian may be said to have been slain, and if not to have redeemed himself by his own blood, yet be worthy of all that blessing, and honour, and glory that shall be conferred upon him in the world to come.'⁶¹

This statement is quite unworthy of Fuller as Crisp was being perfectly Scriptural in what he said and Fuller's taunting contribution shows that Fuller does not know what Crisp meant by *being in Christ* and working *by Christ*. Paul, writing to the Galatians in chapter 2:20 says what Fuller was quite ignorant of, indeed, he points out the very thing that Fuller ridicules and which Cotton Mather had so warmly received: 'I am crucified with Christ: nevertheless I live; yet not I, but Christ liveth in me: and the life which I now live in the flesh I live by the faith of the Son of God, who loved me, and gave himself for me.' Paul says to the Galatians, 'Bear ye one another's burdens, and so fulfil the law of Christ.' (6:2), and obviously expected them, in union with Christ to accomplish it. What would Fuller make of Philippians 4:13, 'I can do all things through Christ which strengthens me?' Nor was Paul idly boasting when he told the Colosians that he was fulfilling the Word of God (1:25). In fact Crisp was obviously referring to Romans 8:3-4 where Paul says, 'For what the law could not do, in that it was weak through the flesh, God sending his own Son in the likeness of sinful flesh, and for sin, condemned sin in the flesh: That the righteousness of the law might be fulfilled in us, who walk not after the flesh, but after the Spirit.' Concerning the 'blessing, and honour and glory' Fuller feels Crisp should have consequently claimed for himself, does not

Matthew 26:21 teach us that the faithful steward will hear the great 'Well done' as he enters into the joy of the Lord? Such talk, Fuller declares is 'carrying principles to extreme'.[62] What would then Fuller make of Romans 8:17 which declares that we are joint-heirs with Christ in both His sufferings and His glory?

Fuller is eager to quote Witsius as his authority but no Calvinistic writer emphasised the unity of Christ with His Bride as much as he did. He also emphasised unity in suffering, both Christ's sufferings for the Christian and the Christian's necessary suffering for Christ's sake. He also stresses the Christian's partaking of Christ's sufferings in the two-way imputation. In his chapter on *Justification* in *The Economy of the Covenants,* Witsius emphasises that the elect:

> are so closely united to him by faith, as to be *one body*, 1 Corinthians 12:13 and which is still more indissoluble, *one spirit with him*, 1 Corinthians 6:17 nor are they only united, but he and they are *one* [63], and that by such an unity or oneness, in which there is some faint resemblance of that most simple oneness, whereby the divine persons are one among themselves, John 17:22-23. But in virtue of this union or oneness, which the elect have with Christ by faith, they are accounted to have done and suffered whatever Christ did and suffered for them.[64]

Being partakers in Christ is not mere imagery
Fuller argues against calling a Christian 'a fulfiller of the Law' because he believes if Christ's obedience had really been imputed to believer's then we might as well call Christ a 'transgressor of the Law' because our disobedience was allegedly imputed to Him. Here both Fuller's logic and inadequate Bible-knowledge are running away with him. First, Crisp never claimed that he could fulfil the law in Adam, in the old man, but only when the Second Adam enabled him in the new man. Second, Fuller's idea that Christ could be called a transgressor is not as shocking as Fuller thinks it is. The prophet Isaiah says in crystal clear language that Christ was smitten of God and *numbered amongst the transgressors*. What Fuller fails to understand, and this pervades Crisp's sermons which brought crowds to Christ, is that the work of Christ on the cross is past history and completed. Christ has borne our sins in His body on the tree and has triumphed over the grave. Thus, there are no Biblical grounds for claiming that Christ is still numbered with the transgressors but there are strong Biblical grounds for claiming that those for whom He died are still partakers of the Body of

Christ i.e. we are the Church of which He is the living Head (1 Corinthians 10:16-17); we are partakers in Christ's sufferings (2 Corinthians 1:5 ff.); partakers in Christ Himself (Heb. 3:14); partakers of the Holy Ghost (Heb. 6:4), and even partakers in God's holiness (Heb. 12:10).

Christ's righteousness is not transferable and thus not receivable for Fuller
As strongly as Fuller affirms that there is no actual partaking of sin and righteousness in the Biblical doctrine of imputation, he also emphasises that 'neither sin nor righteousness is *in itself* transferable'.[65] We thus never really receive Christ's righteousness for our own. Fuller is here thinking in terms of the old man, whereas Crisp, whom Fuller is still criticising, was speaking in terms of the new man in Christ. Partaking of Christ or union with Christ, however, does bring with it a transference of righteousness as we grow in grace and in a knowledge of our Lord and Saviour Jesus Christ. Paul says in Romans 6:6 ff., 'Knowing this, that our old man is crucified with him, that the body of sin might be destroyed, that henceforth we should not serve sin. For he that is dead is freed from sin. Now if we be dead with Christ, we believe that we shall also live with him. . . . Likewise reckon ye also yourselves to be dead indeed unto sin, but alive unto God through Jesus Christ our Lord . . . for sin shall not have dominion over you.' The explanation Paul gives for this is that, 'Being then made free from sin, ye became the servants of righteousness.' Thus we see that the believer is capable of serving righteousness but only because he is wedded to Christ whose righteousness becomes his own. Indeed the very purpose of being wedded to Christ is so that we might do Christ's works of righteousness. Paul says in Romans 7:4, 'Wherefore my brethren, ye also are become dead to the law by the body of Christ; that ye should be married to another, even to him who is raised from the dead, that we should bring forth fruit unto God.' This is contrasted with our former state when we brought forth 'fruit unto death'. The very purpose of the atonement was for Christ to be united with the Bride of His choice and to purify her in Him. This is surely the meaning of Ephesians 5:25-30 where the Apostle says: 'Husbands, love your wives, even as Christ also loved the church, and gave himself for it; That he might sanctify and cleanse it with the washing of water by the word, that he might present it to himself a glorious church, not having spot, or wrinkle, or any such thing; but that it should be holy and without blemish . . . For we are members of his body, of his flesh, and of his bones.' Here union with Christ is shown to be not a mere moral metaphor but an actual identification with the very flesh and blood of Christ who represented His Church in His own body on the cross.

All this is denied by Andrew Fuller who maintains that no righteousness is transferred but merely the effects of Christ's righteousness are given us i.e. forgiveness and mercy in the form of pardon. Thus the atonement and the new birth do not change the sinners' conduct in any way. The sinner does not become a new creature. Paul however, argues in Romans 3:22 ff. that the righteousness of Christ is not only there for us i.e. so that we can profit from its effects in accomplishing our salvation but is 'upon all that believe'. Surely this must be more than a mere 'as if' state. We are talking about believers who have had their sins propitiated by the shedding of Christ's blood, and have become objects and partakers of Christ's faith. We are talking about believers who give God the glory for what they perform in His name and have the love of God shed abroad in their hearts by the Holy Spirit who is given to them. We are talking about believers who have the Law of God written on their hearts and can say, 'How shall we, that are dead to sin, live any longer therein?' If there is no putting on of Christ to be seen in the believer, no 'partaking of the divine nature of Christ' then the lack of fruit in that person's life will give him—and others —cause to believe that he is none of Christ's. Christ changes His people!

Nevertheless, we find Fuller, in his criticism of Crisp, emphasising that the doctrine of imputation and union with Christ cannot possibly have anything to do with a transfer of character. The believer remains the same sinner that he always was.[66] The only difference is that he is pardoned. In fact, all Fuller's theological jargon, whether he is referring to his metaphorical atonement, imputation, reconciliation, redemption or justification all boils down to the one word 'pardon'. The sinner is pardoned; and that is that. The hymn writer says, 'Ransomed, healed, restored, forgiven.' Fuller can only truly say 'Amen' to the last of these four features of salvation. His doctrine of pardon and forgiveness, however, falls short of the Biblical norm as no true restoration Christ-wards takes place but only Adam-wards.

No gospel that makes men righteous

Although Fuller emphasises that mankind fell in the realm of morals alone, surprisingly, he finds no moral change in the believer after conversion although the Bible tells us that faith without works is dead and we shall be known by the fruits of righteousness that we produce. Such fruits, according to Scripture, are the practical outworking of Christ's righteousness indwelling the new man. When Paul says to the Philippians, 'Let that mind be in you which is in Christ Jesus,' he is speaking about the Christian's new character. From where or from Whom does the believer obtain the wherewithal to change his character? Paul tells us in the same passage, 'For it is God which worketh in you both to will and do his good pleasure.' The Christian has thus a new character in Christ. This character is not an attribute of the crucified old man but is developed through the renewal which took place when he was bought and possessed by Christ and was made a new creature in Christ. God in Christ works in the believer. The Scriptures use very vivid language in describing how man receives a new mind. Ephesians 4:22 ff. says: 'That ye put off concerning the former conversation the old man, which is corrupt according to the deceitful lusts; And be renewed in the spirit of your mind; And that ye put on the new man, which after God is created in righteousness and true holiness.' For Fuller, this is highly figurative thinking that has no actual bearing on the quality of life now present in the believer. For the Scriptures, it is a concrete, objective fact to be taken seriously, otherwise the supposed believer is deceiving himself.

Christ's righteousness not brought into His union with His Bride according to Fuller

If there were no transfer of righteousness; if Christ did not bring His righteousness into His union with His Church, the believer would be left unrighteous. There would then be no gospel to preach that would be worthy of acceptance by seeking sinners. The gospel that is worthy of all acceptation is the gospel that makes a man righteous before God. Christ did not come to have us merely *considered* righteous, He came to *make* us righteous. Paul tells us clearly that this good news is true and that 'now being *made* free from sin, and *become* servants to God, ye *have* your fruit unto holiness, and the end everlasting life' (Romans 6:22). This testifies strongly to our union with Christ and to the fact that His righteousness triumphs in this union. This union is not merely one of moral character but, because of Christ's indwelling the believer, his whole personality and form is changed. The Apostle says in 2 Corinthians 3:18: 'We all, with open face beholding as in a glass the glory of the Lord, are *changed into the same image.*' Thus, to argue that union with Christ is a mere 'as if' formality with no practical outworking in the life of a believer, is to argue contrary to Scripture.

Fuller stresses rightly that Abraham's righteousness 'did not become meritorious, or cease to be unworthy'.[67] His proof of this, however, would seem to contradict him as he stresses again and again that it was belief prior to righteousness which brought on righteousness.[68] One might say, as many did, that Fuller held to 'unrighteous belief'. Fuller, however, stresses that the righteousness which Abraham did eventually receive was only an 'as if' righteousness, so it 'could not be *properly* imputed, or *counted*, by

Him who judges of things as they are, as being so.' This would mean that God never *counted* His elect as being His Son's perfect Bride which is the very meaning of the doctrine of imputation in Scripture. If the sinner is not counted as truly righteous by God, then we must doubt whether Christ's sacrifice truly blotted out his sins. A person not counted as righteous by God is one whose sins have not been blotted out. This is why a large question mark must be placed beside the whole of Fuller's theology. Just as his doctrine of righteousness never gets beyond the 'as if' stage, so his doctrine of the blotting out of sin is equally merely on the level of what never actually happened but was accepted by God as if it did happen. The Bible, however, stresses that the believer, *in the new man*, is capable of true righteous acts, and is expected to be 'filled with the fruits of righteousness, which are by Jesus Christ, unto the glory and praise of God' (Philippians 1:11). Thus, the very fact that Christ indwells those whom he properly counts as righteous, because He has atoned for them, enables them to do real works of righteousness and not merely live 'as if' they performed such works. Naturally this is not to their own merit but to the One who has saved them in order to show forth fruits to His glory.

Fuller's doctrine of holiness separated from actual union with Christ
This brings us to one of the most difficult points in understanding Fuller's system. Fuller does actually demand of his readers that they live holy lives, bringing forth fruit worthy of their calling. There is no doubt about this as witnessed by his work *The Gospel its own Witness* against the Deist's lack of personal holiness. However, in separating the doctrine of the practical outworking of a believer's righteous service from his union with Christ, Fuller leaves only three other possibilities for man's growth in sanctity. He either believes that the whole doctrine of righteousness, sanctification and holiness is merely a make-believe, 'as-if' sham, leaving no essential difference between the new man in Christ and the old man in Adam, *or* he believes man's own personal inherent longing to do good is strengthened after conversion *or* he believes that the holiness which God demands of the saints can be worked out by their observance of the Law. Actually Fuller, as this book clearly demonstrates, combines and relies on all three methods and thus opts out of the Reformed Faith altogether.[69]

The atonement was truly an at-one-ment
It is a Biblical truth that Christ's purpose in choosing His Bride was to unite Himself with her as a major step so 'that he might fill all things'. This is the plain teaching of Ephesians 4:10-16 which goes on to say:

And he gave some, apostles; and some, prophets; and some, evangelists; and some, pastors and teachers; For the perfecting of the saints, for the work of the ministry, for the edification of the body of Christ: Till we all come in the unity of the faith, and of the knowledge of the Son of God, unto a perfect man, unto the measure of the stature of the fullness of Christ: That we henceforth be no more children, tossed to and fro, and carried about with every wind of doctrine, by the sleight of men, and cunning craftiness, whereby they lie in wait to deceive; But speaking the truth in love, may grow up into him in all things, which is the head, even Christ: From whom the whole body fitly joined together and compacted by that which every joint supplieth, according to the effectual working in the measure of every part, maketh increase of the body unto the edifying of itself in love.

Union with Christ is not merely witnessing some 'effects' or receiving some 'benefits' of Christ's moral triumph over death as Fuller affirms. It is being a new creature in Christ. It is being one with our blessed Redeemer.

5. Servants to Righteousness unto Holiness

Fuller criticised his predecessors' doctrine of holiness

Fuller was most critical of the holiness doctrine of his fathers in the faith such as John Gill and John Brine from whose writings he concluded— quite wrongly—that they held to 'two kinds of holiness, one of which was possessed by man in innocence, and was binding on all his posterity—the other derived from Christ, and binding only on his people'.[70] Fuller, believing his own faulty conclusion, was then of the opinion that 'Those exhortations to repentance and faith, therefore, which are addressed in the New Testament to the unconverted, I supposed to refer only to such external repentance and faith as were within their power, and might be complied with without the grace of God. The effect of these views was, that I had very little to say to the unconverted, indeed, nothing in a way of exhortation to things spiritually good, or certainly connected with salvation.'

Such statements coming from the pen of Andrew Fuller were not shared by his biographer and fellow-Fullerite, Dr. John Ryland, who argued that Gill was perfectly orthodox in his view of Adam before the Fall.[71] Ryland, obviously conscious of the fact that Fuller looked to Gill as holding two different standards of morality and thus provoking Antinomianism, says;

'Dr. Gill, Mr. Brine, and Mr Toplady utterly reprobates that pernicious sentiment'.[72] Gill, Brine and Toplady, if they emphasised anything, it was not that man could gain an alternative holiness by returning to the pre-fall standards of Adam, which, incidentally, actually became the 'one holiness only' teaching of Fuller, but that Adam's posterity had no clue whatsoever as to what constituted a holy life, because of the Fall. Here Fuller was certainly in strong disagreement not only with Gill, Brine, Toplady but with the whole of Bible-believing Christianity!

Fuller's doctrine of holiness is the least convincing part of his system
No Fullerite doctrine is so unbiblical as his doctrine of sanctification and holiness. In fact Fuller completely reverses the Biblical norm here. William Cowper aptly says of the true heaven-sent gospel preacher:

> By him the violated law speaks out,
> It thunders; and by him, in strains as sweet
> As angels use, the gospel whispers peace,

The terrors of the Law are preached to show man how his sin has slain him and the gospel comes as balm for his self-inflicted wounds. Fuller thinks otherwise. As the Law has nothing to do with the covenant of works, the Law speaks alike to both sinner and saint, urging them to love God *the same as if they had never apostatised'.*[73] Thus Fuller's Gospel that he claims is worthy of all acceptation is to tell men to behave as if they were not fallen. After all; they have the natural and moral abilities and powers to do so! To this, Baptist historians of the Old School, C. B. and S. Hassell say:

> Many of Mr. Fuller's expressions, in regard to the ability and power of the un-renewed mind, go far beyond the Arminianism of James Arminius, John Wesley and Richard Watson, who declare that the un-renewed will and all the other faculties of the un-renewed mind are dead in trespasses and sins. Paul declares that 'the world cannot receive the Spirit of God;' and Christ declares that 'the world cannot receive the spirit of truth;' and that 'no man can come to Him except the Father draw Him.' What then shall we think of Mr. Fuller's fine-spun metaphysics about un-renewed human ability? How can any believer in the Scriptures believe a word of it? It is the superficial declaration of the Roman Catholic Council of Trent that Divine commands necessarily imply human ability - *just as though man had never fallen.*[74] Though man has fallen and become unable

to obey the commandments of God, the nature and law and requirements of God are unchanged and unchangeable.[75]

Thus Fuller can teach that the so-called moral law (his word for the Decalogue) contains all that is necessary to encourage a man to believe and take up his moral obligations. It is no wonder that Fuller rejected the teaching of Thomas Boston and the Marrow Men who emphasised that there are three rules to be followed: the rule of the Law, the rule of faith, and the rule of Christ, under which are the first two rules. No wonder Fuller rejected the teaching of William Huntington who maintained with true New Testament reasoning that if the Old Covenant had sufficed, there would have been no need for the New.

Not a new man in Christ but a restored old man in Adam

This teaching is symptomatic of Fuller's restoration view of salvation. It is not that the believer is a new man in Christ but that he is a restored old man in Adam. Adam's holiness, in Fuller's eyes, is the future holiness of those who are in Christ and when once a man is born again, he gains the status he would have had if Adam had not sinned.[76] Fuller, of course, completely ignores the fact that Adam's fall was physical and spiritual and death came to him physically when he sinned spiritually. Adam actually sinned in thought, word and deed. If converted man were again Adam-like, he would not see corruption. Sanctification thus in Fuller's interpretation is centred around the complete old man. It is being in Adam as Adam ought to have remained. But here is the snag. Adam's faith was untried and when it was put to the test, it failed. If we were given such a holiness, it would be a temporary thing indeed. William Button, son of one of John Gill's deacons, touched Fuller on this very spot, accusing him of believing that the righteousness we have in Christ is the same righteousness as we would have if we were still naturally holy and merely rejected the inclination not to believe. 'Natural holiness', Button tells Fuller, 'was liable to be lost; but spiritual holiness (i.e. that derived from Christ's righteousness in the new man) never was liable to, never was, never can be, lost.' Fuller replies that Button's argument is beside the point and does not prove that the natural principle in both is different. Holiness is holiness, no matter how long it lasts. Thus the holiness which the fallen angels lost is the same holiness as the elect angels keep. Fuller illustrates this on the human level by saying: 'A principle the same in nature may be produced in one subject, and left to the conduct of that subject to preserve it in being; while, in another subject in different circumstances, its existence may be infallibly secured by the promise and power of God.'[77] Fuller must argue in this way as he believes that the natural law, reflecting true holiness, is a standard irrespective of and prior to the revealed will of God and fully clear to all men. The awareness of that standard is there but not the inclination to keep it. This inclination is provided by Christ's demonstration of God's 'displeasure' at sin and 'amiability' towards sinners on the cross to motivate man to live up to his inherent standards.

Rather than Button's crucial argument being beside the point, Fuller's distinction between temporary and permanent holiness is fully irrelevant to the gospel story which promises eternal holiness to the elect and this is the only holiness accepted before God and thus the only true holiness possible. Fuller leaves out of consideration that Adam was a probationer. Born again believers are not probationers but have already had their rights to eternal holiness paid by Christ and entered into the Lamb's book of life. Adam failed as a probationer but Christ has kept Adam's probation and our probation for us in his life of obedience and has redeemed us from the debts accrued through our natural, fallen lack of holiness by his sacrificial, vicarious death on the cross. Here we see that it is not John Gill who has two views of holiness but Andrew Fuller himself.

The beauties of Christ are looked forward to in vain in Fuller's presentation of holiness

Fuller's many books and essays on the holy life make dreary reading indeed. Whether one takes his *The Holy Nature and Divine Harmony of the Christian Religion*, *The Nature of True Virtue*, *Morality not Founded in Utility*, *The Great Aim of Life* or *The Goodness of the Moral Law*, or any of his other moral essays dealing with that holiness without which no man can see the Lord, one looks for the work of the Holy Spirit or the indwelling of Christ in the believer in vain. This led William Rushton to complain that one heard from Fuller 'as little of the earnest and the witness of the Spirit as if we were Sandemanians.'[78] Most of Fuller's moral essays do not refer to the work of the Spirit once and Christ is left aside with an occasional general reference to 'the religion of Christ' or some such vagary as if Fuller were merely dropping the name of the Giver of holiness for formality's sake. There is much talk about man's striving for the common good and happiness, and very much talk about virtue but He who provides goodness, true happiness and virtue is quite left out as Fuller is dealing with his favourite topic, human agency.

It will thus come as no surprise that Fuller's doctrine of holiness and sanctification is based on a high view of man's human tendency towards and ability to embrace legal goodness. This we find in Fuller's lengthy treatise on holiness which fills Part I of his *The Gospel Its Own Witness or*

The Holy Nature and Divine Harmony of the Christian Religion Contrasted with the Immorality and Absurdity of Deism. This book which claims to portray Christian holiness against the immorality of Bolingbroke, Paine and Hume etc. fails completely in its aim. Though it is a book on holiness one has to read through page after page of kitchen gossip and muck-raking in which the sexual sins of the learned and famous are paraded before the reader's eyes. One is reminded of Paul's words in 1 Corinthians 5:1 concerning sins which are 'not so much as named among the Gentiles'. Fuller has no such inhibitions and seems to believe that in painting a picture of lasciviousness he is obeying his gospel of a moral deterrent and frightening man from sin. Such portrayals as Fuller gives can only serve to entertain man's fallen lusts—the opposite of making him holy.

One looks in vain for the beauties of Christ, held up against this sordidness. No antidote is offered. In fact Fuller rarely mentions Christ in the 57 paged work. There is only one reference in the whole book to the life of an upright Christian, who is depicted as reading the Bible, worshipping God and engaging in Christian conversation. We are not told what made him thus and how these exercises relate to holiness. There is only one exhortation to believe in Christ but, again, not to how this promotes holiness. The fact that the Holy Spirit is mentioned but once in the whole 7 chapters speaks volumes regarding Fuller's doctrine of holiness. This is a quote from Philippians 2:1 (if any fellowship of the Spirit) which is one of a number of quotes bearing the majority of Fuller's references to Christ which are merely listed but which are sadly not expounded, nor their sources given. We are merely told that they reflect motives which induce Christians to practice morality.

Every man is supposed to desire a good which has no limits

Fuller's final chapter in his holiness treatise is entitled *Christianity a Source of Happiness* in which he outlines his philosophy that fallen man has a basic desire to do good and this draws him to the goodness of Christ in whom he finds his heart's desire for happiness. This basic desire in man, which Christ utilises in drawing the sinner to Himself, is obviously a purely selfish desire. This does not worry Fuller at all! His point is that such a desire can be satisfied in Christianity rather than in other philosophies. Of fallen man, he says, 'Every one who looks into his own heart, and makes proper observations on the dispositions of others, will perceive that man is possessed of a desire after something which is not to be found under the sun—after a good which has no limits.'[79] Echoing what he says in *The Gospel Worthy of All Acceptation*, Fuller claims that the gospel call as illustrated by Isaiah 55:1ff., 'Ho, every one that thirsteth, come ye to the waters, and he that hath no money; come ye, buy and eat; yea, come, buy wine and milk without money and without price,' meets this necessity of fallen man. This invitation, which Fuller argues is a gospel-offer, is not what Christians usually take it to mean but 'The thirst which they are supposed to possess does not mean a holy desire after spiritual blessings, but the natural desire of happiness which God has planted in every bosom.' He can thus conclude, 'The whole passage is exceedingly explicit, as to the duty of the unconverted; neither is it possible to evade the force of it by any just or fair method of interpretation.'[80] A gospel which claims that it is the duty of all men to titillate natural desires and does not appeal to and for holy desires is a pseudo-gospel and as such unworthy of the Christian and can never produced that holiness without which no man shall see the Lord. The Bible makes it plain that the purer the Gospel light, the purer the Gospel life.

Fuller's *Nature of True Virtue* is not founded in Christ

Any one panting for holiness as the hart pants for water will only find polluted wells in Fuller's moral essays *Nature of True Virtue* and *Morality not Founded on Utility*. There is not one mention of Christ nor the Holy Spirit in either work. There is some talk of virtue produced by love and benevolence but this is always expressed from the side of man. Fuller's conclusion on how to live a virtuous life is:

> It is not necessary to true virtue that it should comprehend all being, or 'distinctly embrace the welfare of the whole system.' It is sufficient that it be of an expansive *tendency*; and this appears to be Edward's view of the subject. A child may love God by loving godliness, or godly people, though it has yet scarcely any ideas of God himself. It may also possess a disposition the *tendency* of which is to embrace in the arms of good-will 'the immense society of human kind;' though at the time it may be acquainted with but few people in the world. Such a disposition will come into actual exercise, 'from particulars to generals,' as fast as knowledge extends. This, however, is not 'private affection,' or self-love, ripening into an 'extended benevolence, as its last and most perfect fruit;' but benevolence itself, expanded in proportion as the natural powers expand, and afford it opportunity.[81]

Fuller is here criticising the definition of virtue in a sermon of Robert Hall's on 'Modern Infidelity' in which the preacher objects to definitions of the same by Jonathan Edwards. One can hardly imagine Gospel preachers feeding their flocks with this kind of food, but the sermons of the New Baptist School of this generation abound in such abstractions. Imagine a person who has learnt that he loves God only because God has loved him and given him His Son and His Spirit to indwell him and make him holy. This person then enters into a conversation with a Fullerite who tells him that he is a heretic to believe that God must take the initiative and give him divine love so that he might love back. Imagine that holy man's surprise when his condemning judge says to him, 'Let benevolence in you expand in proportion as your natural powers expand. Then, and only then, will you become a virtuous man!'

An eleventh and twelfth commandment

In his *Answers to Objections* concerning his theories propounded in *The Gospel Worthy of all Acceptance*, Fuller takes up what he had left out in that book, i.e. the work of the Holy Spirit. Rather than preach positively on the Spirit, however, showing how He is the Comforter who Christ has sent to the heart of the believer, Fuller merely quotes the Spirit as an influence to enable man to do his duty. Again, he draws wrong conclusions from his false antitheses. If saving faith is not the duty of sinners, he argues, then 'we must conclude either, with the Arminians and Socinians, that 'faith and conversion, seeing they are acts of obedience, cannot be wrought of God; or, with the objector, that, seeing they are wrought of God, they cannot be acts of obedience. But if we need the influence of the Spirit to enable us to do our duty, both these methods of reasoning fall to the ground.'

Here Fuller makes a whole series of theological, Biblical mistakes.

a. He does not make exactly clear whether he is referring to fallen man's duties or believers' duties or the duties of saints and sinners alike. A duty to serve the law as the responsibility of fallen human nature is not the same as exercising faith dutifully as a born-again believer. To confuse the rule of law with the rule of faith is to see no difference in the New Covenant and the Old.

b. Faith and conversion are never *ipso facto* acts of obedience sponsored by man's innate initiative. Nor are they ever required to be so. Nor are they an extension of the legal code of Moses, the eleventh and twelfth commandment, to be obeyed by all. They are gifts of grace which can only be enacted when that grace has been given. Fuller seems actually to be saying that the sinner is duty bound to exercise grace before he is converted and has any grace to exercise. He is thus as quite off the gospel mark as the Arminians and Socinians.

c. All true Christians acknowledge that faith and obedience are wrought by God but it is then and then only that duty-faith begins. Duties before conversion are law-duties. Faith before conversion does not exist. When man is motivated by the Spirit, he sees that his own works cannot bring him to Christ. This is when Christ starts to take over his life, not merely influencing him but living in him and writing the law on his heart. When this takes place, acts of faith and obedience become essential features of the New Creature's walk with God.

d. Seeing that faith and obedience are acts of God, they automatically become acts of obedience for the saved as it is Christ who is working in us, making us perfect in every good work to do His will (Hebrews 13:21). This He does through the atoning blood of the everlasting covenant which blotted out our sins, restored us to God, imputed Christ's righteousness to us and gave us the gift, not the mere outside influence, of the Holy Spirit, in fact, made us partakers of that Spirit in the mystical union of the body of Christ.

From the sublime to the ridiculous
This writer must confess to be rather privileged in matters of good literature on holiness as he has spent many happy hours contemplating on the God of Israel with the book of that title written by William Huntington. Here the work of the Holy Spirit is outlined in an almost matchless way. Whereas Fuller speaks of the conversion of the Prodigal as one returning to where he knows he was better off with the promise of pardon as a bonus to encourage him, Huntington deals with the subject on a far higher and God-honouring level. He sees the Prodigal as becoming a holy being with Christ dwelling in him. Of the Prodigal's conversion, Huntington says:

> The voice of God the Father's love in the heart is—'Yea, I have loved thee with an everlasting love; therefore with loving-kindness have I drawn thee.' Jer. 31:3.
> The voice of the atonement of Christ, in the believer's conscience, is, pardon, peace, and reconciliation with God. And these are better things than spoken by the blood of Abel, Heb. 12:24.
> And the distinct voice of the Holy Ghost in the hearts of all believers is, 'Abba, Father,' Gal. 4:6. This divine teaching, my dear brother, is attended with a holy claim upon God as our own God; and God will own and acknowledge such. To such God speaks, 'Thou shalt call me thy Father, and thou shalt not turn away from

me,' Jer. 3:19; which is what no man can do, in truth, without the witness and voice of the Spirit of adoption; for it is he that cries, 'Abba Father.' Such souls, also, claim Jesus for their own, with an infallible witness in their own souls of the truth of it; which no man can do, in truth, without the Spirit of God; for 'no man can say that Jesus is the Lord (with application) 'but by the Holy Ghost,' 1 Cor. 12:3. Hence it is plain that the Spirit makes us, as he did the prodigal, arise and go to our Father; which, when spoken by the Spirit, is what God will ever own and honour, as he did in that parable - 'This is my son.' And, though at times unbelief prevails, yet the Spirit subdues it again and again, as he did in Thomas, 'My Lord and my God!' These plain truths, my dear brother, clearly reveal this sublime mystery; and these things the children of God have in their own experience; and it is such experience as this that worketh hope. This is submitting to divine revelation, and not being wise above what is written. And whatever appears dark to us in the word of God we must pray the Lord to shine upon it, that we may know the mind of the Spirit in it; for it is in his light that we see light.[82]

With such passages in mind, I turned to the promising title of the *Inward Witness of the Spirit* [83] in Fuller's works, hoping against hope that here, at least, would be some uplifting and comforting teaching on the Spirit to assist the believer in his holy walk. The essay is an exposition of Psalms 85:8 and 35:3 'I will hear what God the Lord will speak: for he will speak peace with his people, and to the saints: but let them not turn again to folly.' 'Draw out also the spear, and stop the way against them that persecute me: say unto my soul, I am thy salvation.'

At first sight, one wonders what such passages have to do with the inward witness of the Spirit, as Fuller starts by arguing that the texts prove that God bestows prosperity on His people. This is the true meaning, Fuller argues, of 'God will speak peace unto his people.' Fuller goes on to say that 'There is no doubt but that true Christians do possess, though not without interruption, peace of mind, joy in the Holy Ghost, and a solid, well-grounded persuasion of their interests in eternal life.' This is welcome information. One would suppose that Fuller was now about to outline what he means by the indwelling of the Spirit and how this helps the believer in his union with Him and in his holy service to Him. Such people, longing for the Spirit's indwelling holiness must remain disappointed. This is the only reference to the Holy Spirit in the sermon and Fuller goes on to argue that Christians who hold this view misunderstand what is meant by it. They have relied on the truth being a matter of revelation and Christian

experience which is the greatest of errors, according to Fuller. Those who
trust in Scripture and their own experience of its truths in this way, Fuller
emphasises, have been 'deluded into great errors, to the dishonour of God
and the ruin of their future peace.' Fuller adds that he has seen more than
a few evils attached to such a view.

The wolf running amok

Here, as so often, in Fuller's exegesis, he strives to teach truths by shocking
his hearers and forcing them to leave their old views of piety, going to
great stretches of exaggeration regarding their position to do so. He tells
them that they are letting their hearts rule their heads. They are putting
revelation before reason. He preaches as a wolf amongst the sheep, rather
than a good shepherd who feeds his sheep with heavenly food. If God
does not speak to Christians by the revealed Word and the indwelling of
the Spirit, how does He communicate with His people? Fuller answers with
the full weight of Grotian rationalism and Socinian scepticism behind him.

First, we can only know God's working in us by 'inference'. Here we
have the Grotian *a posteriori* view again. Faith is not an exercise in using
the gift of love to God, it is that which comes through inferring what is
fitting or not. It is obvious that Fuller looks down his nose at those believers
who can say with Paul, 'I live by the faith of the Son of God, who loved *me*,
and gave himself for *me*'(Galatians 2:20). The apostle's words to Timothy
might also appear suspicious to Fuller when he says, 'Henceforth there is
laid up for *me* a crown of righteousness, which the Lord, the righteous
judge, shall give *me* at that day' (2 Timothy 4:8). He is so far from a belief
in the inward witness of the Spirit in man, bearing witness with his spirit
that he is a son of God that he deems such testimonies presumptuous. The
Scriptures only speak to characters (we would say 'types' nowadays) and
only if we can ally ourselves by inference with such 'characters' can we
speak in such a personal way of what God has done for us. There is never
a direct personal appeal to a person from the Scriptures. One wonders, as
so often, what has happened to Fuller's doctrine of the work of the Holy
Spirit here. Fuller does not reveal if he considers Paul to be one of these
'characters' from whom we can infer like experiences with ourselves or
whether Paul himself was merely taking on the role of another character as
Fuller expects the Christian to do. Be this as it may, Fuller is adamant in
insisting that God, through His Word, does not speak directly to individuals
but such individuals can only infer their own salvation by comparing
themselves with Bible patterns. Again, he boils Christian assurance down
to reason rather than revelation. The sinner is left on his own in judging
what is 'moral' and what is 'positive', what is 'carnal' and what is 'spiritual'.

Second, all this talk about Bible revelation and religious impressions is all unimportant secondary material to Fuller. He seeks to force his hearers attention away from the means God has used to the mere rational fact that belief is present. Thus he can say, 'It is very indifferent by what means we are brought to embrace the gospel way of salvation, if we do but cordially embrace it.' Again we are confronted with Fuller's *a posteriori* Grotianism. Inference through hindsight.

After all this philosophical, though certainly not convincing, logic, Fuller again takes on the role of the orthodox pastor, even appealing to the use of the heart. He closes his sermon with the words, 'Believing on the Son of God, we are justified; and being thus justified, we have peace with God, through our Lord Jesus Christ'. Romans 5:1.

In carefully choosing a Biblically promising title, the *Inward Witness of the Spirit,* which nowhere finds echo in his sermon, and in ending on a pseudo-Biblical text which Fuller has altered to suit his theology, Fuller believes he has done the work of an evangelist. His effort is, however, a caricature of the pastoral calling of a preacher and he misuses the Spirit's name to promote a gospel without means, based on pure rational inference to fulfil its end. Hardly the stuff to promote true holiness!

Romans 5:1 actually reads, 'Therefore being justified by faith, we have peace with God through our Lord Jesus Christ.' Paul is speaking of faith given by Christ's agency (v1) through the outworking of the Spirit (v5), entrusted to sinners by the Father (v8) as a ground of justification, not the act of believing which procures justification. The apostle is certainly not speaking of prosperity when he refers to 'peace' but he is clearly talking about hope in the glory of God even in tribulation. This is all procured, Paul argues, by Christ's atonement. Rather than experiencing God by in-ference, we read that 'the love of God is shed abroad in our hearts by the Holy Ghost which is given to us as we have been reconciled with God.' The Gospel, when it comes to a person, comes personally. The Spirit does not reach us by a gospel of inference but by illuminating our hearts and granting us grace to experience God's direct and undeserved love in Christ.

6. False Prophets, False Teachers and Damnable Heresies

Fuller condemned Baxterism and Socinianism confessing that the former made him ill[84] and the latter shocked him by its arrogance and infidel nature.[85] Any study-in-depth, however, of Fuller's relationship to Arminianism will shows that where Fuller differs from the Remonstrants, it is not from a Calvinistic position but a position to the far side of Arminianism. His is a position much akin to Baxterism, though it goes beyond that system, and finds common identity with Socinianism on at least ten major issues.

Baxterism and Fullerism

Actually, though he denies that he is a Baxterian, Fuller, as Abraham Booth strove to explain to him,[86] comes very near to Baxter's theology, especially in his teaching that substitution does not fulfil the law but is 'above the law'. Though Fuller argues that his universal sufficiency of the atonement is different to Baxter's 'universal redemption', in reality, it is very much the same, differing only in the terminology used. Baxter speaks of universal redemption with regards to its foundation in the atonement. This, too, is universal for Fuller in that it is sufficient for all and sundry, should they apply for it. When Fuller speaks of redemption, however, he dodges the issue by meaning its application to believers only and not to its being worked out in the atonement. Fuller accuses Baxter of Neonomianism but he is no less a Neonomian himself. In arguing that the Ten Commandments are all that is necessary to teach a man gospel obligations, he is robbing the Law of its condemning and commanding powers and thus creating a new law robbed of its sting for saints and sinners alike and a new gospel which is merely an accommodation to the weakened law. For Fuller his new law is applicable to saints in just the same way as sinners as it tells them that they ought to love Christ as if they had never apostatised. What is this but the Neonomian doctrine of 'sincere obedience'? Fuller, however, goes further than Baxter in his Neonomianism as he emphasises that redemption does not entail Christ's fulfilment of the Mosaic Law in all respects but merely in a token fulfilment of its spirit. In this way, Fuller even makes Christ a Neonomian.

Doing something towards salvation

Fuller claims that Baxter demands evangelical works before he can be justified. This is Fuller's duty-faith teaching in a nut-shell. Indeed, Fuller's teaching concerning man having his full moral powers and natural abilities intact and his duty to use them savingly goes far beyond any Baxterian views of 'evangelical works' before justification. Fuller demands a work of faith on the part of the sinner before righteousness and justification can be given him. What is this initial step then if it is not works-righteousness, however 'evangelical'? Fuller criticises Baxter for teaching that the unconverted can 'do something towards their conversion'. Is not this the Fullerite doctrine of the agency of man working side by side with the purpose of God? In most of his works, Fuller emphasises and dwells at length on man's natural abilities and claims that there are no natural impossibilities for man to co-operate with God in salvation. A man who emphasises so much that man 'could if he would' in matters of faith, can hardly criticise Baxter for saying that man 'could do something' towards his conversion. Baxter is criticised for believing that Calvinists and Arminians are reconcilable, 'making the difference between them of but small amount.' Here Fuller dodges the issue. He says that he 'should rather choose to go through the world alone rather than be connected with them,' i.e. Arminians. This is not the point. Fuller has very obviously striven to reconcile Calvinism and Arminianism by combining what he feels is the best of their various gospels in his own system. He has thus no need to be directly connected with the Arminians as he has produced his own mixed version of the gospel to take him safely past the Scylla of Calvinism and the Charybdis of Arminianism.

The five points of Calminianism
Baxter's gospel was indeed what has become known as Calminianism. Kenneth Good lists the Calminians' Five Points as being:

1. Depravity - all are born with a nature which is sinful, but none is born under a curse or wrath of God for Adam's transgression. There is no such thing as total inability to believe. All men can believe if only they will to do so.
2. Election - no one but the elect will be saved, but God's choice of the elect is determined by His foreknowledge of what each person will do when he hears the gospel. There is no such thing as sovereign election upon God's free will alone.
3. Redemption - Christ died equally for all men without discrimination of any kind. No one's salvation was guaranteed at Calvary, but anyone may be saved by the atonement if he so wills. There is no particular redemption.
4. Grace - God provides grace equally for all and this is available to anyone who wills to be saved. There is no such thing as 'irresistible grace'.
5. Perseverance - All the believers are eternally secure, and none of the saved will ever be lost. However, this is based essentially upon what Christ does *for* them rather than what Christ does *in* them.

Though Good presents Fuller as the most orthodox of Five Point Calvinists, it is obvious that, in reality, he is more of a Calminian than Good suspects. Indeed, Fuller is further away from true Calvinism than the Arminians in several respects. Where he errs, it is at the far side even of Calminianism. Concerning depravity, we have seen how Fuller rejects the idea of its totality and looks upon sin in a metaphorical sense. Otherwise, he is in entire agreement with the first of the Calminian points. Indeed the whole purport of his *The Gospel Worthy of All Acceptation* is that 'There is no such thing as total inability to believe. All men can believe if only they will do so.' Rather than being Calminian, Good's first point is strictly Arminian.

On the matter of election, Fuller, in keeping with orthodox Calvinism, would certainly maintain that none but the elect will be saved. Few Arminians, however, would disagree with this. The difference between the two schools of thought rests on how this election takes place. For Fuller and the Arminians, it is not a decree worked out in the mind of God before the foundation of the world but election takes place on the believer's acceptance of the gospel. Here again, Good's second point is basic Arminianism.

Good's third Calminian point is again orthodox Arminianism which is less radical than Fuller's own view of redemption. Whereas Arminians believe that redemption was worked out in the atonement and then applied to those who believe, Fuller sees no true redemption in the cross at all but a token demonstration against sin. Rather than view Christ's redemptive death as being 'for all men without distinction of any kind', Fuller does not view it in relation to paying the debts of sin of any man at all but as an abstract method of dealing with sin itself. Fuller would argue that he believes in particular redemption but he uses the term metaphorically, excluding limited atonement, looking upon the particular nature of redemption as being merely in its application. There is, of course, no absolute, practical, physical redemption either general or particular in Fuller's theology as it merely applies to an acceptance of God's moral government of the world through a right use of natural and moral powers which have not changed since before Adam first sinned.

Whereas Fuller would agree with the first part of Good's fourth Calminian point concerning the availability of grace, he would argue that grace, when applied to the saved, is truly 'irresistible'. He sees, however, this grace as being appropriated through the natural abilities of man which makes it thus less than grace. As man is never dead to a knowledge of God, the saving grace of God is less in that it does not need to equip him with that knowledge and the ability to use it. Thus man's agency renders the necessity of salvation being 'all of grace' less absolute.

Regarding perseverance, Fuller, at first sight, is a typical Calminian. However, he is very reluctant to bring this factor, along with election and predestination that engendered it, into his gospel preaching. Fuller criticised those who stressed that none could pluck them from the Father's hand as 'Antinomians' and seemed to believe that the doctrine tended to make

Calvinists spiritually proud and believe they were no longer accountable before God. He thus tended to argue that these doctrines belonged to God's secret will and preachers should disregard them in presenting their gospel.[87] They were, at best, for the ears of believers only.[88] He could not accept as, say, Zanchius that these doctrines were an essential part of the gospel and some of its main comforts. This misunderstanding of the gospel on Fuller's part was again due to his faulty understanding of the old and new man and his insistence that human agency must always balance off God's purpose with man.[89]

Arguing that the full gospel is for believers only in his controversy with Dan Taylor, Fuller says, 'Hence it is that the chief of those scriptures which we conceive to hold forth a limitation of design in the death of Christ, or any other doctrine of discriminating grace, are such as were addressed to believers.'[90] This contradicts Fuller's argument that all are in a natural position to accept the gospel and exercise duty-faith savingly. Fuller ties himself in evangelical knots by at times arguing for a 'common call' to faith which is to be preached to all as all have theoretically the natural abilities to accept it and an 'effectual call'[91] which is 'peculiar to all Christians' and a work of grace alone. This is all part of his argument that the gospel to be preached to all men is the gospel of the *sufficiency* of Christ's death, whereas the gospel to believers is the *efficiency* or *efficacy* of Christ's death. Thus Fuller's gospel of man's universal natural and even moral powers to perform spiritual things is a sham gospel which he knows has no saving efficiency or effect in preaching. When we free Fuller from the entanglements of his own system, we find that in both his own conversion and last words that he was a debtor to grace alone. If he had stuck to this truth in his preaching and dropped all his humanistic talk of man's abilities and powers, he would have had a gospel worthy of all acceptance. In seeking to stir up men to accept the gospel based on the wrong motives, he completely confused the issue.

Confusing law with gospel
Fuller accuses Baxter of virtually confusing what is legal with what is evangelical, i.e. law with gospel. This of course is one of the very severe criticisms with which Fullerism itself is faced. In their *History of the Church of God*, the Hassells argue concerning the churches propensity to accept the 'doctrines and fables of men', 'Andrew Fuller becomes a wonderful standard. He takes repentance and faith out of the covenant of grace, and puts them under the law, in the sense that he makes them man's duty, and not gifts of grace,'[92] This criticism must hold as Fuller argues that the law

provides us with all the obligations necessary to believe in Christ savingly and the gospel merely brings with it the encouragement to perform them.

Though Fuller is adamant that he is not a Baxterian, it is obvious that his beliefs often coincide with Baxter's and are as often even less Biblical. When examining the views of Fuller and his co-defendants of his position, this soon becomes evident.

Robert Hall and Baxterism

Especially Robert Hall's works are revealing. Taking up Tom Nettle's eulogy of Fuller as being the Baptists' Luther, one can say that Hall was to Fuller what Melanchthon was to Luther, especially in his systematising of his beliefs. Hall can thus say in conversation with a friend, 'I believe firmly in "general redemption": I often preach it, and I consider the fact that "Christ died for all men" as the only basis that can support the universal offer of the Gospel.'—'But you admit the doctrine of election, which necessarily implies limitation. Do you not think that election and particular redemption are inseparably connected?' 'I believe firmly,' he rejoined, 'in election, but I do not think it involves particular redemption; I consider the sacrifice of Christ as a remedy, not only adapted, but intended, for all, and as placing all in a saveable state; as removing all barriers to their salvation, except such as arise from their own perversity and depravity. But God knew that none would accept the remedy, merely of themselves, and therefore, by what may be regarded as a separate arrangement, he resolves to glorify his mercy, by effectually applying salvation to a certain number of our race, through the agency of his Holy Spirit. I apprehend, then, that the limiting clause implied in election refers not to the purchase, but to the application of redemption.'

Here, it is interesting to note, Hall's friend asks him to produce a book which 'he regarded as the Scriptural doctrine on the subject, stated and illustrated.' Hall thus recommended Bellamy's *True Religion Delineated*. It was Bellamy's natural religion and rationalism that Fuller leaned on when writing *The Gospel Worthy of All Acceptation*.

Fuller and Socinianism

Warfield points out how Grotianism was influenced by the moral government theory of the Socinians taken over from Abelard. He was particularly thinking of the Socinian view of Christ's affecting the minds of sinners positively through considering his life of faith and the manifestation of God's love in it, encouraging man to go and do likewise. Joseph Bellamy, whose writings were republished by Fuller, led this Grotian New Divinity School.[93] It is interesting to note that Hall's biographer, Olinthus Gregory, defends Hall against obvious Latitudinarianism[94] by stressing that what he taught was also taught by the Reformers and Puritans. This is also Fuller's argument in the *Gospel Worthy of All Acceptation*. The quote from Hall above, as the many quotes already given from Fuller's works show clearly how baseless such an argument is. Hall, following Fuller, was basically a Baxterian working under strong Latitudinarian and humanistic principles. Though present day evangelicals are again putting forward Bellamy as an antidote against what they call 'false Calvinism', it would pay them to read the warning words of Warfield[95] which describe how the New Divinity men, hiding in the shadow of Jonathan Edwards, 'recast' the established faith and changed both its 'aspect' and 'substance' until it was the 'exact antipodes of Edwards'.

Indeed Warfield quotes Atwater and Ridderbos approvingly as they maintained that Edwards gained his chief celebrity in demolishing the very views which the New Divinity School held. Warfield shows how the New Divinity eventually down-graded into a system which taught 'the Pelagianising doctrines of the native sinlessness of the race, the plenary ability of the sinner to renovate his own soul, and self-love or the desire for happiness as the spring of all voluntary action.'[96]

Warfield sees clearly the evils of the New Divinity School but obviously feels that they are so rationalistic and unbiblical that they cannot possibly live long in a Reformed Calvinist society. He can thus say that when Edward A. Park died in 1900 'the history of "New England Theology" seems to come to an end.' He would have been shocked to find that in 1995 perhaps the bulk of the evangelical Establishment in Britain and the U.S.A. are mistakenly putting forward Fullerism and the New Divinity Theology as 'true evangelical Calvinism'.

The fact is that Fuller equalled if not outstripped the New England School in his tendency towards Socinianism. This is seen especially in Fuller's doctrine of Scripture, sin, the fall, the work of Christ and the role of God in salvation. In all, there are ten major features of Fullerism which reflect Socinianism so exactly that they can be regarded as one and the same heresy. Here then are the Ten Moral Guides of the Fullerite-Socinian School:

1. Scripture

Socinians hold that not all Scripture is of the same importance, indeed, it is not all divinely inspired in the sense that it reflects God's own will and character. Only the essential parts of Scripture are of immediate divine inspiration and these are mainly doctrinal matters. Fuller's view of moral and positive obedience comes very near this teaching as also his continual emphasis on the spirit of a Bible word rather than its letter. To the Socinian, the Old Testament, though part of the Bible, is purely history and spiritual truths, i.e. essential doctrines, are scarcely to be found there. Fuller is extremely ambivalent in his attitude to the Old Testament, now showing himself as extremely legalistic, now arguing that the Old Testament has only positive rules of a mere temporary nature which need re-interpreting to find the spirit in the letter. At times, it seems that he finds the whole gospel wrapped up in the Old Testaments 'positive' wording. Fuller argues, however, that the Old Testament dispensation knew only a 'work to rule' way of life and, though he discusses the law much, he neglects to discuss the promises. He thus tends to have a very unsure view of the Old Testament Church, which hardly comes into his teaching, as also of the covenantal relationship of Christ to His pre-Calvary Bride. His doctrine of the atonement does not look back to the saints of the Old Testament but is merely a future deterrent. Fuller, of course, totally rejects a literal interpretation of key Scriptural terms such as justification, imputation, reconciliation and righteousness and teaches a figurative view of the Bible that, at times, runs into the wildest allegorising.

2. Reason and revelation

Reason is, for the Socinian, man's 'spiritual eye' and is his judge in all controversial matters. Few theologians argue from the earthly to the spiritual more than Fuller and he is continually writing of common sense, reason, inference and a knowledge of the nature and fitness of things to guide the Christian in discerning what is truly moral and what is merely positive; what is right in itself or what is merely right because God says so for the moment. Fuller agrees fully with the Socinians that the truths of revelation are above reason but not contrary to it but this still leaves reason as the final judge as it alone determines what is contrary to itself or not. Just as the Socinian believes that true philosophy and true religion always agree, so Fuller argues that the philosophically acceptable principle of 'right reason' is the touchstone of religion.

3. God's knowledge

Socinians argue that God does not know in such a way that whatever He knows will surely come to pass. They mean by this that God never uses His knowledge to force things to happen or not happen. If this were so, whatever happens or does not happen would be merely because of God knowing it into existence or oblivion and thus everything existent would be a product of sheer fatalism or necessity. Applying this to the doctrine of salvation, they affirm that if God did know things into existence and they happen necessarily so, it would mean there could be no real sin and no real guilt.

It is obvious that Fuller's double emphasis of 'no necessities' and 'no impossibilities' arises from this view of God. His idea of an atonement which does not of necessity atone for any one and his idea of a fall that does not make it impossible for the sinner to realise his state and duty to do something about it are typically Socinian points of view. Fuller leaves these factors outside of God's knowledge, indeed, even God's foreknowledge is rejected as Fuller sees conversion as not being secured in the mind of God and effected through the atonement but in the repentance and faith exercised by whosoever will. Christianity must remain, in Fuller's system, the gospel of surprises. Fuller, however altered the Socinian doctrine in two ways. He argued that, though there is no *necessity* in man's conversion or perdition, there is a *certainty*. He also did not see the *necessary* relevance of punishment and guilt at all in God's plan of salvation as the whole problem was circumlocuted by the *demonstration* effect of the atonement rather than its *expiatory* effect.

4. The Trinity

The Trinity is alleged by Socinians to be irrational, that is contrary to reason and thus it must be unscriptural. They believe that it is not one of the lesser, non-essential teachings of Scripture—it is not there at all! 'Now surely', modern Fullerites will say, 'we are not to suppose that Fuller denied the Trinity!' The answer must be, 'No.' But who would deny that Fuller presents us with a Trinity of irrationality and un-scripturality second to none? His doctrine is not that of the triune God, Father, Son and Holy Spirit who took counsel before the world began to elect a people for Himself. The God of the Scriptures, we are told in those Scriptures, elected us in Christ before time began and in God's knowledge and experience in eternity Christ was offered for our sins, i.e. before the foundation of the world. This is discarded totally by Fuller who sees God the Father secretly ignoring the atonement as a means of securing salvation and applying election directly to those who believe. Meanwhile God the Son is setting His human life on the atonement as a means of releasing all or anybody, as the case may be, from sin. At the same time the Holy Spirit is not only encouraging one and all but even *warranting* one and all that if they keep one eye on the ten commandments and one eye on Christ's exemplary death and what they infer from both, they are of the elect. The Spirit stands behind the would-be believer, urging him on as there seems to be no doctrine of the indwelling of Christ and the Spirit in Fuller's system and certainly no doctrine of a union with them. One cannot help concluding that a caricature of a

Trinity is just the same as no real Trinity. A god whose own will contradicts his own revelation is not the God of the Bible. Even if Fuller pays lip-service to the Godhead, he certainly does not attribute to either Person His Scriptural role. Indeed, Fuller portrays God as a Being subservient to what the human mind believes is the nature and fitness of things. He also believes that the will of God in revelation is secondary and subordinate to Natural Law. Thus Fuller's view of God is not a fraction sounder than that of the Socinians.

5. The image of God in man

Fuller believes that God's image in man consists of man's reason, conscience and immortality and is not lost in the fall. The Socinians substitute mind for conscience and drop mortality as they believe man is only as immortal as God makes him in salvation. Practically speaking, however, Fuller and the Socinians agree. The outcome of this teaching, as seen in Fullerism, is there is no true fall and no true absolute depravity as God's image in man is always there for God to appeal to directly. There is something of God, e.g. His image, in every man. This common feature of Quaker theology is shared by Fuller and the Socinians. In order to understand this teaching better it is necessary to examine Fuller's and the Socinians teaching on Adam.

6. Adam and the fall

The sin of Adam, according to the Socinians, did not cause his posterity to lose their freedom to chose between right and wrong. There is no original sin and each man is condemned for his own sin alone. There is no federal sharing of Adam's sin; there is no being in Adam as there is no true being in Christ. There would be no point in calling a man to repent and believe, they argue, if he were captive to original, i.e. Adam's, sin. Man's inclining to sin has nothing to do with Adam. If it were so it would not be sin because sin implies guilt and it is impossible to be guilty of another's sin.

There is much here that reminds us of Andrew Fuller. He does not believe that there is any true imputation either from Adam to man, from man to Christ or from Christ to man. Guilt cannot be transferred, neither, accurately speaking, can punishment. Only the effects and the affliction caused by it can be experienced by another. Although Fuller admits that man has some connection with Adam because he was the first to sin, he views unfallen Adam as a proto-type example of how man could be if he repented and believed. Fuller does not see the New Adam as this proto-type in any sense and salvation projects us back to the earthly Adam rather than forwards to the heavenly Christ.

Both Fuller and the Socinians as a result of their denial that Adam's sin was imputed to his posterity, can blandly believe that man has not lost the image of God in him. It is still intact whatever Adam might have done! This is why one can appeal to man's reason in presenting Scriptural revelation to him as he has the mental wherewithal to separate the wheat from the dross, the spirit from the letter, the essential from the inessential. Fuller goes, however, further in his radicalism than the Socinians. They look upon man as following in Christ's footsteps in the life and walk of faith, gradually becoming more Christ-like whereas Fuller teaches a restitution theory in which man becomes the Old Adam restored.

Fuller in his *The Gospel Worthy of All Acceptation*, argues just like the Socinians that God could not require repentance and faith of man if he were not in a position to respond to His commands, invitations and offers. Dead men cannot stand up and walk. Here there is no idea of the Biblical teaching that even whole valleys of dry bones can be made to walk, the dead to be resurrected, the blind to see and the deaf to hear. Luke tells us dramatically in chapter four that when Christ first set out to bring the good news to man, he read from the book of Isaiah to show that he was the Servant of God whose work was to heal and restore sight to the blind and deliver the captives.

7. Satisfaction seen as being at variance with the gospel
The idea of satisfaction in the atonement is quite contrary to the Socinian view of the gospel. They believe that satisfaction logically rules out salvation being a free gift which is given by a gratuitous God. As it stands to reason that the guilt and punishment of one cannot be borne by another, so it is obvious one cannot be obedient in place of another. Thus Christ obeyed for Himself and could not obey on behalf of others. Christ's sacrifice was thus not to appease God's wrath against sin but to demonstrate to man what obedience is and to show him that, using his own abilities, strengthened by Christ's example, he could go the same way. He would thus emancipate himself from sin. Indeed, redemption for the Socinian is nothing but an emancipation from sin where no price is paid. It is interesting to note how often Fuller uses the idea of 'encouragement' to illustrate the work of the gospel. This is the very term, with its synonyms, that the Socinians use. The gospel merely encourages us to return to God.

How are sins thus forgiven in Socinianism? One might equally ask how they are forgiven in Fullerism. They are not forgiven via the cross directly but indirectly. God was so impressed by Christ's obedience that after His death, the Father gave Christ the power to forgive sins as a reward. Christ

keeps us from sin by presenting His love and obedience to us and showing
to us how He was able to resist temptation.

This is a more radical view than Fuller's but the basic elements are the
same. The atonement saves no one *absolutely* in Fullerism but always
conditionally on accepting the atonement's influence. What one learns
from the atonement in moral obedience is the true atonement, not the
decree of God whether 'in God's mind' or outworked in history on the
cross. Atonement is by application not by satisfaction; it is by exemplary
demonstration not by penal expiation.

This latter view is at the heart of Socinianism with its teaching that the
virtues of the atonement are in its appointment and application by God.
This is, of course, election but not atonement. Election is worked out in the
atonement but it is not the atoning factor itself. The atonement in Fuller's
system has no direct, specific, logical or soteriological connection with its
appointment or application. It is equally sufficient for one as it is for many,
indeed, for all. It appoints and secures nothing of itself in God's plan of
salvation as any efficacy the atonement might be attributed with is in the
appointment of the believer alone.

In fact, both the Socinians and Fuller are appalled by the idea of a
penal, vicarious redemption in which debts are paid and accounts are
balanced. If debts are paid, there can be no forgiveness as there is then no
reason or need for forgiveness. All has been settled! God's salvation,
however, is freely given without demanding anything of man or Christ.
Thus we see Fuller denying that man's debts are taken over by Christ and
denying that man's guilt is completely blotted out. It is all unnecessary as
salvation has nothing to do with former guilt but everything to do with
present moral obedience.

8. No imputed righteousness

The Socinians teach that God does not impute Christ's righteousness to
sinners but, for Christ's sake, treats them as if they were like Him. This, of
course, is Fullerism pure and simple. It is the gospel of make-believe. Fuller
emphasises that if our sins were really imputed to Christ then Christ's
death would have been a just action on God's part and Christ would have
been treated according to his deserts which would have not helped the
sinner in any way. Similarly, if Christ's righteousness were imputed to the
believer, he would be able to claim his deliverance as a matter of right and
not of grace.[97] This is because Fuller cannot accept any literal substitution
or satisfaction in any sense. He has no doctrine of God's justice being
wrought out in Christ on our behalf and no teaching that Christ works out
for us the privilege of being right with God and thus judged righteous. In

arguing for more grace, he is actually denying true grace. This does not mean that true righteousness is impossible to obtain, according to the Socinians. Repentance is the gateway to righteousness. Repentance means abandoning sin and, because of this, earning God's forgiveness. Repentance is imitating Christ and thus becoming like Him. Thus the Socinians see a Christ-like righteousness in believers but not the righteousness of Christ. As shown above, repentance is the gateway to atonement with God in the theology of Andrew Fuller and, no matter how pious this appears to be, it can only be named by its correct name - a substitute for the righteousness of Christ.

9. Christ suffered for non-essentials
Warfield in his work on the atonement mentioned above stresses with Herzog's major article in the *Schaff-Herzog Encyclopaedia of Religious Knowledge* that the Socinians viewed Christ's 'sufferings and death as merely those of a martyr in the cause of righteousness', or, as Warfield adds, 'in some other non-essential way'. Here, too, we find many echoes of Fuller. In comparing Christ to the officer who has his hand blown off in the battle fray - seemingly quite accidental, Fuller paints a caricature of the real sufferings and death of Christ, apart from the plain fact that he fully ignores the reason for Christ's 'affliction'.

Due to none essentials taking the place of essentials, Fullerism and Socinianism make inessentials of essentials. A typical example is the idea of sacrifice itself. As shown when comparing Fuller's view of the Old Testament sacrifices with his similar view of Christ's becoming a sin-offering, he believes that Christ's sacrifice is of even less efficacy than the Old Testament shadows of it as they were sacrifices of sin-transfer which, Fuller believes, Christ's was not. This is the old Socinian and Remonstrant heresy of *acceptilatio*, i.e. that the sacrifice of Christ was only expiatory in its side-effects and was not more so than that of bulls and goats but the point is that it was accepted as if it had been more by God. There is thus no power in the blood of the Lamb of God to save! There is only executive power in God's deciding to accept it as such. This is a blasphemous insult to both God's justice and mercy. It is a central doctrine of Fullerism.

10. The upkeep of God's moral government
The principle design of the atonement in the Socinian system is to reveal God's displeasure (not wrath) against sin in His upkeep of His moral government. This is obviously an important factor in the redemption story and is an equally obvious intention and outcome of Christ's sacrificial death. Yet this cannot be all the cross provides, nor can it be the essential

factor of redemption. God shows His wrath and hatred (displeasure is far too weak a word,) of sin in the law and the Old Testament dispensation. This same law provides also for God to exercise moral suasion as the wages of sin is death and justice, even without the atonement, would take its natural course and God's moral government would not suffer in any way. Sinners are punished in the old dispensation as they are in the new. If a declaration of God's moral government is the sole aim of the atonement, then it is little wonder that Fuller and the Socinians see Christ's death merely in its symbolic function, akin to part of the function of the Old Testament sacrifices.

Christ is not a new law-giver bringing a new code of obedience to keep the administrative wheels of God's executive power turning. The old law is good enough for Christ as it reflects the eternal nature of His Father and is the law He fulfils and establishes. Christ came as a Saviour to atone from sin through taking upon Himself the punishment and guilt of His elect so that they might go free so that full mercy can be combined with full justice. Fuller's terms of atonement are far less than the Biblical terms and in keeping with those of the Socinians. The atonement for the sins of the elect is not Christ's primary task; it is very dubious whether Fuller sees this as a true moral task at all but just another 'positive' executive device. Christ's task, for Fuller, is to bring new conditions to bear on man so that he might be morally reformed and return to God via a path that was hitherto closed to him. This again shows Fuller as the Neonomian he is at heart as he always emphasises that it is the act of believing which is imputed to us for righteousness and not Christ's obedience. Neonomians teach that 'faith in Christ is the principle part of that obedience which is required by the new law, and this is accepted for righteousness, instead of that perfect, un-ceasing obedience, which the Law of ten commands requires.'[98]

---

[1] Taken as a handy summary from *Lessons from the University of Life*, a review article by Clifford Pond in the August, 1995 issue of Evangelicals Now, p. 21.

[2] My emphasis. See *Six Letters to Dr. Ryland Respecting the Controversy with the Rev. A. Booth*, *Works*, vol. II, p. 709.

[3] P. 128.

[4] *Works*, vol. I, p. 41.

[5] This is, of course, merely the subjective view of this author who finds that Taylor left a good testimony.

[6] See Fuller's *Reply to Mr Button, Works*, vol. II, p. 420 ff. and *The Reality and Efficacy of Divine Grace*, vol. II, p. 512 ff.

[7] Quoted from J. A. Jones' *A Sketch of the Rise and Progress of Fullerism*, Earthen Vessel, Sept. 2, 1861, p. 234.

[8] *Works*, vol. II, pp. 373-374.

[9] Ibid., p. 697.

[10] Ezekiel 18:4, 20 and Romans 6:23.

[11] See *Conversation on Imputation, Works*, vol. II, p. 682.

[12] *Works*, vol III, pp. 720-721.

[13] *The Gospel Worthy*, Vol. II, p.373 ff. Fuller outlines the atonement here as a moral victory over crime.

[14] Vol. II, p. 781. See also *The Gospel Worthy, On Particular Redemption*, pp. 373-374, Line beginning 'If any man has a taste for moral excellency,' p. 352.

[15] Revelation 4:11.

[16] See especially Fuller's *Change of Sentiments, Works*, vol. II. p. 709 ff. and his *Imputation, Works*, vol. III, p. 720.

[17] *The Myth of Common Grace.*

[18] Taken for the BOT's edition of John Owen's *Works*, 1967, vol. 10, p. 25.

[19] Pp. 368-369 in the chapter entitled *Man and God.*

[20] *Are Baptists Calvinists?*, p. 76.

[21] *Works*, vol. II, p. 690.

[22] Ibid., p. 691, also p. 708.

[23] My emphasis.

[24] *Works*, vol. II, p. 489 fn. Fuller gives Vol. I, Chapter IX as his source but the passage is to be found in Book II, Chapter IX of *The Economy of the Covenants.*

[25] My emphasis.

[26] *Works*, vol. II, 707.

[27] Ibid., p. 489.

²⁸ Ibid., p. 714 ff.

²⁹ Ibid., p. 707.

³⁰ Ibid., p. 710.

³¹ Ibid., pp. 699, 701.

³² *Works*, vol. II, p. 689. Cf. also p. 707. This phrase occurs often in Fuller's writings with small variations.

³³ *Help for the True Disciples of Immanuel*, London, 1841, pp. iv-v.

³⁴ Fuller's emphasis.

³⁵ My emphasis. Note that our being a debtor and God being a creditor is, as always, sheer metaphor to Fuller.

³⁶ *Works*, vol. II, p. 690.

³⁷ Ibid., p. 692.

³⁸ *Works*, vol. II, p. 498.

³⁹ Ibid., p. 495.

⁴⁰ Ibid., p. 494.

⁴¹ See Gill's various expositions of Song of Solomon, chapter 5 and Revelation chapter 3. See also my chapter on *The Voice of the Beloved* in *John Gill and the Cause of God and Truth*.

⁴² See *Justification: The Doctrine of Imputed Righteousness*, *Works*, vol. II, p. 709 ff., especially p.720. See also *Six Letters to Dr. Ryland Respecting the Controversy with the Rev. Booth*, *Works*, vol. II

⁴³ *Conversation on Particular Redemption*, *Works*, vol. II, pp. 695-696.

⁴⁴ My emphasis.

⁴⁵ See *Works*, vol. II, p. 680 ff. and p. 702 ff.

⁴⁶ *Conversation on Substitution*, *Works*, vol. II, p. 689.

⁴⁷ John 1:29, Hebrews 9:28, 1 Peter 2:24.

⁴⁸ *Works*, vol. I, pp. 17-18.

⁴⁹ *The Moral Nature and Fitness of Things Considered*, *Sermons and Tracts*, vol. 3, pp. 488-489.

[50] *The Economy of the Covenants*, Book III, Chap. IV, vol. I, p. 324 ff.

[51] See ibid, especially *Of Election* XIII and *Of Justification* p. 491 ff.

[52] *Works*, vol. II, p. 338.

[53] *Remarks on God's Justifying the Ungodly*, vol. iii, p. 715.

[54] Vol. iii, pp. 714-719.

[55] My emphasis of the words Fuller leaves out.

[56] See Hervey's *Works*, *Letters to The Rev. Mr John Wesley*, sometimes also called *Aspasio Vindicated*. See also my *Whose Righteousness Saves Us*, BLQ, July-September, 1991, pp. 436-442.

[57] *Andrew Fuller (3)*, BQ, p. 225.

[58] Hervey's *Works*, *Letters to Rev. Mr. Wesley*, Letter X, p. 553.

[59] *Vital Christianity: A Brief Essay on the Life of God in the Soul of Man; Produced and Maintained by a Christ living in us And the Mystery of a CHRIST within Explained*, Boston 1741, p. 4.

[60] *Conversation on Imputation*, vol. II, p. 685.

[61] *Works*, vol. II, p. 685.

[62] Ibid., p. 685.

[63] Witsius' emphasis.

[64] Vol. I, Book III, Chap. VIII, p. 403.

[65] *Works*, vol. II, p. 686.

[66] *Works*, vol. II, p. 688.

[67] *Works*, vol. II, p. 703.

[68] *Works*, vol. II, p. 703.

[69] See Fuller's attack on the doctrine of imputation which he calls typically a *Defence of the Doctrine of Imputation*, in his essay on *Justification*, *Works*, III, p. 709-722. Here Fuller distiguishes between a righteous man, i.e one who is in an 'as if' state and a sanctified man, i.e. one who is in a 'real' state.

[70] *Memoir, Works*, vol. I, p. 15.

[71] Fuller as good as concedes this in *Answers to Objections*, *Works*, vol. II, p. 367.

[72] See Ryland's *Life and Death of the Rev. Andrew Fuller* where Ryland corrects Fuller's assessments of Gill concerning Adam in his innocent state. Fuller modifies this criticism of Gill in his *Gospel Worthy of all Acceptation*.

[73] My emphasis.

[74] The Hassells' emphasis.

[75] *Church History*, p. 339.

[76] *Works*, vol. II, p. 369-371, p. 443 ff. (All of Section VIII and IX).

[77] See *Reply to Mr. Button*, *Works*, vol. II, especially p. 445.

[78] *Particular Redemption*, p. 14.

[79] *Christianity a Source of Happiness*, *Works*, vol. II, p. 52.

[80] *Works*, vol. II, p. 344.

[81] Ibid., vol. II, p. 818.

[82] Letters to the Rev. J. Jenkins on the Trinity collected under the title *Contemplations on the God of Israel*, Collingridge, vol. II, p. 227.

[83] *Works*, vol., I, p. 624 ff..

[84] See *Baxterism*, *Works*, vol. II, p. 714 ff.

[85] *Works*, vol. II, pp. 109, 171, 220. See especially *The Calvinistic and Socinian Systems Examined and Compared As to Their Moral Tendency*, vol. II, p. 108 ff.

[86] See *Six Letters to Dr. Ryland Respecting the Controversy with the Rev. Booth*, *Works*, vol. II, especially p. 702.

[87] *Works*, vol. II, p. 374.

[88] Ibid., p. 495.

[89] See Fuller's *Perversion of the Doctrines of the Gospel*, *Works*, vol. II, pp. 761-762.

[90] *Reply to Philanthropos*, *Works*, vol. II, p.495.

[91] *The Reality and Efficacy of Divine Grace*, *Works*, vol. II, p. 544.

[92] P. 310.

[93] Otherwise called the New England School.

[94] Gregory, after dealing with Hall's view of redemption, goes on to deal with his view of the Church in which direct allusions to Latitudinarianism are made. Hall's view of

the Church, however, cannot be separated from his view of redemption. Nor can that of the Reformers and Puritans.

[95] See Warfield's *Edwards and the New England Theology*, *Works*, vol. ix, pp. 515-538.

[96] Ibid., p. 536.

[97] *Works*, vol. I, p. 290.

[98] Quoted from Rushton, *Particular Redemption*, p. 95.

Part IV
Andrew Fuller and the Gospel's Evangelistic Witness

1. Appraisals of Fuller as an Evangelist

His indebtedness to the New Divinity School view of evangelism
Warfield explains concerning the New Divinity School how, 'the inheritance of the party from Edwards showed itself much more strongly in the *practical* than the *doctrinal* [1] side. Its members were the heirs of his revivalist zeal and of his awakening preaching; they also imitated his attempt to purify the Church by discipline and strict guarding of the Lord's Table.'[2] The Princeton theologian goes on to argue how the Bellamy school pressed to extremes in these matters which caused a great disturbance in the churches who, nevertheless, gradually allowed the New Divinity School to dominate them though that theology was continually suffering change.

Exact parallels can be drawn in Fuller's theological development and in the troubles he brought to the Particular Baptists in particular. The weaker he became on doctrine, the more earnest he campaigned for evangelistic work which would spread his views. This has caused many a Fullerite to believe honestly that until the time of Fuller in England, at least, no evangelisation or missionary work of note had taken place. This idea is given pre-eminence rather than the theological facts which show Fuller becoming more and more confused and pseudo-philosophical in his doctrine. Kenneth Good can therefore inform his readers that concerning evangelism:

> In his study and prayer on this subject Fuller was directed to the writings of Jonathan Edwards from which he received considerable help and pertinent instruction. He emerged from these

mental and spiritual conflicts fully convinced that it was God's will that the gospel should go everywhere indiscriminately. As a consequence he wrote the epochal treatise *The Gospel Worthy of All Acceptation* to express these views and arouse the churches. This publication shook the Baptist churches in both England and America to their foundations. It was a devastating blow to Hyper-Calvinism and the beginning of a great missionary movement.[3]

Though Good acknowledges that Fullerism brought a radical reshaping of Calvinism, he considers this merely a matter of externals, obviously believing that doctrine comes second to outreach. He can therefore write:

> Probably the most externally significant modification of Calvinism to be observed in the English speaking world took place through the ministry of Andrew Fuller. Evaluated in the perspective of history it could be said that he rescued the Particular Baptists of England from what may well have been self-destruction and oblivion.[4]

Thomas Nettles, though a Baptist himself and well versed in Baptist history, states quite dogmatically in his *Preface* to the Sprinkle Publications edition of Fuller's works, that 'there was no Baptist Awakening except the one in which Fuller played a formative role.'

Fuller's theology thought to be a driving force in evangelism

Most modern exponents of Fullerism, however, will not accept that Fuller was any weaker in his theology than in his evangelism and teach that it was Fuller's theology that drove him to be so evangelistically minded. Thus A. C. Underwood can affirm of Fuller, 'Indeed it may be said that he was the soundest and most creatively useful theologian the Particular Baptists have ever had.'[5] Michael Haykin, on several occasions, enthusiastically expresses that he regards Fuller as a theological genius and indeed claims that Spurgeon looked upon him as 'the greatest theologian of the nineteenth century'.[6] W. T. Whitley stresses the practical nature of Fuller's theology and says of him, 'He stands as a fine type of the Baptist for the nineteenth century and in this period as the ablest theologian yet produced.'[7] Thomas Armitage called Fuller 'a profound thinker and ready debater'[8] and speaks of 'his immortal work', viewing him as 'one of the lights and leaders of the world.' Fuller's enthusiastic modern exponent, E. F. Clipsham subtitled his four detailed and lengthy studies on Andrew Fuller and Fullerism in the *Baptist Quarterly* (xx, 1963-64) *A Study in*

Evangelical Calvinism and compared him with Whitefield and Wesley as a great theologian who, apparently unlike the former two, provided the theological basis for evangelical outreach at home and missionary endeavours abroad.

Faced with such exuberant praise of Fuller's theology and evangelical acumen, anyone challenging Fuller's credentials runs the risk of being regarded as a Philistine indeed. Yet all is not gold that glitters. Just as Warfield saw that the New Divinity School's emphasis on evangelism stood in no sound relationship to orthodox doctrine, so it has been shown in the previous chapters that any evangelisation based on Fuller's theology must be regarded at best as a mere humanistic effort to better man's morals and at worst a complete travesty of the gospel, neither of which can possibly produce an evangelism such as that outlined in the Acts of the Apostles.

Fuller praised by the unorthodox or those less particular in doctrine
Thus, when one examines closely the eulogies uttered in Fuller's praise, one soon finds that they are either uttered by those who obviously lack theological discernment or who are less than orthodox themselves or by those who are prepared to close an eye to faulty teaching in view of Fuller's zeal for evangelism. The end, they believe, justifies the means. Thus when Nettles' praise of Fuller, quoted above, is looked into, facts appear which would challenge the objective veracity of his statement. Nettles, for instance, praises John Gill as being a contender for the faith and for preserving the orthodoxy of the Particular Baptists and yet can see little difference between Gill's theology and that of Fuller's. He seems to forget that it was Fuller's reaction to 'Gillism' which prompted Fuller to turn his back on the orthodoxy expressed by such fine preachers and evangelists as Davis, Gill, Brine, Hervey, Toplady, Beddome, Wallin, Martin, Button and Booth and adopt a less Biblical position. Nettle's just does not seem aware of Fuller's unorthodoxy and in his chapter *On the Road Again* in his book *By His Grace and for His Glory*, he attributes to Fuller orthodox doctrines such as satisfaction, substitution and propitiation which Fuller clearly does not hold. The tiniest peep behind Fuller's façade of metaphor shows that he held to a token satisfaction, a mere moral substitution and an 'as if' propitiation based on a figurative interpretation of redemption. Though Underwood tells us that Fuller 'dealt the mortal blow' to the system of Calvinism he sought to change, the Baptist historian is obviously no friend of Calvinism himself, preferring an ecumenical liberty of thought and preserving 'the spiritual rights of the common man' which entails offering 'a high-churchmanship without clericalism, and sacramentalism without sacerdotalism'.[9]

Fuller's 'theological genius' seen as resting in his New England Grotianism

Turning to Michael Haykin's glowing reports of Fuller, one finds that the Professor of Church History identifies the Home Trio of the Baptist Missionary Society,[10] Sutcliff, Fuller and Ryland, fully with the moral government theory of Grotius and its New England development, sincerely believing that Grotianism and the New Divinity School represent 'Evangelical Calvinism' against the supposed 'False Calvinism' of pre-Fullerite years. This school of thought is, erroneously, closely associated by Haykin with the theology of Jonathan Edwards as in the minds of most modern Fullerites. It is, however, so vastly opposed to Edward's overview of theology that one wonders if Haykin is associating rank Fullerism and Grotianism with the noble name of Edwards to give it an aura of respectability. It is either this, or Haykin has quite misunderstood Edwards and sees him as teaching Haykin's own highly indistinct theology. Warfield is, again, able to help us here. In his *Edwards and the New England Theology* he writes (p. 535):

> The younger Edwards (Jonathan Edwards' son) drew up a careful account of what he deemed the (ten) 'Improvements in Theology made by President Edwards and those who have followed his course of thought.' Three of the *most cardinal* [11] of these he does not pretend were introduced by Edwards, attributing them simply to those whom he calls Edwards' 'followers'. These are the substitution of the Governmental (Grotian) for the Satisfaction doctrine of the Atonement, in the accomplishment of which he himself, with partial forerunners in Bellamy and West, was the chief agent; the discarding of the doctrine of the imputation of sin in favour of the view that men are condemned for their own personal sin only—a contention which was held in extreme form by Nathaniel Emmons, who confined all moral quality to acts of volition, and afterwards became a leading element in Nathaniel Taylor's system; and the perversion of Edward's distinction between 'natural' and 'moral' inability so as to ground on the 'natural' ability of the unregenerate, after the fashion introduced by Samuel Hopkins—a theory of the capacities and duties of men without the Spirit, which afterwards, in the hands of Nathaniel W. Taylor, became the core of a new Pelagianizing system.

Furthermore Warfield points out that the New Divinity men were already denying the real vicarious suffering in Christ's atonement by the

1780s, i.e. during the period Fuller is thought to have come under their influence, and were in general giving up the doctrine of imputation not only of sin but also in justification and teaching that 'all holy Motive operates as terminating in personal Happiness.' Warfield is quoting Ezra Stiles but adds that this was, 'A very fair statement of the actual drift'.[12]

Such is the background both in time and doctrine in which Michael Haykin approvingly places the evangelistic and theological 'genius' of Andrew Fuller![13]

The confusion in tracing Fuller's sources

Arthur Kirkby in his very readable Ph.D. thesis *The Theology of Andrew Fuller and its Relation to Calvinism*, argues that Edwards' influence on Fuller was far less than is generally claimed and came far later than pro-Fuller writers have imagined. He sees the main influence as coming from Calvin's works. E. Clipsham in the above mentioned articles feels that the evidence Kirkby gives is quite inadequate and sees Edward's direct influence as being by far the stronger. Clipsham's view is, however, less well-documented than Kirkby's work. It is customary for Fuller's supporters to confuse the influence Bellamy and Edwards had on Fuller, believing that they held the same doctrines. This is very apparent when studying through Haykin's above-mentioned book, especially chapter seven entitled *Sutcliff's Friends: Andrew Fuller*. Convincing evidence for a direct influence by Edwards on Fuller has still to be produced and this author is very sceptical whether such material will ever be produced as Fuller's theology is so radically different from Edwards'. The argument seems to be based on the mere presumption that Fuller read much of Edwards. This author has read much of Fuller but would hate to think that this would brand him as a Fullerite. Edward's *Humble Attempt to Promote Explicit Agreement and Visible Union of God's People, in Extraordinary Prayer for the Revival of Religion*, for instance, which sparked off the Prayer Call of 1784 was sent to Ryland by John Erskine in April 1784 and probably passed on to Fuller soon after. *The Gospel Worthy of All Acceptation*, however, was completed around 1781. According to Fuller's diary, he only started to read Edwards' sermons in 1789-90. It must also be stressed here that Edwards received the impetus for his call to prayer from earlier British Independent believers who had started such a project at the very beginning of the century. The Anglicans led by Romaine and Hervey had maintained a similar evangelistic call to prayer in the 1750s. Baptist John Gill emphasised the Christian duty to evangelise the world, albeit 'as the Spirit leads' around this time, too.[14] Thus this prayer for evangelical outreach, seen as Fuller's 'trumpet blast' which heralded a new awakening in evangelical strategy, was by no means a Fullerite venture. Indeed, of all the major British and American denominations, not to mention the Continental churches, the Fuller, Ryland and Sutcliff band of 'evangelical Calvinists', once sound Baptists, were very late in promoting a widespread evangelistic call to united prayer.

Five, Four, Three and Two Point Calvinism
As Grotius was as anti-Calvinistic and anti-Dissenting as one can possibly imagine and a hater of the Puritans, it is extremely difficult to understand why such writers as Haykin, a Baptist church historian, is prepared to accept that the new orthodoxy for Particular Baptists should be rooted in the rationalism of a man who denied all the Five Points of Calvinism. More puzzling still is the fact that Haykin claims that Fuller's Grotianism represents true 'Evangelical Calvinism'. Obviously, doctrine is here not the deciding factor but methods and means, of which Grotius was an expert, of spreading the gospel of moral government. Kenneth Good in his book *Are Baptists Calvinists?* appears to argue that the Five Points are not above discussion for Baptist Calvinists and he even speaks of Four, Three and Two-Point Calvinists. Even the doyen of Good's Calvinists, Andrew Fuller, however, is demonstrably not a Five, nor even a Four-Point man at all, in spite of Good's assertions to the contrary, so we are left with a Calvinism either void of meaning or as an elastic umbrella term to include anything both this side of Arminianism and beyond its far side.

Calvinism humanised
Whitley, in his admiration of Fuller, is quite clear where he is to be placed theologically. Arguing that Fuller 'humanised the older Calvinism,' he quotes a verse by Maria de Fleury,[15] a vowed opponent of the Calvinist path, on the correct way to preach the Word and goes on to say, 'This new temper may be traced to the influence of one man, Andrew Fuller, adding, 'He became to Baptists what Baxter would fain have been for Presbyterians.'

Maria de Fleury made a name for herself in defending Fullerism against William Huntington's orthodoxy, calling him a Master of the Black Arts, an Antinomian who finds lying as natural as breathing and one who has a familiar spirit and is a conjuror void of any grace of God.[16] In her efforts to label Huntington an Antinomian, though he defended the eternal nature of the Mosaic Law, de Fleury laid open her full disregard for the Law's eternal nature as a reflection of God's holy character. This is, of course, so typical of Fullerites who believe that their notions are 'above the Law'. Hooper in his work *The Celebrated Coalheaver*, came to Huntington's defence by saying of de Fleury, 'she had far better never have taken up her pen against him: for he turns the charge of Antinomianism against herself and friends, and proves that what he was in name only, they were in fact.'[17] One of the friends who had supported de Fleury was John Ryland Senior who gradually saw through both de Fleury and Fuller when his own son Dr. John Ryland began to follow their ways. Speaking in the early 1790s, shortly before his death, on the confusion of law and gospel in duty-faith Fullerite theology, Ryland was heard to say, 'Robert Hall, his son, and Fuller were busied on it. The devil threw out an empty barrel for them to roll about, while they ought to have been drinking the wine of the kingdom. That old dog, lying in the dark, has drawn off many good men to whip syllabub,[18] and to sift quiddities,[19] under pretence of zeal for the truth.'[20]

William Huntington's criticism of Fullerite Antinomianism

Whitely's recommendation of Fuller is hardly convincing as he compares him with a woman who confusingly taught that a Christian should be placed under the Law yet believed, as Fuller, that the covenant of works had been annulled for both sinner and saint alike. He also compares him with Richard Baxter who was at best a Calminian. This is hardly the stuff that Calvinists are made of! Huntington, a vowed opponent of Antinomianism, as witnessed by his many articles against it, corrected Fullerite de Fleury on the Law by saying:

> I read that the old veil of ignorance is done away in Christ; but I never read that the law was done away. Christ came to fulfil it; the apostles preached to establish it. Christ is a just God and a Saviour; and all Adam's race, saints and sinners, must and shall appear before the judgement-seat of Christ. And he will appear as a just God with the book of the law, and pronounce the curse from thence upon the bondservant, for it is a covenant of works to him. And he will appear with the book of life as a Saviour, and pronounce the blessing of life from that, as a covenant of grace. Thus the pharisee and the believer will both be judged according to their works. He that is of the works of the law will be tried by the book of the law; and he that is of the works of faith will be tried by the law of faith, and be proclaimed a good and faithful servant.[21]

Armitage is perhaps the most exuberant of historians in using epithets in Fuller's praise, though he quite ignores his theology. All we read is that he 'brought about a reform', he 'presented the truth in a new light' and he 'put a new phase upon Calvinism' which 'has not only moulded his own denomination, but has spread its leaven through all other Calvinistic bodies.'[22] This hardly provides material on which to base a balanced judgement and indeed, is alarming to those who see in Fuller's novelties and influence a salt which has lost its bibline savour.

2. Doing the Work of an Evangelist

Fullerism: Neither evangelical nor Calvinism

Clipsham, in arguing that Fuller was the founder of 'Evangelical Calvinism' actually links the title to a teaching which is neither Calvinist nor in any way remarkable for its evangelical outreach. In fact, if being evangelical as a Calvinist includes evangelising according to Calvinist beliefs, as it ought, then Clipsham has no grounds whatsoever for claiming that Fuller was an evangelical Calvinist. Indeed, Clipsham does not seem to think that he is in conflict with the Reformed faith in any way when he argues that Fuller rejected the debt-paying function of the atonement and followed Grotius, whom Clipsham openly calls an Arminian. He explains that Grotius saw the atonement as 'a satisfaction to the general justice of God, establishing the authority of the divine law, supporting the divine government, at the same time making it possible for God to exercise his mercy in the pardon of sinners.' If Clipsham were to analyse Fuller's doctrines of satisfaction, general justice, divine law and divine government, he would find that his definitions were bubbles of metaphorical air that had no basis in concrete Biblical theology which provides the Church with the only yardstick for gospel-preaching. When Fuller argues, for instance, that imputation, too, is merely figurative, Clipsham accepts this without question. Clipsham's work on Fuller reveals what little theological care is taken in accessing the value of Fullerism in evangelisation. In Clipsham's work, one discovers with amazement that Fuller is called a Calvinist because, in his central doctrine, he follows an Arminian whom most Arminians would suspect of being a Socinian.[23]

The claim that Fullerism makes better and more successful evangelists is false.

Many Calvinists of the Old School cannot accept such rosy pictures of Fuller which clearly contradict the sombre facts of his own writings and the glorious facts of the gospel of salvation. They would also argue that far from being less evangelistic and having less outreach and filling their churches less, men of the Old School of Calvinists could rightly divide the word of God and win souls to Christ with a display of gospel preaching that was far more true to the Bible and true to the principles of the Reformation than Fullerism with all its novelties. Especially the Particular Baptists need not be ashamed of the stalwart men in their pre-Fuller ranks. This must be emphasised as the Fullerites sought first and foremost to promote the Baptist image by steering Baptists clear of their pioneer fathers. Such men of God from a number of denominations such as Crisp, Davis, Gill, Brine, Romaine, Toplady, Hervey, Wilson, Noble, the Wallins, Beddome, Button, Huntington, Philpot, Doudney, Hawker, Gadsby, Warfield, and the great Dutch preachers such as Kohlbrügge were all excellent evangelists, pastors and preachers though far from the Arminian-cum-Socinian theology of Fuller. Indeed, when considering the very men that Fuller and modern Fullerites accuse of not preaching the Fullerite gospel, one sees how much more successful they were in presenting the whole counsel of God to sinners and saints alike.

Tobias Crisp and spiritual evangelism
Fuller is especially scathing in his criticism of Tobias Crisp (1600-1643) who was a seeker and healer of souls second to none. He preached the whole gospel to the whole man as revealed in the doctrines of grace outlined in Scripture and in the witness of the New Testament saints. People flocked from miles around to hear him preach and testified that Crisp's doctrine was 'spiritual, evangelistic, particularly suited to the case of awakened sinners, greatly promoting their peace and comfort. His method was familiar and easy to be understood by persons of the meanest capacity and was particularly adapted to the condition of his hearers.'[24]

Many of Crisp's fellow ministers, including nominal Reformed evangelicals, could not understand why Crisp was so much more successful than themselves. They raised the cry that Crisp was a poacher of souls as their own members were prepared to ride 12 miles and more to hear Crisp rather than walk round the corner to their local church. As this accusation was tantamount to admitting that possibly something was wrong with their own witness, other methods of criticism were devised. Crisp was accused of taking the doctrine of imputed righteousness literally and believing that Christ truly bore our sin and was actually *punished* in our stead. He was also accused, oddly enough by the same people, of denying the need for righteousness and affirming that as one was safe and secure in Jesus, one could live as one wished. The former accusation showed again the strong impact of Dutch Grotianism on British Reformed doctrine. Grotius looked upon the imputed righteousness of Christ as a mere metaphor, bringing with it no actual transformation from outside (i.e. from God) into the life of the believer. It was a mere *pro-forma*, arbitrary arrangement between God and man. Robert Traill tells us that Arminian influence was so strong at the time that it had become respectable evangelicalism to teach that Christ's atonement merely prepared the way for a salvation which was to be secured by good works. Those who did not believe this were termed 'licentious'. These ideas strongly contradicted each other as Arminians looked upon the Law as reflecting the eternal nature of God and were thus, in this respect, orthodox, whereas the Grotians looked upon the Law as a temporary device of God to exert moral influence on man which in no way reflected God's eternal character. Crisp answered these groundless accusations in such sermons as *Free Grace the Teacher of Good Works* and *The Use of the Law*. None of Crisp's works were published during his life-time, however, and the rumours grew, especially as his critics were slow to check their own theories by actually hearing Crisp preach.

Dr William Twisse (1575-1646), moderator of the Westminster Assembly of Divines and author of works on the Christian's moral obligations, on hearing the criticism, made a special study of Crisp's teaching and witness, finding him absolutely orthodox. He suggested that the only reason why Crisp was unpopular amongst ministers was 'because so many were converted by his ministry, and so few by ours.'[25] Concerning those who accused Crisp of Antinomianism, Mr Lancaster, his publisher, said 'that his life was so innocent and harmless from all evil, and so zealous and fervent in all good, that it seemed to be designed as a practical refutation of the slander of those who would insinuate that his doctrine tended to licentiousness.'[26]

Crisp's preaching, as his life, testifies to his purity of religion. Expounding Matthew 25:44 on the Christian's duty to God and man, Crisp says:

> We do not perform Christian duties in order to our being delivered from wrath; but we perform them because we are delivered. A man will work for Christ who has tasted of Christ's loving-kindness: he stands ready to shew forth the praise of that glorious grace which hath so freely saved him. Such a man is as glad to work for Christ's sake, as if he was to work for his own salvation. There are many ingenious persons in the world, who will be more ready to serve a friend that has already raised them; than to serve a master, that they may be raised. This is the true service of a believer. His eye is to the glory of Christ, in regard to what Christ hath already done for him: and not in expectation of anything Christ hath yet to do. He looks upon all, as perfectly done for him in the

hand of Christ, and ready to be delivered out to him as his occasions
may require. The work of salvation being thus completed by Christ
and not to be mended by the creature; the believer having now
nothing to do for himself, all he doth, he doth for Christ . . . Salvation
itself, therefore, is not the end proposed in any good work we do.
The ends of our good works are, the manifestation of our obedience
and subjection; the setting forth the praise of God's grace and
thereby glorifying him in the world; the doing, good to others with
a view to *their* profit; and the meeting the Lord Jesus Christ in the
performance of duty, where he will be found, according to his
promise: these are some of the special ends, for which obedience is
ordained, salvation being settled firm before.

Crisp also said:

There is no believer who hath received Christ but he is created
in him unto good works, that he should walk in them. He that
sprinkleth clean water upon them, that they become clean from all
their filthiness, puts also a new spirit within them, and doth cause
them to walk in his statutes and testimonies. So I say that
sanctification of life is an inseparable companion with the
justification of a person by the free grace of Christ. But I must
withal tell you that all this sanctification of life is not a jot of the
way of that justified person unto heaven. It is the business a man
hath to do *in* his Way, Christ.

The cause of criticism was the new theologies which saw no need to
preach the terrors of the Old Law with its call for absolute obedience or
eternal destruction, warded off by Christ's perfect righteous sacrifice and
His righteousness being imputed to the elect. Followers of such errors,
were named Neonomians because they held that 'evangelical righteousness'
could be obtained through following the New Law of 'faith, repentance
and sincere obedience'. If these three commandments were kept for life,
the sinner would be saved. Louis Berkof concludes, 'The covenant of
grace was changed into a covenant of works.'

As Crisp preferred God's Law to the New Law he was called an
Antinomian - a lawless man. Crisp's enemies had cunningly combined the
errors of Amyraldism, Grotianism and Arminianism to form a new pseudo-
evangelicalism. This Neonomian stance split evangelical churches down
the middle and the modern cleft between free-gracers and free-willers shows
that sadly this cleft remains. On the Neonomian side one finds Presbyterian

Dr. Daniel Williams (1644-1716), whose lop-sided criticism of Crisp even influenced Benjamin Brook's brief biography of him and also the Lorimers' Hall Western Association Baptist Conference of 1704 in which 13 churches denounced Crisp's doctrine of the imputed righteousness of Christ as tending to 'overthrow natural, as well as revealed religion'. On the Crisp side, we find such outstanding evangelicals as Twisse, Traill, Toplady, Hervey, Gill, Ryland Senior, Whitefield, Boston, the Erskines, John Brown of Whitburn, Huntington, those Anglicans who hold Article 13 dear and many modern Particular Baptists, in fact, all true Reformed men. Modern critics of Crisp are invariably Fullerites who have quite a different view of the law, grace and the indwelling of Christ in the believer.

Richard Davis: A great evangelist
Independent pastor Richard Davis (1658-1714) has long been viewed as one of the fathers of Hyper-Calvinism though his evangelistic efforts were second to none. Oddly enough Peter Toon in his *The Emergence of Hyper-Calvinism in English Nonconformity 1689-1765*, also argues that Davis was a pioneer Hyper-Calvinist but the long list of Hyper-Calvinist proofs he delivers concerning how they cramp preaching, teaching and evangelism do not apply to Davis at all. Davis taught young Gill 'If you know Christ well, it is no matter though you are ignorant of many other things; if you are ignorant of Christ other knowledge will avail but little.'[27] This helped the young boy to come to a knowledge of the truth and see the centrality of preaching Christ. Gill praised Davis 'very powerful and evangelistic Ministrations' with his zeal for soul-winning.[28] This alleged Hyper-Calvinist evangelised through eleven counties, founding churches wherever he went. He trained weavers, carpenters, tailors and farmers to go out into the highways and byways to bring sinners to Christ. In so doing, he earned the animosity of many sleepy pastors in an 80 mile radius of his Northamptonshire church who woke up to find that Davis was doing their evangelistic and pastoral work for them. Michael Haykin soft-pedals on Davis' theology when explaining that he evangelised the Olney area and made the subsequent work of Baptist John Sutcliff all the easier. Actually Davis contradicts all that Haykin has to say about his High Calvinists who are shown as being antagonistic to evangelism and as causing congregations to shrink. On the other hand, Fullerites are all good and the only true apostles of evangelical expansion. Haykin, like the New Divinity School which he continually praises, is obviously more interested in inheriting Edwards' zeal for evangelisation rather than his doctrine. Haykin thus treads on very thin doctrinal ice by emphasising the 'vigorous preaching' of Robert Robinson and his 'extremely fruitful ministry till his

death'. According to Underwood, whom Haykin uses as his authority, Robinson surprised even Joseph Priestley by his ridicule of the Trinity. He died supplying a Sabellian pulpit and his biographer, William Robinson, says, 'He was one of the most decided Unitarians of the age'. Perhaps Haykin has not read Fuller's own severe *Strictures on Some of the Leading Sentiments of Mr. R. Robinson.*

The beauty, eloquence and power of James Hervey's preaching
Fuller is also severe in his criticism of James Hervey who was greatly influenced by Gill and Brine. Though an invalid throughout his entire ministry and though he often could only preach in a reclining position, his church was always full to bursting point and drew in hearers from many miles around. There is hardly a saint in the history of the church who better utilised every minute of his frail life to the glory of God and the extension of his Kingdom. The following is a typical transcript of Hervey's words to the many who gathered around his table at meal times:

> The Weather being wet and tempestuous, brought on our Remembrance that cheering and comfortable Passage, where it is said of CHRIST JESUS; *He shall be for a Place of Refuge, and for a Covert from Storm and from Rain.*
>
> How, or in what Respects, shall CHRIST answer these desirable Purposes? - Because, He is our Surety. He has put Himself in our Stead. He has undertaken to answer all Accusations, that may be brought against Us; and to satisfy all Demands, that may be made upon Us.
>
> Has the Law of GOD any Charge against Us?—It has. The Law saith, *Cursed is He that continueth not in all Things that are written in the Book of the Law to do them.* And instead of continuing in ALL, We have continued in none. We have not *perfectly* kept any, but repeatedly broke all the Commandments. Broke them, if not in the outward Act, yet in our Hearts—If not in the Sight of our Fellow-Creatures, yet before the all-seeing GOD—If not in the literal, yet in the spiritual sense of the Precepts. Therefore, the Law pronounces Us accursed: and the Law cannot be broken. Heaven and Earth may pass away, sooner than one Iota or Tittle of its Commands shall be unfulfilled, or of its Threatenings unexecuted. To rescue Us from this dreadful condition, the blessed JESUS said; 'Upon me be their Curse. I am content to be treated as an accursed Creature. Let all that Ignominy and Wrath, which are due to the vilest Transgressors—let it all fall upon me.'

Had the *Justice* of GOD any Controversy with Us?—It had. Justice solemnly declared, *The Soul that sinneth, shall die*. All We have sinned, and dealt wickedly. Death therefore is our due: Death temporal, spiritual, and eternal.—But our adorned Redeemer put Himself at our Head; became responsible for all our Provocations; and said, as it is most sweetly recorded in the Book of Job, Deliver them from going down into the Pit; I have found a Ransom. 'Here am I; prepared and determined to expiate their Iniquities: though it cost me Tears and Groans, Agonies and Blood.'—Accordingly, the Sword of inflexible Justice awoke; sheathed itself in his sacred Heart; and took full Vengeance on the Royal and Immaculate LORD, that it might spare his mean and sinful Servants.

The *Authority* of GOD had a Demand upon Us; That We should keep the divine law, or else never expect a Title to eternal Life. *This do, and Thou shalt live*; is a Decree, that will never be repealed.— It was impossible for our *fallen* Nature, to perform the heavenly Commandment, in all the Extent of its Requirements. Therefore, our ever-gracious Master became our Surety. HE, who gave the Law, was made under the Law. HE, who is Ruler over all, subjected Himself to our Obligations: in our Place, and in our Stead, He fulfilled all, that the Law commanded. On purpose, that He might answer that amiable Character, THE LORD OUR RIGHTEOUSNESS. On Purpose, saith the inspired Writer, That by *his* Obedience *We* might be made righteous. Rom. v. 19.

In these Respects, the LORD JESUS is a Refuge and Shelter. A *Refuge*, ever open and free of Access to all Sinners: a Shelter, inviolably secure and never to be penetrated by any Danger. Lot was safe, when He fled to Zoar. Noah was safe, when He was shut up in the Ark. The Prophet was safe, when Chariots of Fire and Horses of Fire were all around Him. And are not they equally safe, who fly to this divinely excellent MEDIATOR? Who are interested in his atoning Death, his justifying Righteousness, his prevailing Intercession? They may boldly say; they may rejoice and sing; *We have a strong City*, in our Redeemer's Grace and Love. *Salvation*, Salvation itself, hath GOD appointed for *our Walls and Bulwarks*.

All this is pure gospel and quite the opposite in many instances to the doctrines and preaching of Andrew Fuller. The latter was quick to point out that those whom he deemed 'High-Calvinists' were slow to do good works and to labour for the spiritual and bodily needs of the unsaved. On this topic, John Ryland Senior says of Hervey:

His love and compassion for the poor, rose to such an astonishing degree, as I never discerned in any other human being: he appeared to be nothing but bowels of mercy: he had a powerful disposition to feed them, to clothe them, and instruct them in the true method of salvation, by our Lord, Jesus Christ: he did but just allow himself the necessities of life, in order that he might have the more to bestow on the people of God, and ministers of Christ. He kept no money by him, any longer than he could dispose of it to some good use; yet he made no account of the money that he gave away; he tried to forget every thing he did, and could not bear to have any body mention any charitable action he had done.[29]

The young Ryland, a budding educationalist, and his wife had ample opportunities to hear Hervey preach as they stayed with him often and sat under the word he preached. Of those times Ryland writes:

In the course of six years that I visited him twice a year; what astonishing charms of eloquence have I heard from him at family worship, as well as in the pulpit. Never did I hear from any other man such new turns and elevated range of thought and passion as I have heard from him times more than I can recollect, in the parlour, at family devotions. In a word, they were some of the best divinity lectures that ever were given to young students . . . He knew as well as any man the best figures which contained a beauty, or expressed a painful or pleasing commotion of the soul, and he seized with ardour the most glowing images of all things. He relished the most daring and striking ideas, and painted them in so lively a manner, as though you saw them before your eyes . . . his manner of addressing the understanding and conscience, the imagination, memory, and passions of his different kinds of hearers, were unboundedly new; and he could afford to blot out, and throw away riches, superior to other authors.[30]

Writing on Hervey's eloquence as a preacher, Ryland says:

We have very able divines, who have stated the great doctrines of the Gospel, and improved them in a masterly manner. Witness Dr. Waterland, Dr. Abraham Taylor, Dr. Calamy, and Mr. Sloss, on the Trinity. Dr Owen and Mr. Hurrion on particular redemption. Mr. Richard Rawlin on Justification, by Christ's righteousness. Dr. Doddridge's sermon on Regeneration. Edward Polhill, Esq. on

Christ, as the mirror of the divine perfections, and vital union with
Christ. The Rev. Thomas Hall, on Final Perseverance. Dr. Gill on the
Resurrection of the Dead: With many other great and good authors; but in point of eloquence and beauty, Hervey exceeds them
all.[31]

Hervey did not only reach thousands through the preached word but
literally hundreds of thousands through the written word, his books
running into several editions a year and being translated into a number of
Continental languages. The Anglican saint showed that the high doctrines
of grace, if experienced in person, led effectively to the preaching of the
gospel in fervent love for sinners.

Evangelists to the very marrow

Fuller, in his *The Gospel Worthy of All Acceptation* is also critical of the so-
called Marrow Men[32] for their teaching regarding salvation and justification
as a sovereign gift of God rather than something to be grasped at through
personal motives. The spirituality and evangelistic prowess of these men
can be illustrated in the life of Ralf Erskine (1685-1752). In Scotland at the
beginning of the 18th century, there was a wide-spread belief that all men
receive a common grace to be improved on. This could develop into saving
grace which, in turn, could be neglected and rendered ineffectual. This
view was coupled with Neonomianism, the teaching that faith became
savingly effective through keeping the New Law of 'sincere obedience'.
When Edward Fisher's *Marrow of Modern Divinity* was re-published,
men such as Hog, Boston, Watson and the Erskines saw in it a refutation
of these errors. The Scottish Assembly regarded the book as a plea for
Antinomianism and branded those who supported its teaching, popularly
called the Marrow Men, as heretics. Then the Assembly legalised the
appointment of ministers via patrons rather than the vote of church members
and as the Marrow Men protested against this move they were gently but
firmly thrust out of the denomination. Both sides accused the other of
acting contrary to the church confessions. The Assembly genuinely
thought the Marrow Men were making justification the goal of faith rather
than Christ and showing disrespect to those placed in authority. They, in
turn, felt that the Assembly mistook anti-Baxterism and anti-Neonomianism
for Antinomianism and showed too much respect for 'persons of quality'.
After much inner conflict, Ralf Erskine believed he ought to identify himself
with the Secession and entered into his diary on Wednesday, 16th February,
1737, 'I gave in an adherence to the Secession, explaining what I meant by
it. May the Lord pity and lead.' The great majority of Erskine's large

congregation wasted no time in leaving the Established Church with their pastor and erecting a new place of worship.

Ralf Erskine's ministry was so blessed that revival broke out and the worshippers filled the church and church-yard. After the service prayer and thanksgiving went on in small groups sometimes all night long. One seeker arose at two in the morning to pray outside in secret only to find the whole town on its knees. The entire countryside hummed like a gigantic hive of bees as hundreds of penitent sinners poured out their petitions to God under the dome of heaven. The seeker writes marvelling at the fact that he could hardly find a place to pray though it was raining steadily. Professions were so numerous and the Lord's Table so crowded that Erskine and his brother pastors began to soundly catechise the people to remove the chaff from the wheat, only to find the former hardly present. Erskine's sermons are extant in which he portrayed hell so that his hearers felt they were already there and then he portrayed heaven's open doors in Christ and admonished his hearers to flee from the wrath to come. This method produced genuine conversions. Such manifestations of the work of the spirit, according to Fuller's criticism, ought never to have taken place in the ministries of those with whom Fuller disagreed. It is extremely dubious whether anything approaching such a work of evangelisation as carried out by the Marrow Men was ever evident in the preaching of Andrew Fuller, John Ryland Jun., Robert Hall and other pioneers of the Fullerite system.

The Life, walk and triumph of faith in a balanced ministry
This section would not be complete without a reference to William Romaine (1714-1795). Though Fuller himself, appears to have said little in criticism of this great evangelist and pastor, modern Fullerites are severe and harsh in their criticism of him as a noble contender for a life of faith. In his Banner publication *No Holiness, No Heaven,* Dr. Richard Alderson presents Romaine under the heading *A Dangerous Imbalance* as maintaining a most one-sided ministry.[33] True to the Fullerite method of comparing 'essential' Scripture with 'inessential' passages, and quoting John Angell James, Alderson argues that Romaine emphasises too much that Christ is our righteousness and too much that faith should be in Him for justification. He finds that there is too much of Paul in Romaine and too little of James. Romaine, he argues, has leaned too much on the Epistle to the Galatians and too little on the Sermon of the Mount. Thus the unity of teaching in Scripture about which Romaine wrote, is rejected as being an 'unbalanced' thing. It is typical of this school of thinking that the teaching of the Apostle James is centred upon as opposed to that of Paul. This is why Fuller

always assumed the figure of James in his *Dialogues* and allowed those whom he conquered in debate to adopt the characters of other New Testament writers. This reminds one of the Tübingen Liberal theory that Peter had a different gospel to Paul, only amongst Fullerites it is usually James against the rest.

After such unbalanced criticism, Alderson uses Angell James as his spokesman to back up his interpretation of the Apostle James in saying of Romaine:

> What was the consequence? Just what might have been expected: he prepared the way for theoretic Antinomianism, and many of his hearers when he died became the admirer of that notorious personification of spiritual pride, presumption, and arrogance, William Huntington. For what is Antinomianism? The gospel abstracted from the law and resting upon a basis of sovereign mercy, instead of being founded upon the principles of moral government.

This is Hyper-Fullerism at its worst. Though Fuller often confused justice with mercy, he never went to the extreme of arguing that the gospel rested merely on the moral government theory irrespective of sovereign mercy, though obviously later Fullerites took Fuller's teaching to its logical conclusion. A brief look at the life and work of William Romaine will show how successful he was as an evangelistic preacher and how modern cries of Antinomianism and Hyper-Calvinism against him are completely and utterly erroneous. It is also strange that Richard Alderson should quote J. A. James against Huntington in a book on holiness of all things. James is well-known for his executive understanding of Scripture. To him the revealed Word points to a universal divine management which relegates a theological understanding of sovereignty and mercy to mere means to an end. J. A. James's end would strike more than casual readers as being highly legalistic. Indeed, in quoting J. A. James at length to show that the gospel is more law-centred than Christ-centred and abides more by the rectoral principle than it is dependent on sovereign mercy, Mr. Alderson leaves himself wide open to the charge of being dangerously imbalanced himself in a way Romaine never was.[34]

Philip Schaff, the church historian, said that Romaine 'stood forth as *the main pillar of Evangelization*,[35] which was reviving in the Church of England after the reaction against Puritanism consequent upon the Restoration a hundred years before.'[36] This is no exaggeration as whatever Romaine preached, lectured, wrote or said in conversation witnessed to blessings in Christ. Imagine, for instance, attending a lecture by Romaine in his capacity as Professor of Astronomy and hearing him declare, 'Were dying sinners ever comforted by the spots on the moon? Was ever miser reclaimed from avarice by Jupiter's belts? or did Saturn's rings ever make a lascivious female chaste?' Well might the secular historian W. H. E. Lecky say in his history of the 18th century, 'Few contemporary clergymen exercised a deeper or wider influence, or displayed a more perfect devotion to the cause they believed to be true.' Both Schaff and Lecky agree that Romaine's contemporary fame 'rests chiefly on the extraordinary popularity of his preaching'. J. B. Owen goes even further and says that as a preacher and writer 'none ever attained a greater popularity; and, what is infinitely more important, none were ever more signally blessed with proofs of usefulness in his ministry.'

Romaine was ordained as an Anglican minister in 1736, a year before obtaining his Master's degree at Oxford. He became chaplain to Sir Daniel Lambert and through him gained access to the pulpit of St. Paul's Cathedral where, at 27 years of age he preached a sermon on Romans 2:14 ff. against Latitudinarian ideas of natural religion and reason, stating plainly that the only religion suitable to his hearers' fallen condition was the religion of Divine revelation and grace. As such a display of gospel preaching was anathema to what was really a fore-taste of Fullerism in Anglican vestments, Romaine was banned from taking up a pastorate. Romaine felt called to preach to the metropolis and thus turned down lucrative offers to move elsewhere. Whitefield even offered Romaine £600 a year to pastor a Philadelphian church. Instead, Romaine accepted two lectureships in London on £18 per annum. This did not prevent him, however, from raising hundreds of pounds a year for charity.

Romaine became immensely popular in his new form of preaching, telling sinners that it was useless looking to a right use of their own senses to comprehend and accept Christ's salvation. They must accept their complete and utter impotence and, in this state of inability, draw near Christ who accepts all those who bring their yoke to Him. Much as the common people were glad to hear that there was hope in Jesus, the office-bearers in the churches where Romaine lectured were appalled. Here was a learned man telling the people frightening Bible stories instead of patting them on the back and informing them that God had given them the privileges of reason and natural ability so that they might assist Him in the moral rule of His world and thus earn eternal rewards. They strove to hinder Romaine in every way possible, at times preventing him physically from entering the pulpit and at times locking the doors of their churches so that the vast crowds could not enter whenever Romaine was to preach. When Romaine won the backing of his Bishop and gained entry into churches, their false ministers refused to lighten them up on winter evenings so that Romaine preached holding a candle whilst his large congregation sat and stood in physical, but by no means spiritual, darkness.

In 1750 Romaine was appointed assistant morning preacher to St. George's, Hanover Square, one of the most fashionable churches in London. For five years he 'preached Christ crucified among those who are least disposed to receive him.' His sermons carried titles such as *A Method for Preventing the Frequency of Robberies and Murders*, showing how the reformation of manners demanded by the Latitudinarian clergy could only be accomplished by converted men and women. Soon the rich left the church and the poor took their place and the clergy were once more up in arms. One nobleman said that the theatres were only too glad to welcome the poor but the Church did their best to ban them. Romaine was also banned from his post in 1755, the year he married. In 1752 he had been appointed Professor of Astronomy at Gresham College but as he was very free in finding loopholes in the Newtonian view of the cosmos which was held as 'gospel' by scientists, he soon lost this appointment. Romaine also preached at Oxford University but, though welcomed by the students, the Vice-Chancellor was 'deeply offended' by his words and dismissed him in 1757. Such events never seemed to weigh Romaine down. As one door closed, he waited cheerfully and calmly until the next one opened.

Now Romaine became curate to St. Olave's, Southwark, in an area supporting a dozen Dissenting churches, including John Gill's, only a matter of yards away. Indeed he took it in turns with Gill to visit ailing James Hervey in Mile Lane who became a firm friend of both. Now supported by a wife, Romaine kept an open breakfast table where all could join in the meal and share in Romaine's message. Though over forty years old, he was still only a curate but the younger clergy who came to visit Romaine looked upon him as a father in Israel.

The year 1757 was a notable one for Evangelicals as Romaine sent out the first of three calls for prayer. A weekly hour of prayer was to be set up nation-wide for the spread of the gospel, to 'advance the fame of Christ' and support Evangelical ministers who were prayed for by name. At first, Romaine knew of only eight Evangelicals in all Britain but when he issued his second extended call in 1779 at least 80 Evangelical ministers were preaching the true gospel up and down the country. Romaine circulated a tract listing seven reasons why the prayer life of the Church was of vital importance in the cause of revival.

Soon Romaine was moved on again and ministered a short time at St. Bartholomew's and Westminster Chapel besides doing itinerant work all over the country, in particular in Yorkshire. Wherever he went, Romaine was adored by the poor and hated by the senior clergy who used rights of patronage to get rid of him. Finally in 1764, though he refused to canvas as the other nominees, he was chosen by a great majority of the parishioners to the rectory of Blackfriars. The two candidates who lost pressed for a second election, which also turned out in Romaine's favour. They then took their unworthy cause to the courts who confirmed the result of the election. Romaine told his new church that he looked upon them as a nursery which it was his duty to water and feed until they could be planted out and work for Christ in their various spheres. He confessed openly that it was his duty to create in his flock a knowledge of themselves—their vileness, and a knowledge of Jesus—His glory.

Finally settled down in his own congregation, Romaine's work prospered and his church had to be extensively enlarged. As most of his parishioners moved out of the city in the summer months, Romaine found time to do itinerant work throughout the country. He is said to have never avoided an opportunity to preach nor to have failed to take on an appointment because of illness.

Romaine published little, his main calling being to preach. He did however produce one book on the *Life, Walk and Triumph of Faith* which has become a Christian classic. Critics such as John Angell James and Alderson, see in this book an exaggerated stress on the work of Christ in these areas of faith to the detriment of man's responsibility. It must be remembered, however, that Romaine's calling was to a denomination that had tended to ignore the Biblical doctrines of imputed righteousness and the inner work of the Holy Spirit; in fact all that had to do with living a holy life through the indwelling Christ. This had been substituted by the teaching of Grotius, Toland and Tillotson with their high view of man as one who, though fallen in part, is not subdued by sin and has the natural capacity to climb to his former glory. This is pseudo-holiness at its worst. Any reservations one might have in thinking Romaine leaves out human responsibility are put to flight when one reads his published letters which are packed with experimental, practical advice concerning how to walk with and serve the Lord. As Cadogan says, Romaine's writings are 'the effusions of a good man, full of faith and the Holy Ghost, and as a little history of heaven upon earth.'[37]

When Romaine realised that his earthly tabernacle was to be replaced by a heavenly eternal one, he wrote 'I have lived to a blessed time. All that is worth enjoying has been freely given to me. By the quickening grace of the Spirit, brought into oneness with Jesus, and to partake of the Father's love in Him,—all is mine . . . These are the prospects which faith, looking back, opens to the Christian with delight; and thereby renders my present condition a subject of praise and thankfulness.'

The only conclusion one can come to after reading Romaine's life and testimony is that if he is accused of Hyper-Calvinism and Antinomianism, it is obvious that his accusers either do not know what the words mean or they have no idea of what balanced preaching entails.

3. John Gill and pastoral evangelism

Gill's highly successful lengthy ministry

As John Gill is looked upon by modern Fullerites as the bogeyman of evangelism or the prophet of How-It-Should-Not-Be-Done, it is essential that this man's work for the Lord should be examined in detail. Michael Haykin, in describing 'God's preparation for a great work', meaning the era of Sutcliff, Ryland and Fuller, refers to Gill and Brine and quotes Ryland Junior as saying Baptist preachers, 'were too much restrained from imitating our Lord and his apostles, in calling on sinners to "repent and believe the gospel".'[38] Haykin, however, negligently attributes what Ryland says of Lewis Wayman to Gill and Brine. He also does not mention that Ryland, in a lengthy footnote to this section, exonerates Gill from the main charges of Hyper-Calvinism. It is also worthy of note that Ryland shows how Brine sought to mediate between the two extremes on the negative and positive side of the Modern Question. All this, and the fact that Ryland is as critical of the Countess of Huntingdon's men for their suspected tendency towards Antinomianism as he is of the older Baptists seems to have quite escaped Haykin's browsing through Ryland. Indeed, when reading carefully through Ryland and viewing his controversy with Huntington, it is obvious that Ryland does not know quite where to place traditional Calvinists, of whom, as his earlier works show, he was enthusiastically one.

Haykin, following Cramp, makes the wrong choice in picking Gill out as one who 'abstained from personal addresses to sinners by inviting them to the Saviour, and satisfied himself with declaring their guilt and doom.'[39] Such a judgement has nothing to do with the facts. Cramp's account of this period is very sketchy and the fact that he presents John Newton as George Whitefield is an indicator that he should be read with discernment. Even so, Fullerites who quote him both exaggerate what he says and write as if Gill and his followers perpetually emptied churches. Haykin, for instance, quotes Cramp as saying that 'When his (Gill's) example and teaching were followed by many of his fellow Baptist ministers, the Baptist cause in England began to *plummet.*' Cramp, however, in the reference Haykin gives, clearly distinguish between Gill's ministry and that of those who followed him and he does not refer at all to 'plummeting' numbers.[40]

Most modern, negatively-biased assessments of Gill are based on what happened at Carter Lane in the dying months of a great evangelist, pastor and scholar. During this period of his ministry, after he had been ill for two years, only preaching once a week and his loving flock refused to accept his resignation and find a new pastor, Gill's church shrunk to around 150 members. This was, however, after over 50 years of blessed and successful ministry and this decreased number still made Carter Lane one of the largest Baptist churches of the time. It is interesting to read how modern traducers of Gill accuse him of emptying his church yet these very men have both emptied churches themselves and even been thrown out of them by their dissatisfied members. Even today, few Baptist pastors, whether Particular or General can boast of the success in numbers Gill had over the whole of his ministry. He also served one and the same church from 1719 to 1771. Modern pastors seem to have a seven year's itch[41] and rarely serve the same flock for a lifetime. Gill's faithful flock would not give up their pastor, though he was at death's door, but most of the young people, who had not these attachments went where they could obtain more regular preaching. However when Gill took over the Goat Yard pastorate in 1719, its membership grew by leaps and bounds until the building, according to John Rippon, Gill's successor, was filled to bursting point. Even a writer such as Curt Daniel, who is convinced that Gill was a Hyper-Calvinist, believes that Gill drew in a over a thousand worshippers.[42] Incidentally, Daniel's sole reason for dubbing Gill a 'Hyper' as he terms him, is that he does not find Gill using the term 'free offer'. The days of shibboleths have not ended!

The importance of Gill's preaching

In spite of the glowing facts of Gill's successful ministry, his modern traducers are prepared to go to great extremes and use all their dialectic skill to prove the opposite. Peter Naylor, in his book, *Picking up a Pin for the Lord*, combs through Gill's sermons to find what he has the audacity to call 'a good example' of his preaching to prove that there was no 'hope of glory' in Gill's message and he did not preach Christ.[43] Naylor alights on a few words, torn from their context, which state, 'Attend the means of grace, and may the Lord call you by it, in due time, that you may fear and serve your father's God, and fill up his place in the world and the church.' implying that this is all there was to Gill's gospel. Actually these words were not part of the body of a sermon at all but words addressed personally

to the children of John Davenport after preaching at his funeral on Job
30:24. Anyone familiar with this printed sermon and Gill's exposition of Job
30 in his commentaries will note how utterly unfair it is to portray Gill as if
he had no burden for the conversion of sinners. Naylor gives Ivimey as his
source rather than the original sermon, yet Ivimey quotes John Rippon,
Gill's successor who maintained that Gill, 'came into the pulpit, at times,
with an heavenly lustre on his countenance, in the fullness of the blessing
of the gospel of Christ, enriched, and generally enriching'.[44] So fervent
was Gill in his preaching that, during the sermon, handkerchief after
handkerchief was passed up to the pulpit by a loving congregation so that
Gill could wipe his perspiring face.[45]

Ryland Senior not only maintained that the very reason why the
Particular Baptists kept up their numbers and sound theology was because
of Gill's influence but in 1753, when the Baptists in general were at a low
ebb, his statistics give Gill the largest membership of any church in London
only rivalled outside of London by Benjamin Beddome's church in Burton-
On-the-Water. Unlike Gill who did not live to experience the fall-away in
doctrine due to Fullerism, Beddome (1717-1795) lived to experience the
down-grading and kept his distance from it. A successful evangelist
himself, he could not understand why Fuller was keen on sending people
abroad when they had not proved their calling at home.

Gill set as his aim to preach those two aspects of the gospel which
Fullerites always deny Hyper-Calvinists preach, 'repentence and faith'.
This is stressed by both Rippon and Ivimey. He was most successful, not
only in his home church but in the lectures he gave to a large audience of
mixed denominations at Great Eastcheap and other lecture halls. He was in
great demand as a speaker, evangelist and preacher at ordination ceremonies
and—though he disliked the task thoroughly—at funerals. When one
compares Gill's sermons with Fuller's it is like descending from the mountain
tops of Biblical exposition to the dark valley of philosophical speculation.
Fuller's sermons remind one of village hall further-education lectures on
philosophy and the good life and are very often void of application or
appeal in any way.[46] Gill's sermons are rich with instruction on the ways of
the Lord, now speaking to the sinner, now addressing the saint. His
language, especially when dealing with the eternal love of Christ for His
Bride, reaches the lyrical and he is full of teaching concerning the indwelling
of Christ and the work of the Holy Spirit, not influencing a man from
outside, which seems to be the best Fuller can do, but transforming him
from within.

It is very difficult to conceive that anyone familiar with the ministry of
John Gill could accuse him of being without vigour in preaching the Gospel

to sinful man. Thomas Wright called Gill 'the profoundest preacher', claiming that 'Dr. Gill's voice rose clear and distinct above the babblement of the day.' Wright ranked Anglicans Berridge and Hervey, and Baptists Gill and Brine as preachers of the pure Gospel and men who 'were baptised with the Holy Ghost and with fire, setting their faces as a flint—men with whom religion was a transporting passion.' Wright's portrait of young theology student Toplady is very moving. He describes how, in an effort to receive the very best, Toplady would hear Gill preach in Southwark and then dash off to hear Whitefield at Tottenham Court Chapel. Toplady's friends could not understand how one training for Holy Orders could spend so much time listening to a Baptist but Toplady knew that he was receiving the pure Word of God.[47]

Gill's chapel was renowned throughout the country for the power of gospel preaching which was maintained in it and John Rippon, who succeeded Gill in the pastorate and William Button who published his sermons tell of the influence of his message of joyful Christian experience which spread far and wide amongst the Baptists and influenced 'all the evangelical denominations at home and abroad'. Furthermore Gill was one of the very few Baptist preachers who took a very active part in working with Anglican Calvinists who were pioneering the Great Awakening in the middle 18th century. James Hervey, Augustus Toplady, Erasmus Middleton and Henry Venn[48] were only a few of the many members of the establishment who received ever new impulses from Gill's sermons and theological works and they snatched up his books with the print fresh on them whenever they could. Toplady was not too proud as an Anglican to sit under Gill's ministry, always taking the opportunity to make copious notes. The great many quotes in Toplady's works from Gill's sermons are testimony enough of the power he found in them. Toplady also quoted extensively from the East Cripplegate and Lime Street lectures. Wesleyan critics were quick to spot the unity of heart that there was between Gill and Hervey. They poked fun at Gill for making Anglicans (thinking of Toplady) and criticised Hervey for supporting Baptists (thinking of Gill and Brine). Venn distributed Gill's printed works amongst his friends. Hervey highlights time and time again the beauty of Gill's language in spreading the good news of Christ's love for sinners. He found especially Gill's teaching on the perseverance of the saints 'full of weight, rich with consolation, and worthy of a place in our memories and in our heart. May our own meditation fix them in the one, and the Spirit of our God implant them in the other!'[49]

Augustus Toplady has left us with one of the earliest eye-witness accounts of Gill as a preacher. Of his mentor he wrote:

As a minister, his deportment in the pulpit was grave and solemn. His language plain and expressive: His method natural and easy: His reasoning strong and nervous: His addresses affectionate: His matter substantial, clear and consistent, well digested, and delivered with great fluency and accuracy, which failed not to command and fix the attention of his hearers. In prayer, he poured out his soul with great freedom and fervency, with much importunity, familiarity and liberty; and, like another Apollos, was mighty in the Scriptures, and had the tongue of the learned to speak a word in season.

Universal offers of grace not conducive to evangelism
When one reads such words from such trustworthy eye-witnesses as Toplady, one sees how incredible are the statements of modern Fullerites who deny any such testimonies out of apparently sheer bigotry. Erroll Hulse, for instance, in his booklet *The Free Offer* says in stark contrast to the overwhelming evidence, 'Gill's church on the other hand shrunk and we are not surprised. When Gill declared, "that there are universal offers of grace and salvation made to all men, I utterly deny",[50] he was expressing with accuracy the deficiency of all his writings and works. Valuable though they may be in many other ways they are destitute of pleadings with sinners to repent, believe and be saved.'[51] Needless to say, Hulse does not explain that Gill is not arguing against invitations and exhortations to believe in Christ, as he points out in Section X, p. 15 of *The Cause of God and Truth*. In the context Gill is condemning Arminian Whitby's ideas of a 'come and get it' approach to a universal atonement which guarantees salvation for all providing they take the initiative and grasp it. Further-more, in the same context, Gill is actually emphasising evangelism's impor-tance and scope within the world-wide strategy of the Holy Spirit, and *as He leads*, not denying it. Hulse clearly confuses Gill's use of the term 'universal offer' with his own pet term 'free offer'. The former refers to a universal offer of the full gospel, which must then, of course, include election and predestination, warranting such salvation *for all at all times*, whereas the latter is normally understood as 'preaching the gospel freely to *all as the Spirit leads*. This is the clear teaching of the Synod of Dort which refers to 'affording an offer of salvation to sinners without distinc-tion' adding 'to whom God in his good pleasure sends the gospel' The former gives every man a mandate over his own salvation and is thus not preaching the gospel at all. The latter is preaching the gospel properly. The 'universal offer' theory, if held by a professing Calvinist, would mean that he sincerely believes that God offers salvation to some to whom He will not give it. If this is not a blasphemous thought, it is difficult to con-

ceive what is. It is certainly as far from Calvinism as east from west. As the word 'offer' is highly ambiguous, as Gill explained in his preface to Davis' hymnbook, and modern Fullerite evangelists often give the word a free-will connotation bordering on the 'universal offer' theory, it is perhaps best to use a more Biblical and apt phrase.

The idea that Gill did not earnestly plead with sinners to repent cannot have been obtained from Gill's works and contemporary testimony. It obviously belongs to the category 'mistaken rumour'. It also shows that Fullerites have a quite unbiblical view of repentance. Gill emphasised that a sinner must feel his own vileness and guilt before he could turn to Christ for cleansing. This is, according to Cramp, not part of the gospel which is why he castigates Gill for preaching 'guilt and gloom'. Fullerism teaches sinners to love Christ as if they had never sinned, believing that, encouraged by the promise of salvation, the sinner is fully able to do so. There is little coming to Christ in anguish and torment, confessing one's absolute filthy nature in Fullerism. The vileness of the sinner and cleansing in Christ is soft-peddled as no true vileness exists where man is not truly fallen and no true cleansing exists where no true redemption and satisfaction has taken place.

Gill preached the whole counsel of God
When Toplady discussed all the truths that Gill preached, which are all the truths that Fullerites deny that he preached, he concluded with the words:

> He did not shun to declare the whole counsel of God, and kept back nothing that might be profitable to the people; constantly affirming, that those who believe should be careful to maintain good works. His ministry, by the blessing of God, was very much owned, and greatly succeeded to the *awakening, conversion, comfort, instruction, edification and establishment*[52] of many, who enjoyed the opportunity of attending upon it.[53]

Toplady's thankful praise to the testimony Gill gave him is far from exhausted. He also puts to flight any groundless criticisms that Gill was a Hyper-Calvinist who rejected good works and tended towards Antinomianism:

> Those who had the honour and happiness of being admitted into the number of his friends can go still further in their testimony. They know, that his moral demeanour was more than blameless: it was, from first to last, consistently exemplary. And, indeed, an

undeviating consistency, both in his views of evangelical truths, and in his obedience, as a servant of God, was one of those qualities, by which his cast of character was eminently marked. He was, in every respect, a burning and a shining light—Burning with love to God, to Truth, and to Souls—Shining, as 'an ensample to believers, in word, in faith, in purity'; a pattern of good works, and a model of all holy conversation and godliness.[54]

Preaching wrath and forgiveness

Gill, contrary to the beliefs of a host of critics, often ended a sermon with a rousing plea to sinners to flee from their danger. In his sermon on *The Character and End of the Wicked, Considered*, based on 2 Samuel 23:6-7, Gill concludes by addressing the sinners amongst the gathered saints directly with the words, 'If any of you are seeking to flee from the wrath to come, which is revealed from heaven against all unrighteousness and ungodliness of men; and should be asking, Whither shall we flee? . . . There is no other way of escaping the wrath to come, due to the sons of Belial, but by fleeing for refuge to lay hold on the hope set before you in the everlasting gospel; by fleeing to Christ, turning to him, the strong hold, as prisoners of hope; and, being justified by his blood, you shall be saved from wrath, through him. It is he, and he only, who delivers from wrath to come.'[55]

It is no wonder that Fullerites continually insist that Gill does not teach fleeing from the wrath to come as they have quite a different view of God's wrath than Gill. Rather than view God's wrath as being vindictive in the Biblical way, they emphasise its lovely and amiable (sic!) nature[56] in accordance with 'the nature and fitness of things' and 'common sense and practice of mankind'. They even see hell as a place where the sinner may positively ponder on the good things he has lost. The condemned sinner has an eternity of recollection and reflection before him![57]

Preaching on Matthew 11:28, 'Come unto me, all ye that labour and are heavy laden, and I will give you rest.' Gill puts to flight all criticism that he taught the sole importance of 'bare ordinances' and that the Gospel should only be preached to the converted. The saint proclaims freely the Gospel exhortation to come to Christ:

> Christ having signified, that the knowledge of God, and the mysteries of grace, are only to be come at through him, and that he has all things relating to the peace, comfort, happiness, and salvation of men in his hands, kindly invites and encourages souls to come unto him for the same: by which is meant, not a local coming,

or a coming to hear him preach; for so his hearers, to whom he more
immediately directed his speech, were come already: and many of
them did, as multitudes may, and do, in this sense, come to Christ,
who never knew him, nor receive any spiritual benefit by him: nor is
it a bare coming under the ordinances of Christ, submission to baptism, or an attendance at the Lord's supper, the latter of which was
not yet instituted; and both may be performed by men, who are not
yet come to Christ: but it is to be understood of believing in Christ,
the going of the soul to him, in the exercise of grace on him, of desire
after him, love to him, faith and hope in him: believing in Christ, and
coming to him, are terms synonymous, John vi. 35. Those who come
to Christ aright, come as sinners, to a full, suitable, and able, and
willing Saviour; venture their souls upon him, and trust in him for
righteousness, life, and salvation, which they are encouraged to do,
by this kind invitation; which shows his willingness to save, and
his readiness to give relief to distressed minds.

The myth of the old Particular Baptists empty chapels and great revival under Fullerism

Hulse gives no sources for his contradiction of the evidence in arguing
that Gill emptied his church, indeed the myth which is firmly believed
amongst Fullerites is that Gill took over a large thriving church from
'moderate' Benjamin Stinton and then proceeded to frighten the members
off. The opposite is the case. Such critics should cast their eyes on their
own ranks.

Fuller never reached the membership the best of the Old School
Calvinists had in their worst years in his very best years as a pastor.
Though he addressed thousands on his commercial, missionary fund-
raising campaigns,[58] far from home, his home churches around Kettering
and Northampton, which were the most influenced by the new teaching,
remained relatively small. The way Fuller spent his years travelling for
hundreds of miles on fund raising expeditions shocked the more spiritual
minded of his brethren. Fuller would even accept invitations from the
pulpits of churches which he openly criticised as being less than Christian
to beg money of these supposed less than Christians to finance his society.[59]
The fact that with all his efforts Fuller was only able to raise a fraction of
the capital needed to assist the church at Serampore which, through God's
grace, was quite able to look after itself, puts a question mark to the whole
principle of expecting what one considers the world to finance what one
considers the Lord's work. It also questions the Dissenting principle of

the independence of a local church.[60] Huntington was able to raise many hundreds of pounds for his church-centred work by merely commenting in a few seconds on the need to his flock. He was appalled by the idea of misusing pulpit time in fund-raising and preaching sermons with a view to financing an institution. He was also shocked by the idea that churches called upon him to preach, knowing that he would draw in the crowds and thus fill the collection boxes.[61]

4. The True State of the Fullerite 'Evangelical' Churches

A heart-breaking disappointment

In 1814 Fuller took sober stock of the state of the Baptist churches in Northamptonshire.[62] He looked back over the past 50 years of which the last 30 had seen a growing interest in evangelising according to the new system of warranting and offering salvation to all as opposed to those who had gone before who had allegedly not even preached to sinners. The results must have been a heart-breaking disappointment to Fuller. Even though a great many Anglicans in the district had become Baptists after the deaths of James Hervey and Abraham Maddox who had filled their churches with believers, Fuller says that the average membership was fifty with a number of churches reaching 70. No church had more than 'about three hundred hearers'. Though Fuller says that half the present number of churches have been established within the previous 50 years, he does not say whether this growth had been at the beginning of this period, i.e., before Fullerism had developed, or within the last few decades. Fuller's following essay *On the Decline of the Dissenting Interest* would suggest that the picture had not been too rosy in more recent years. In that article Fuller confesses that the Evangelicals of the Church of England, who were at that time still committed to the doctrines of grace, had experienced real growth.

In spite of the facts, modern Fullerites still speak of 'the most vibrant force for change on behalf of evangelical Calvinism' which is supposed to have made Old Calvinism 'a dead issue'.[63] This force is imagined to have spread, conquering in all directions. Baptist pastor John Stevens was an eye witness of this 'outreach' and could testify that it was certainly not the Word of Life which was being spread abroad but strife, contention, split churches and wishy-washy teaching. Commenting on Fuller's desire to clean up what he called the dunghills of Baptist doctrine and the effect of this purging, Steven writes:

> I well remember that in places where there had been but one church before, that one soon became divided into two; and no small

contention arose amongst many who had dwelt in quietness together, before what then obtained the name of Fullerism was known among them. Thus the inertness gave place to agitation and dissention, and many humble quiet souls became sorely unsettled and distressed in diverse places. Hence the Baptist churches, instead of becoming 'perfect dunghills', became extensive swamps of a very fungous quality. To prove this we need only refer to the Circular Letter of the ministers and churches of the Midland Association.

Stevens quotes from this Association letter to thirty-six churches who appear to hold to the sufficiency and universality of the atonement; that it is equally provided for every *rational* creature; a public satisfaction for the relief of mankind indiscriminately; that men have the faculties to make themselves new hearts and return to the Lord and a host of other strange doctrines that are almost unbelievable. Stevens then goes on to say:

> The preceding extract amply shews the fruits of Mr. Fuller's treatise, with others of the same description published since his time; and also proves that the Baptist churches are indeed very greatly changed, and certainly not for the better since the days of Dr. Gill and John Brine, and others who laboured with them in the gospel of God. It is now but a short distance further for the Midland ministers to go, and they will have arrived through moderate Calvinism to the depths of Pelagianism; which are only a little way from Socinianism; where, having once found a sojournment, it will be but a further step to Deism. May the Holy Spirit enlighten their minds, impede their progress, and bring them to a settlement in the spiritual knowledge of Christ and his glorious gospel. Charity would fain hope that the thirty-six churches are not all so deeply fallen from grace, (Gal. v. 4.) as the Circular Letter would represent them to be. If they do really approve of the faith set at the head of the Letter, and the Letter itself, in which that faith is openly denied, they must be an unenviable people![64]

By 1889 the Northampton Association had renounced verbal inspiration and denied there was, 'one rule of holiness, and obedience for all saints, at all times, in all places.'

Stevens saw the Fullerites joining with Arminian churches and boasting that they were living out true evangelistic thinking. He shows great scepticism regarding their claim that the church has been asleep for 1800 years and confesses that never in that history was universal atonement so much spoken about as in his day. It is thus no surprise to read in the *Earthen Vessel* of September 2, 1861 a warning article under the heading *A Sketch of the Rise and Progress of Fullerism, or Duty-Faith. That Gangrene now rapidly spreading in many Baptist Churches*. The author of this article, J. A. Jones sought the Lord's face to undertake a lasting work in spreading the gospel and was moved to support Anglican David Alfred Doudney in his republication of Gill's works.

The sober statistics that Fuller gives and the vivid picture that Stevens and Jones paint from within the Baptist churches explode the myth that the Old School Baptists were ineffective in reaching sinners but the New School men preached to all so that sinners were now converted, were baptised and joined local churches in great numbers. Sadly, the leaders of the New Theology had an even smaller membership than the leading Old School Calvinists whether in the town or country. A direct comparison with the so-called High-Calvinists or Hyper-Calvinists who were contemporary with Fuller shows that a good number of their churches, especially those connected with the Calvinist Independents and William Huntington, were far larger than those of the Fullerites. William Huntington was preaching to between two and three thousand until his death in 1813. In fact as an old tree he was bearing his most prolific fruit. Indeed the life, teaching and preaching of men such as William Huntington and William Gadsby who felt that Fullerism was a wolf in sheep's clothing shows how earnest was their evangelistic zeal and how fervent their soul-winning work for the Lord. Huntington was the means of establishing, or encouraging the establishing of numerous churches besides grounding some 30 ministers from the various denominations in the faith.[65] William Gadsby is known to have founded between 45 and 50 churches made up of members who chiefly came to know the Lord through his ministry. Such preachers of grace as J. C. Philpot, John Kershaw and John Warburton were excellent evangelists. The Fullerite theory that those whom they call High-Calvinists or Hyper-Calvinists did not preach the gospel properly needs to be exploded for the libellous and evil myth it is. Typical of this myth is the claim Fullerites will not give up in face of the overwhelming evidence that evangelical stalwarts such as Gill, Toplady, Hervey and Huntington refused to invite sinners to Christ. The chief name picked out here is invariably Huntington who scarcely wrote a letter to believers and unbelievers alike without painting Christ's mercies in the most beautiful of Scriptural colours. Hear him, when elderly and infirm, speaking to an elderly infirm lady whom he greets with the words, 'Dear Friend, Fellow-sinner, and Fellow-sufferer, Grace and peace be multiplied through our Lord and Saviour Christ Jesus,' and goes on to say:

There is not one word in all the everlasting gospel against a sensible, lost, and undone sinner, who feels his need of Jesus, and seeks him with all his heart, no, not one word. Christ himself invites the weary, the thirsty, the heavy laden, and all that are willing, to come to him, and to take the water of life freely; and declares, that whosoever cometh he will in no wise cast out; and his gospel is not yea and nay, but yea and amen. Be of good cheer, he is the resurrection and the life, and whosoever believeth on him shall never die. Grace and peace be with thee.

W. Huntington[66]

Robert Hawker exalted Christ in the crowds

Anglicans such as D. A. Doudney who printed and distributed Gill's works and Robert Hawker, Vicar of Charles, Plymouth who could not stomach the false teaching of Fullerism were also extremely successful in winning souls for Christ though they ministered in the supposed hey-day of Fullerism. Well did John Kent write on hearing of Hawker's death in April, 1827:

No more the hallow'd fane of Charles shall hear
Salvation flow from his melodious tongue;
Christ, in his glory, was exalted there,
While the vast area crowding thousands throng.

There did he preach to man's apostate race,
While in his breast divine affections glow,
The glories of Jehovah's sov'reign grace,
And awful glory of the fiery law.

Through Britain's isle, to climes beyond the west,
Such pastors, O thou God of Jacob send;
Who, with the spirit of Elijah blest,
Shall for the faith delivered thus contend!'

Suspicious of the fund-raising sermons of the missionary movement, though he strongly approved of world-wide church-planting and evangelism, Hawker accepted an invitation to preach for the London Missionary Society. He chose Romans 10:14-15 as his text and spoke on 'The Work of the Holy Ghost essential to give success to all missions for the Gospel.' He did not misuse the opportunity to preach the gospel to canvas for money and afterwards argued against the glorification of fund raising in sermons as if the more money that was raised, the more souls would be converted. He called such efforts 'wretched divinity'. Hawker was shocked to find the new missionary societies organising themselves on a commercial basis and was compelled to withdraw from membership of such societies. He was also alarmed at the watered down, anti-Trinitarian gospel of Fullerism that was being preached on the mission field and stressed that if missionaries hoped for blessing on their ministry, they should not only preach the redeeming love of Christ but also the electing love of the Father and the renewing grace of the Holy Ghost.[67]

Fuller's ministry not according to Christ's precepts and example
Perhaps the reason why Fullerism was not immediately successful, though it preached easy-believism, boiling down the gospel to the appeal, 'love God as if you had never apostatised,' was because the teaching brought a great deal of unrest in the churches and many left churches that had previously been sound in Biblical doctrine because of new Fullerite ideas. In this they followed what can only be called the sect-producing work of their New Divinity brethren. When one considers all Fuller's written works, the vast majority of them are taken up with defending his theories and arguing that his colleagues are unsound, rather than preaching the gospel. Dissenting members who refused to leave Fullerite churches or change their doctrines were excommunicated. The change in Fuller's theology created havoc amongst pastors, turning brother against brother. Huntington's words of defence of one who was excommunicated from Dr John Ryland's church for sticking to traditional Calvinism, are worthy of being quoted at length. Huntington's main point was that in emphasising giving a Gospel invitation to all sinners, the Fullerites were ignoring the evangelistic duty to preach the Law. Sin must be known as sin before grace can be understood as grace. Any neglect of this was sheer Antinomianism to Huntington who thus says:

1. This doctrine can never be established by the practice or example of Jesus: for though he called all that laboured and were heavy laden to come to him, and those that were sick, that were hungry, and thirsty, &c. yet it is clear that he always sent the curious, the pharisaical, and the whole-hearted inquirer; to the law. 'What is written in the law? how readest thou? This do, and thou shalt live.' 'If thou wilt enter into life, keep the commandments.' And, if they asked Which? he replied, 'Do not kill, do not steal, do not commit adultery; and Honour thy father and mother.' This sending them to

the law to work, is a sufficient proof that Christ made not his gospel the rule of these men's duty. Mr. Ryland and Mr. Fuller act contrary to Christ, who is the best example; for it is clear that the Saviour went a different way from them, in making the two tables of the law, not the gospel, the rule of these men's obedience.

2. I think, with respect to the unconverted, sir, that you begin at the wrong end. You tell them, it is the duty of all men to believe; but, as faith is produced in the soul by the Spirit, and is brought forth into exercise by a spiritual birth, I think you should tell the unconverted, that it is their duty first to beget themselves; then to quicken their own souls; then to make a new heart and a new spirit; and then by perfect love, to cast out fear from their hearts; and then their faith would work by their love. A child cannot walk before it is born, nor can any man walk by faith till he is born again. Marvel not at this: before a man can believe, he must be born again.

3. This extorting evangelical obedience to the faith from infidels shut up in unbelief, is a doctrine that cannot meet with the approbation, nor be attended with the impression, of the Holy Ghost; for he is the Spirit of faith, and produces faith: but, by this doctrine the unconverted are set to perform what none but the Spirit of God can effect. A man receives grace for the obedience of faith; but that which is produced by the Spirit's energy, is here made the carnal man's duty. Man is made the agent, where the Spirit is the efficient; and, can it be expected that the Spirit will attend with his seal a doctrine that brings no honour to him? He will not give his glory to another, nor his praise to the unconverted. This doctrine will never add one soul to the household of faith.

4. If it is the duty of all men to believe, they must believe that Jesus died for all men; that he will pardon all men, and save all men. If they believe not this, their faith is vain, and they are yet in their sins; and if all men do believe this, they believe a lie, for the bible affords no such warrant for the universal faith of these unconverted legions. 'I will take you one of a city, and two of a family, and I will bring you to Zion.' Were I to go to the condemned criminals in the cells of Newgate, and tell them, it is their duty, one and all, to believe; that the king will pardon them at the gallows, and that he will save them from death: should I succeed with this doctrine, and bring them all to believe the report, I should think that I had acted as the false prophets did in the days of Jeremiah, make this people to trust in a lie; and, when the rope came to be put round their necks, they

would have just cause to curse my false doctrine, and me also as an impostor and a deceiver. And if all men believe Mr. Ryland's doctrine, they will go down to the grave with a lie in their hand; and he will appear but little better in their sight, when they lift up their eyes in hell, than I should in the eyes of the above criminals, when cast off at Tyburn.[68]

No preacher of righteousness has been so greatly maligned by the present Fullerite establishment as William Huntington. Here was a man who pleaded with hell-bound sinners to flee from the gloom, doom, guilt and punishment which go hand in hand with a life of sin. If ever an evangelical stalwart fulfilled the Fullerite ideal of a man fully intent on serving the Lord as a soul-winner, it was Huntington. Yet it is this fact that causes the ire of the evangelical establishment. Their sense of 'the fitness of things' causes them to believe that as High Calvinists do not preach to sinners, if they seem to do, they are merely performing an empty rite or seeking personal acclaim. They are thus not allowed to join the club. This is the candid opinion expressed in the extraordinary unbalanced attack on Huntington's person in Issue 373, 1994 of the Banner of Truth magazine in which quote upon quote is tailored to suit Fullerism's lop-sided and haughty bias. One must question what view of preaching these apostles of Fullerism have, for instance, when they twist Huntington's solemn appeal to sinners in his *A Watchword and Warning* to mean a personal vendetta against people who disagree with him.[69] What kind of theology do they represent when they argue that the newness of the New Testament is irrelevant (mere evasion) to the meaning of the Old?[70]

The trouble with Fuller's whole concept of evangelism is that it lays his main emphasis on the need for outreach and the accompanying organisation and finance, which are all necessary, though minor, factors in spreading the gospel. In his zeal, he leaves out the main ingredient of evangelistic work. He has no true Biblical knowledge of what a man needs, nor has he a sound Scriptural view of the message which will, through the activity of the Holy Spirit, convict, condemn and convert. Fullerism is praiseworthy enthusiasm spoilt by blameworthy neglect of the gospel which reconciles God to man. There cannot be true evangelism leading to full salvation where God is seen as governed by the Natural Law of His creation and where man is seen as having never lost either the divine witness within him nor the ability to chose God of himself and even act as God's agent in salvation.

5. Conclusion: Our Christian Duty to the Halters between Two Opinions

Dangerous kerb drill
As a small child, I played a fascinating game. Our old street had a kerbstone which grew in height along its length. It had been built this way to make it easier for passengers to climb into the coach at the kerbstone's highest point, level with the coach doors. My game was to walk with one foot on the kerbstone and one foot in the road, and see how far I could hop. This hopping along at two different heights became my daily exercise but my legs never grew long enough to bridge the drop at the highest point and many were my falls when I reached my limit and toppled over onto the rather dangerous road. Needless to say, I always toppled down, rather than up.

The Scriptures tell us in 1 Kings 18:21 that it is impossible to jog along between two opinions; to limp on with your thoughts and hearts at two different levels. This usually ends up by the person who tries to follow two different gospels falling by the wayside. The lower way invariably pulls you down. This was the case with the Israelites who strove to serve God *and* idols and this is the way of modern Fullerite influenced evangelism which strives to follow the doctrines of grace *and* the doctrines of works-righteousness. They erroneously think this is a sensible combination to offer sinners who, they believe, will understand its relevance and may even accept it. As Elijah's Mount Carmel experience taught posterity that salvation was all of God and not of man, so the modern Christian must take up the prophet's mantle to rid the Sovereign gospel from its present-day man-centred, and therefore pagan, perversions.

The 'God does all and man does all, too' theory
The July, 1995 issue of the British *Evangelical Times* carried an extraordinary statement by a leading internationally-known evangelical claiming that it was wrong to say that salvation was half of God and half of man.[71] What true Christian would disagree? Surprisingly, however, the author did not emphasise here that salvation is of the Lord and there is no other Saviour but he made the preposterous claim that salvation, according to the Bible, is 'God doing all and man also doing all.' The writer was not referring to the work of the Incarnate Son of God in His vicarious, penal suffering and death. If this had been a reference to the God-Man, the phrase would have been theologically acceptable, though rather ambiguous. This, however, is not the point the writer makes. He claims that man's responsible use of his own faculties is as efficacious in salvation as

the outworking of God's grace. The necessary corollary to this is that each man is a god-man. This is playing my kerb-side game until it becomes suicidal!

The basic teaching of Andrew Fuller and its results
This, of course, is the basic teaching of Andrew Fuller as he claims that those eternal laws under which God himself is subservient are just as much part of man as they are of God. They are part of the order of creation irrespective of the fall. Team work in salvation is thus called for! The Creator Himself and man as a part of creation are both equally subservient to the Law of Nature, or as Fuller would explain it, 'the nature and fitness of things'. This is what comes of misusing the powers God has given us in an effort to combine the doctrines of grace with the Latitudinarian teaching that man, irrespective of his fallen nature is able to exercise duty-faith savingly. This is what comes of going astray theologically and emphasising human agency shown through repentance and belief rather than God's purpose shown in the atonement. It is an attempt to describe justice and grace in terms of human conceptions of love and mercy.

That Fuller was endued with great spiritual blessings cannot be denied. Both Fuller's conversion and dying experiences testify to a great work of grace in his life. He was most conscious of this and gave God His due glory for the work done in his heart. Instead of becoming a deceiver of men and their leader through his eagerness to develop a philosophy of religion much after the manner of the New Divinity School, which he mistook for Edward's system, Fuller could have used his born-again capacities to live as a bright and shining light, though within a smaller, church-centred circle. In the Fullerite emphasis on pseudo-natural capacities, positive spiritual capacities, in the correct sense of the word 'positive' are neglected. Through emphasising the duties of fallen man, Fuller neglected redeemed man's duties. Moreover, he had not the anchoring in Scripture that Edwards had, nor the spiritual insight and mental capacity to distinguish where God's ways run parallel with the mind of men who are enlightened by those ways and not only walk in them but teach them. He had also a view of the Reformed faith that was, if anything, more jaundiced than that of Bellamy and Hopkins.

The lamp of revelation dimmed by the light of reason
Thus we find Fullerites not only splitting man into his alleged non-fallen and fallen, natural and moral elements but also drawing lines between God's supposed secret and revealed wills; decretive and non-decretive

wills; common and saving grace; special love and universal love; original design and modified design, desires and actions, and also moral and positive laws; each dualistic pair quite self-contradictory. Though no one praised reason so much as Fuller, one can only shake one's head at the unreasonableness of it all. Cowper was true to Scripture and God's view of fallen man when he wrote in *Charity*:

> The lamp of revelation only, shows,
> What human wisdom cannot but oppose,
> That man in nature's richest mantle clad,
> And graced with all philosophy can add,
> Though fair without and luminous within,
> Is still the progeny of sin.
> Thus taught down falls the plumage of his pride,
> He feels his need of an unerring guide,
> And knows that falling he shall rise no more,
> Unless the pow'r that bade him stand, restore.

Seemingly unwittingly, modern Fullerites are following their prophet in his teaching concerning God's alleged conflict with Himself, now arguing according to the Natural Laws which command Him and now arguing voluntarily according to His own will. Usually this conflict is believed to be worked out in a Father-Son debate having serious consequences for the Atonement. This dilemma within the Godhead is illustrated by David Gay in his recent *Banner of Truth* article *Preaching the Gospel to Sinners* (Issue 371-372) in which he claims, 'Jesus said that he often desired that which God, clearly, had not decreed.' This blasphemous utterance would have the Godhead Himself halting along between two opinions. This is no cause for concern, however, for a Fullerite because no decrees of the divine will are eternally binding and God relaxes them or enforces them according to His temporary will. In fact, Fuller follows Grotius closely in teaching that God could and did reject His own Law at times as it was only a demonstration of moral necessity and never an absolute legal necessity.

The difficulties of evangelising Fullerites
It is not easy to witness to Fullerites. Their difference in belief to traditional Christianity, though enormous, is not immediately apparent as they use the same Scriptural vocabulary, though they give most of the terms a figurative, metaphorical or even allegorical meaning. It is just as difficult for them to understand the person who wishes to help them as they hear the familiar terms and understand them in the way familiar to them.

Furthermore, most Fullerites have no idea why they are such. It is the experience of this writer that few, even of their most verbose exponents, have read more than a few misapplied quotes from Fuller in the pro-Fullerite pages of supposedly Reformed magazines. These same people will condemn, say, Gill, Hervey, Toplady, Huntington and Philpot whose works they have hardly touched, merely to keep up their image as 'evangelical Calvinists' as they have heard that these men are extremists. Though they know little of Fuller, many of them know hardly any more of Calvin, Witsius and Owen whom they naively feel are the three pillars of Fullerism. They are, however, more flexible in their discussions concerning these men than when one quotes Scripture to illuminate their minds and souls.

A point of contact
Modern Fullerites have the best reasons for their position. Though they are usually not very well-read in the matters they support, they are impressed by the idea of bringing the gospel to all men and they have accepted this as the good thing it is. They have not thought, however, of the meaning of such words. They have not duly considered what Fuller means by the gospel and what is his theology concerning 'all men'. They have confused 'improper' with 'proper' meanings. This is why they reject Gill and Huntington, because though they have never read them, or read them only to snip out pieces for criticism, they have heard that they are anti-evangelistic and Antinomians. My own personal testimony is that through reading *The Gospel Worthy of All Acceptation* and comparing it with the Scriptures illustrated by Gill on Law and Grace and Huntington and Hervey on imputed righteousness, every vestige, I trust, of Fullerism was removed from my theology as I learnt to 'compare spiritual things with spiritual'.[72] It is thus a very good thing that Sprinkle Publications have re-printed Fuller's works at a reasonable price so that pastors can order them for their church libraries and members can see what Fuller's mock-gospel entails. Gill's and Huntington's works are readily available and the nine volumes of Gill's commentaries have been placed on shareware by courtesy of the Baptist Standard Bearer and are available for the price of a single paper-back. As Fullerism is rapidly strangling the inner core of the evangelical establishment, it is encouraging to hear how many are having their eyes opened by Bible based literature.

Keeping the cross central in one's testimony
Happily, modern Fullerites do not use the airy-fairy philosophical paraphrasing that adorns much of Fuller's writing and camouflages its true intent. They do tend to emphasise duty-faith even more than Fuller and

'the free-offer' which was rarely used by Fuller, has become the shibboleth to modern Fullerites. Those who use the term are judged orthodox, those who do not are 'Hypers', which is their nick-name for Hyper-Calvinists and Antinomians. The facts show that those whom they clothe with these 'theological swearwords' invariably reveal themselves to be quite orthodox brethren with their views based on the cross of Christ. Indeed in witnessing to Fullerites, it is always best to keep the cross central in one's testimony as it is at the cross that Fullerism so miserably fails. As Cowper again says in his poem *The Progress of Error* which condemns so many Fullerite factors, 'There and there only, is the pow'r to save.' Cowper is showing how unchristian it is to believe that Christ, 'Bled, groan'd and agoniz'd, and died in vain.'

When witnessing to Fullerites with Bible in hand, it is useful to go through the key theological phrases of the Bible such as sin, the Fall, the Law, the Covenants, redemption, imputation, atonement, vicarious substitution, justification and sanctification and discuss Fuller's figurative re-translations and re-interpretations with them, emphasising the Bible's literal testimony. They must be shown that all these doctrines centre on the atonement and find their fulfilment there. It will soon be found that most of these terms have been emptied of their theological content of justice, mercy and grace by our Fullerite friends and given a rational, philosophic connotation based on works-faith and works-righteousness. These words are all centred in a moral view of God, man and the world which reflects a completely different gospel to the one commanded by Christ in His Great Commission to be preached to all the world.

Fullerism: A mission-field ripe for the harvest

The Fullerite gospel is nothing but a humanistic message which is designed to appeal to man's fallen nature and is of no saving value. This may seem a severe judgement but when the Fullerite doctrines are examined one by one, this judgement will be seen to be just and, in God's grace, spur us on to a more earnest witness to Fullerites. In the old days when Britain, America and part of Europe were considered 'Christian' and the rest of the world 'pagan', Fullerites emphasised foreign mission work as the culmination of Christian witness. The fields are still ripe unto the harvest but we have no need to go abroad to find work. Fullerism is all around us and this mock-gospel has stormed and captured most of the evangelical para-church bodies, fraternals, conferences and associations which still work under the names of evangelical and Reformed. The hungry sheep look up and are not fed. They look to men at the peak of the evangelical establishment whose words are respected and receive stones to throw at the doctrines of grace rather than receive the Bread of Life. Many are turning Arminian because they see that Arminianism is a more Biblical alternative than Fullerism. Though adherents of the latter claim to be Calvinists, they have been so long in a Fullerite, mock-Calvinist atmosphere that they have forgotten the very existence of true Calvinism and so are not drawn to it.

Awake thou that sleepest!

This is a bleak picture indeed but the history of the church shows that when the Lord's work seems to be dying, new life comes. It came at the beginning of the 18th century when the powerful winds of the Spirit, bringing the doctrines of grace, swept away the dirt and dust of Latitudinarianism, rationalism, Deism and Socinianism. The present day is, spiritually speaking, an exact reflection of that time. As we are approaching the start of a new millennium, may we join in united prayer so that the same Spirit who revived the churches and awakened dead sinners during the greater part of the 18th century will return and do that enlivening work again in our midst. May we all study to show ourselves approved unto God, workmen that needeth not be ashamed, rightly dividing the word of truth. Shunning profane and vain babblings: for they will increase unto more ungodliness and their word will eat as a canker.[73] May we not be disobedient to this heavenly calling in Christ!

---

[1] My emphasis.

[2] *Edwards and the New England Theology, Works*, vol. IX, p. 532.

[3] *Are Baptists Calvinists?*, p. 72.

[4] Ibid., p. 73.

[5] *A History of the English Baptists*, p. 166.

[6] See *One Heart and One Soul*, p. 152 and passim, also p. 127. Haykin does not give the original reference for such a statement and as the words 'the greatest theologian' only are in inverted commas, it seems that Haykin added 'the nineteenth century himself. Fuller, however died in 1815 and most of his works were written between 1780 and 1800 so the reference to the 19th century is rather out of place.

[7] *History of British Baptists*, p. 232.

[8] *A History of the Baptists*, vol. II, p. 584.

[9] See *Larger Horizons and New Problems* in *A History of the English Baptists*.

[10] Followers of Fuller are very sensitive about calling Carey's work the Baptist Missionary Society. They maintain that it was, correctly speaking, The Particular Baptist Missionary Society i.e. indicating that it was Calvinistic in origin. A quick perusal, however, through Fuller's, Ryland's and Hall's letters show that these men called the society merely The Baptist Missionary Society, i.e. to emphasise that it represented all Baptists, which was more than an exaggeration.

[11] My emphasis.

[12] *Works*, vol., IX, p. 535.

[13] See *One Heart and One Soul*. General statements regarding Grotianism and the New Divinity School are found on pp. 53, 139, 209 and 226. Haykin deals positively with Grotian influence on pp. 300-302. Haykin defends the trio's Grotianism against Hawkin's criticism on pp. 348-351.

[14] See my ET article, *John Gill and the Cause of God and Truth*, April, 1994 and my book of that name, Go Publications, 1995.

[15] Also spelt 'DeFleury'.

[16] *The Broken Cistern and the Springing Well*, p. 82.

[17] P. 65.

[18] Dish made of whipped cream and sometimes mixed with jelly.

[19] Speculative discussion over the basic meaning of terms. Ryland is putting his finger on the central weakness of Fullerism, a re-defining of all the major theological words used in describing the work of the gospel. In this they follow Grotius who re-defined theological words so that they found acceptance with as wide a variety of Christians as possible.

[20] *Reminiscences of Ryland*, William Newman, D.D., p. 78.

[21] *The Broken Cistern and the Springing Well*, pp. 82-83.

[22] Op. sit. p. 584.

[23] See *Andrew Fuller and Fullerism: A Study in Evangelical Calvinism* I-IV, BQ, xx, 1963.

[24] Benjamin Brook, *The Lives of the Puritans*, vol. ii, p. 471.

[25] Ibid., p. 473.

[26] Neal's *History of the Puritans*, vol. ii, p. 184.

[27] Taken from Gill's *Preface to Davis' Hymns Composed on Several Subjects*, London 1748.

[28] *Hymns Composed on Several Subjects And on Divers Occasions*, London, 1748.

[29] *The Character of Mr. Hervey*, p. 27.

[30] *The Character of Mr. Hervey*, pp. 5-7.

[31] Ibid., p. 14.

[32] *Works*, vol. II, p. 335 ff.

[33] *No Holiness, No Heaven*, pp. 100-102.

[34] Readers are invited to study Cadogan's and Haweis' testimonies of Romaine in *Life of the Rev. William Romaine, M. A.,* Christian Biography, RTS, for a clear correction to the views supplied by Alderson and James. The story behind Romaine's Prayer Call of 1756 outlined in this work by Romaine himself, shows how fully theologically balanced Romaine was as a Gospel evangelist and praying pastor.

[35] My emphasis.

[36] *Encyclopædia of Religious Knowledge*, vol. III, p. 2058.

[37] *Life of the Rev. William Romaine, M. A.*, Christian Biography, RTS.

[38] Dr. John Ryland's *Memoirs of Mr. Fuller*, p. 5.

[39] *One Heart and One Soul*, p. 17.

[40] See *One Heart and One Soul*, p. 17 and Cramp, *Baptist History*, pp. 435-36, 443.

[41] Judged by a Baptist seminary known to the author which estimated this to be the average length of a pastorate.

[42] *Hyper-Calvinism and John Gill,* published privately 1983, p. 14.

[43] *Picking Up a Pin*, p. 156 ff.

[44] Ivimey, vol. iii, pp. 455-461. See also Rippon's *Life and Writings of John Gill*, p. 122.

[45] Iain Murray has echoed Naylor's unbalanced piece of evidence-sifting in *John Gill and C. H. Spurgeon*, Banner of Truth Magazine, Issue 386. See my refutation of this most careless and inaccurate handling of the subject in *John Gill and his Successors*, Focus, Jan, 1996.

[46] Fullerites will deny this avidly but the proof of the pudding is in the eating. Readers are invited to study carefully the sermons recorded in Fuller's *Works*. Do not start with his sermon in volume II on the *Nature of Virtue*. This will put anyone off wanting to read more.

[47] See Wright's *The Life of Augustus M. Toplady* for details of Gill's influence over the author of Rock of Ages.

[48] The list of subscribers to the various editions of Gill's works reveal a large number of Anglican readers.

[49] Letter CXXX.

[50] *Sermons and Tracts*, III, pp. 117-118, Primitive Baptist Library reprint.

[51] P. 15.

[52] My emphasis.

[53] *Biographia Evangelica*, vol. 4, pp. 454-455, *Sermons and Tracts*, vol. 1, pp. xxxiv-xxxv.

[54] From the short biography appended to Rippon's *Life and Writings of Dr. John Gill*, pp. 138-139.

[55] *Sermons and Tracts*, vol. II, p.126.

[56] *Works*, vol. II, p. 155 ff. See Fuller's defence of his view of vindication on p. 268. The nearest Fuller comes to a clear definition of vindication is when he says it is 'opposed to that punishment which is merely corrective'. See also Clipsham's third BQ article on *Andrew Fuller and Fullerism*, BQ. pp. 222, 225.

[57] Ibid., p. 222.

[58] Fuller's team called this 'preaching for the mission'. It is most discouraging to read the many short entries in the team's letters and biographies which describe preaching engagements briefly as 'preached at so-and-so, collected £ . . .' Commenting dryly on his father's preaching on his first visit to Scotland, his son sums its success up by saying, 'He returned after collecting upwards of 900l'. *Works*, vol. I, p. 69.

[59] See the Rev. T. S. Grimshawe's *A Memoir of the Rev. Legh Richmond*, Seeley & Burnside, 1828, pp. 645-646 for a typical example of Fuller's tendency to criticise the very people before whom he held out his hand for gifts. Notice Legh Richmond's leg pull concerning Fuller's departure from his own 'warranted to believe' attitude.

[60] Fuller, acting as an absent bishop, strove to rule the Serampore church with an iron hand. See *'I throw away the guns to preserve the ship'*, *A Note on the Serampore Trio*, BQ, xx, 1963-64.

[61] See entries under 'Financing of church work' in my *William Huntington: Pastor of Providence*.

[62] *Works*, vol. III, pp. 481-483.

[63] Banner of Truth Magazine, Issue 386, p. 20.

[64] Help for the True Disciples of Immanuel, pp. v-vi.

[65] Issue 378, 1995 of the Banner of Truth magazine carried the unfounded comment that my book *William Huntington: Pastor of Providence*, showed that I 'denigrated' Huntington's evangelical contemporaries 'of all denominations'. In that book, I mentioned numerous men from all denominations who firmly supported Huntington. In a number of letters to the Banner office, I asked this point to be made clear, arguing that the Banner's allegations were highly unfair as they had received ample proof that I in no wise denigrated all Huntington's evangelical contemporaries. On the contrary, I showed how many such men from several denominations turned with joy to Huntington's message of truth. To this end, I quoted Baptists, Independents and Anglicans. I begged the Editorial Director to make this clear in a subsequent issue of the magazine. This plea was ignored and my information suppressed in Issue 380 of the magazine and a selected letter misused to 'prove' that I could come up with no names of contemporaries of Huntington whom I found faithful. I was particularly shocked to find that the Banner refrained from commenting on William Cowper as an exact evangelical contemporary of Huntington's as that magazine had published some five articles from my pen on that great man, whose theology is so very much akin to Huntington's. It would now seem that many evangelical contemporaries of Huntington, because they shared that man's faith, are no longer regarded as 'evangelical' by the Banner of Truth. It is thus not I who denigrate Huntington's evangelical contemporaries but the Banner who denigrates the names of some 30 evangelicals I provided, because, being Huntingtonians, the Banner could not accept them as being evangelical.

[66] *Cleanings of the Vintage*, Letter CXLVIII, Collingridge, vol. V., pp. 192-193.

[67] See a thorough discussion of problems raised by para-church missionary work in *Memoirs of the Life and Writings of the Rev. Robert Hawker, D. D.*, ed. Rev. John Williams, D. D., Ebenezer Palmer, 1831,

[68] *Excommunication*, pp. 147 ff.

[69] See *The Barber: Part III*, CSB Tracts UK, Focus, Number 14, Summer 1995 and also the Huntingtonian Society Newsletter of October 1994 for a rebalancing of The Banner of Truth's numerous recent anti-Huntington articles.

[70] Banner of Truth, Issue 376, Jan., 1995, p. 12. The author of this article professes to be a Boothian but in his eagerness to defend Fuller's liberalism, he seeks to demolish the very arguments that Booth brought against Fuller, especially concerning imputed righteousness and the objectivity of the atonement.

[71] *Spurgeon and the hyper-Calvinists*, subtitled *Iain Murray's well received paper to the Grace Baptist Assembly*, Geoff Thomas.

[72] 1 Corinthians 2:13.

[73] 2 Timothy 2:15 ff.

Appendix:
The Dimensions of Eternal Love

In view of the many Fullerite attacks on the person, testimony and teaching of William Huntington and because of the numerous unfounded and unjust criticisms of him as a Hyper-Calvinist and Antinomian, it will interest readers to see how this man *really* pleaded with souls in his preaching. His method and style may not appeal to everyone as he is most pointed and even personal in his application. However, it will become obvious on reading the following typical example from one of Huntington's sermons that he believes in applying his message directly to the sinner's needs and is careful to bring both law and grace to bear on them. Huntington is an evangelist who stands where the sinner stands, in Christ's stead, as God's own ambassador to fallen man.

This sermon, called *On the Dimensions of Eternal Love* is an exposition of Ephesians 3:18-19, 'That ye may be able to comprehend with all saints what is the breadth, and length, and depth, and height; and to know the love of Christ, which passeth knowledge.' After expounding what this length, depth, breadth and height of the love of God in salvation entails, he goes on to apply his message to the seeking sinner's heart.

I come now to the application; for I reckon that your patience is almost worn out: but, blessed be God, we do not work by the day.

What know you of this love? Is it shed abroad in your hearts by the Holy Ghost? Do you know experimentally the pardon of your sins? Christ said that Mary Magdalen's sins were many, and that they were forgiven her; and she loved much; and, where little is forgiven, the same will love little. Thus you see that love always attends a pardoned soul. And, if you say, 'I love the Lord,' and feel a most cordial affection for Him, for His people, His Word, and His worship; remember your love is nothing but a reflection from His love to you; as it is written, 'We love him, because he first loved us' 1 John 4:19. But perhaps some of you may say 'You are too high; we cannot come up to that experience.' Stay where you are, and I will come nearer to you. Do you find a disinterested love to them that savour most of Christ Jesus in the world? 'Why,' say you, 'is the word disinterested put in? what do you mean by that?' I mean that a hypocrite may love a godly man for what he can get from him, and not for Christ's sake; as Pharaoh loved Joseph for unfolding his dreams, and saving his country from perishing; and as the king of Babylon loved Daniel; and as Potiphar's wife loved Joseph, with the carnal and damnable love of a whore. I ask, therefore, if you love the children of God because their knowledge, their life, and conversation in holiness, appear amiable in your sight? Perhaps you say 'No, I love all people alike, whether they fear God or hate Him; whether they are orthodox or heterodox.' If so, your love has not holiness for its object; it bears no other stamp than merely the impression of the old man. Let me show you the Word of the Lord on this point. 'Who shall abide in thy tabernacle? who shall dwell in thy holy hill? (He) in whose eyes a vile person is contemned [mark that]; but he honoureth them that fear the LORD,' Psalm 15:1, 4. But some will say 'I bless God, I can stand the trial of that pure disinterested love which you describe.' Very well; so far good. 'We know that we have passed from death unto life, because we love the brethren,' 1 John 3:14.

But again, my friends, do you feel sin a plague and a burden to you? Is this your greatest grief; even the unholy motions that are felt from the living corruptions of your heart, because you cannot subdue them, nor keep your thoughts and mind pure, and stayed on the Lord, as you are exhorted to do? Do you say 'Yes' to this; 'I hate the former, and I love the latter.' What says the Psalmist? 'I hate vain thoughts; but thy law do I love.' Psalm 119:113. And again, 'Ye that love the LORD, hate evil.' Psalm 97:10.

Again, brethren, do you find a hatred to erroneous doctrines, which are so dishonourable to God, and destructive to men? I mean such as Arminianism, Deism, Antinomianism, together with all other doctrines of devils? And are your wills brought into subjection to the will of God, so as to consent to wholesome doctrines, even the words of our Lord Jesus Christ? If you say 'Yes;' and conscience says the same, hear the Word of the Lord; 'Through thy precepts I get understanding: therefore I hate every false way,' Psalm 119:104.

But again, some will say 'I bless God, I can say I love Him; for I have been as poor as ever Job was, but His providence has blessed the work of my hands, so that I have abundance laid up in store for my use, while I can see many poor souls destitute of both house and home; yea, and even some of God's people too, who have hardly food to eat, or raiment to put on; therefore God's love has appeared discriminating to me.' Stop, don't you run away; I will come a little closer to you. Your love seems to be more fixed on the providence of God as to the body, than in the discriminating grace of God in Christ revealed to the soul; and has a little of the tincture of those who followed Christ over the Sea of Tiberias for the loaves and fishes, and were sent back with an empty belly and a killing reproof. Suppose God should destroy all your substance, as He did the substance of Job; how then would you stand affected to God? But further; if you were to take your wealth, family, friends, neighbours, with every benefactor, and lay them in one end of the balance, and Christ alone in the other, which, do you think, would gain the draught in the balance of your affections? Nay do not start back at this question. I say, which would then gain the draught? Upon a proper examination, can you say with the Psalmist, 'Whom have I in heaven but thee? and there is none upon earth that I desire beside thee.' Psalm 73:25. If Christ was to put the question to you as He did to Peter, when He said, 'Simon lovest thou me?' could you answer in the affirmative, 'Lord, thou knowest all things; thou knowest that I love thee?' John 21:17.

But again, another may say 'I cannot say that I love Christ; I wish I could: but this I do find, that all the things of this world will not satisfy the boundless desires of my soul; there is a secret anxiety in my mind, which cannot be satisfied by all created and sublunary enjoyments. These are all broken cisterns that can hold no water, (Jeremiah 2:13); they disappoint rather than satisfy me; and increase my thirst rather than supply my wants; therefore I know that my thoughts are hovering about a more satisfactory substance.' Is this your case? Then 'commit thy works unto the LORD [in humble confession and prayer], and thy thoughts shall be established,' Proverbs 16:3. But perhaps you proceed, and say I have heard so much from the pulpit about the amiableness, the suitableness, the sufficiency, the fullness, and the love of Christ to poor sinners, that, if I thought I should have no part or lot in Him, I should view myself of all mortals the most miserable.' You have got love, but it lies in the ashes, covered over with darkness, doubts, fears, and unbelief: be patient, be diligent, and hope for a saving manifestation of pardoning love; for truth has said, you shall not be disappointed of your hope. The disciples going to Emmaus were in your case; but, when Jesus drew near and walked with them, He blew away their ashes, and rekindled the expiring flame, 'Did not our hearts burn within us while he talked with us on the way?' Luke 24:32.

But again, some will say 'My desires are so intense after Jesus, springing from a deep sense of need, and from some glimmerings of His excellent worth, that I cannot rest till I am persuaded of my soul's interest in His eternal love.' Yours is love in the smoke; therefore don't fear, it will not go out; for God says He will not break the bruised reed, though its melancholy jarring sound is not so musical as the voice of doves tabering upon their breasts, (Nahum 2:7). I say, God declares that He will not break the bruised reed, nor quench the smoking flax, till He has brought forth judgement unto truth, (Isaiah 42:3).

'But,' say you, 'I long to enjoy a sense of His atonement in my conscience, and to find an heart felt union with Him, and a joyful love to Him; to say as the spouse does, 'My beloved is mine, and I am his;' Song 2:16 or, with Peter, 'Whom having not seen, ye love; in whom, though now ye see him not, yet believing, ye rejoice with joy unspeakable and full of glory,' 1 Peter 1:8. This joy that you have mentioned is love in the flame; be thankful for the former, but aim at the latter, that you may 'know the love of Christ, which passeth knowledge,' Ephesians 3:19.

Let me show you one great reason why you are kept in perpetual suspense, and tossed about with unbelief, doubts, and slavish fears. Deal faithfully with your own consciences, and try yourselves by what I am going to advance. Your troubles spring from wrong conceptions of God, the fountain of all happiness. Don't you view God as arrayed in terrible majesty, with indignation against you as a sinner? Don't you conceive Him to be an inexorable Judge, comparable to a devouring flame or consuming fire? Are you not afraid day after day, that He will cut you down as a cumberer of the ground, and bring you to judgement, and at the last day expose you before angels and saints as a polluted sinner, with all your secret and unclean sins disclosed to all the host of heaven? If you say, 'Yes, these are my thoughts and my conceptions indeed, you have described my case; and pray how do you find all this out?' Do you leave that to God, and view God speaking to you by me.

You say that what I have said are your conceptions, and therefore you are filled with a slavish fear of God; and this fear is attended with tormenting cogitations; and the workings of your mind are what Job calls tossings, 'I am full of tossings to and fro' Ch 7:4.

If I have mentioned your conceptions aright, let me tell you that you view God in His fiery law; and He is that Judge, that terrible Sovereign, and that consuming fire, which I have mentioned, as considered in His violated law, and out of Christ. And while you conceive thus of God you will be tormented; as it is written, 'Fear hath torment. He that feareth is not made perfect in love' 1 John 4:18.

If what I have mentioned be agreeable to your experiences, you err in your conceptions: I say, as an awakened and quickened sinner, you err in your conceptions; and that holds you down a captive to slavish fear and unbelief. Let us look a little at the back parts of God; seeing we cannot see His face and live, (Exodus 33:20). I say, let us view His back parts, as Moses did. And we will suppose ourselves in the rock Christ, as Moses was in the cleft of a rock at Horeb, when God showed him His back parts; which rock certainly was a type of Christ; and we will endeavour for a while to give credit to what God says in His Word; as it is written, 'In that day the LORD with his sore and great and strong sword shall punish leviathan, the piercing serpent, even leviathan, that crooked serpent; and he shall slay the dragon that is in the sea.' Now we will suppose that this prophecy means destroying the works of the devil in the elect by Christ Jesus, which it certainly does; 'In that day sing ye unto her, a vineyard of red wine. I the LORD do keep it; I will water it every moment; lest any hurt it, I will keep it night and day. Fury is not in me,' mark that, 'Fury is not in me,' Isaiah 27:1-4. But we still proceed to view the back parts of God while we are in the cleft of the rock Christ, and let us hear what God says to us in this situation; 'And the LORD passed by before him, and proclaimed, the LORD, the LORD God, merciful and gracious, long-suffering, and abundant in goodness and truth; keeping mercy for thousands; forgiving iniquity and transgression and sin; and that will by no means clear the guilty' (Exodus 34:6-7) without a Surety, who is Christ, the end of the law for righteousness. Now what do you think of the back parts of God? 'Why,' say you, 'blessed be His holy name, He is better to follow than to meet.' Why then 'be ye therefore followers of God as dear children,' Ephesians 5:1; and you shall not see Peniel, the face of God, till the corrupted veil of mortality shall be swallowed up, and then you will not want to shun that transporting sight. 'Blessed are the pure in heart: for they shall see God' Matthew 5:8.

Again, brethren, if you view God in Christ reconciling the world unto Himself, not imputing your trespasses unto you; but sending His Son to bless you, by turning every one of you from your evil ways; and that the flame of God's wrath is quenched in the Saviour's blood; His sword of justice sheathed in the body and soul of a dear Redeemer; and the law disarmed of its dreadful curse; death disarmed of his sting; the devil himself dethroned and cast down; death plagued; the grave destroyed; the gates of hell barred against every believer, and the doors of heaven displayed to all that ask, seek, and knock; surely these things are sufficient to support a hoping soul. Especially if we consider that our reconciled God is now our most propitious Father; yea the Father of all mercies, and the God of all comfort; our Husband; also our Friend; a present help; our strong hold; our unchangeable Lover; our God, Guide, and Guard; yea, our rich Provider, the strength of our heart, our Justifier, our Saviour, the shield of our help, and our portion for ever. Well, what do you now think of the ever-blessed God? 'Blessed be His name!' say you, 'He seems altogether sweet and lovely, as those Scriptures represent Him which you have quoted.' The Word of God; bears me out in all that I have said. And He is that blessed One to you, if you view Him reconciled in the Mediator, and come to Him by Christ. View Him as I have represented Him from His own Word, and you will find Him the perfection of beauty, and the best of friends; and this will disarm your souls of that slavish fear and torment; and sweetly soften, dissolve, and attract your affections to love Him as the greatest of names, and the fountain of infinite happiness.

But some may say 'What is all this long harangue, and strict scrutiny, about love for?' Because the apostle says, 'Now abideth faith, hope, charity, these three; but the greatest of these is charity,' or love; 1 Corinthians 13:13 and this charity, or love, never fails. Beside, if all your religion springs entirely from the fear of hell, without any hatred to sin, thirst for holiness, love to God, or desire after His favour, all your religion is eye service: it is with you according to the Kentish proverb, 'No longer pipe, no longer dance.' I mean, you move on in your religion no longer than while conscience spurs you, vengeance drives you, or carnal gain or human applause allure you. You are an eye servant; you cannot work but while the whip is upon your back. The very moment that your master Moses lays by the lash of scorpions, you are gone to the ale-house, card-table, ball-room, rout, play-house, or some idle amusement or other. And as soon as Moses comes in, then you set off to the sanctuary again, to offer to God a silly dove without a heart, (Hosea 7:11); or else to mock Him with a dry form of prayer; and every time you perform that task you offer thirty lies to God; and then you wipe your mouth like the whore in the Proverbs, and say 'This day have I paid my vows' Proverbs 7:14. But, if you live and die in that state, God will requite you with the greater damnation.

Let me now appeal to your conscience in the sight of God. If you hear a preacher who enforces the Spirit's work on the soul; that preaches down human merit, will, and power, and insists on the application of truth, the love of the truth, the experience of truth, the enjoyment of the truth, the practice of the truth, or a walk in the truth; who treats much of the life of faith, the joy of hope, the liberty of the Spirit, the enjoyment of love, an heart-felt union with Christ, peace of conscience, and a tender regard for the honour of God; don't you despise and rail against such preachers and preaching? If conscience is to be umpire or arbitrator, will she not say, Yes? As the Lord God of hosts lives, before whom I stand, if you live and die a stranger to all that I have said upon these points, you cannot escape the damnation of hell (Matthew 23:33).

But again; I will come with another appeal to conscience. Are you not fond of hearing a thundering law preacher, who deals chiefly in the vengeance of heaven, and fetches all his artillery from the fiery law of God? And don't you find that discourse is most descriptive of your legal feelings that savours most of death, judgement, destruction, damnation, and the very flames of hell? 'Yes,' say you, 'while this storm is going over my head I am all religion; and while it is preaching I think in my own mind, Oh! how will I watch, and work, and pray, and perform my task when I get home again!' Ay; but before you get your feet over the threshold of your own door the sound of the thunder is gone out of your ears, and all your blind zeal that was awakened, and the working frame that was communicated to your spirit, are gone; and you are immediately taken captive by the devil, and led into some besetting sin; and by that secret sin you are held a prisoner all the year round. This you know is truth; let conscience do her office. 'I cannot deny,' say you, 'but this is the case; and how you find it out I know not.' No, nor are you likely to know: but this I tell you, in the Church of God there are both servants and sons, 'The servant [says the Saviour] abideth not in the house for ever, but the son abideth ever. If the Son therefore shall make you free, ye shall be free indeed' John 8:35-36. If you are a servant you will stick to the rod of Moses, till your spirit and conscience will be hardened like a blacksmith's anvil: but, if you are a son of God by faith in Christ Jesus, the undeserved love of the Father, and the dying love of the dear Redeemer, when preached, applied, and enjoyed, will make your soul like melting wax before the flame, until your softened spirit will become susceptible of every divine impression, and your tender conscience will feel the least sin heavy indeed; every just reproof will be then an excellent oil; yea, one reproof from the lips of the gracious will enter deeper into your heart, as a wise child, than an hundred stripes into a fool, (Proverbs 17:10).

God own and bless the few hints that I have dropped among you, to His own honour, and your eternal comfort.[1]

---

[1] Taken from *On the Dimensions of Eternal love*, *The Works of William Huntington*, vol. II, p. 373 ff. Focus Christian Ministries have recently published a beautifully produced reprint of this sermon at a very reasonable price.

Selective Bibliography

Numerous other works quoted in this book can be found in the index of titles.

Abbreviations:
BHH: Baptist History and Heritage; BHS: Baptist Historical Society; BOTM: Banner of Truth Magazine; BOTT: Banner of Truth Trust; BQ: Baptist Quarterly; BRJ: British Reformed Journal; EP: Evangelical Press; EQ: Evangelical Quarterly; ET: Evangelical Times; EV: The Earthen Vessel; F: Foundations (Engl.); Foc: Focus; GM: Gospel Magazine; GP: Grace Publications; GS: Gospel Standard; JTS: Journal of Theological Studies; NF: New Focus; NTT: Nederlands Theologisch Tijdschrift; RT: Reformation Today; SBHSB: Strict Baptist Historical Society Bulletin; SGU: Sovereign Grace Union.

Primary Literature and Biography
Fuller, Andrew, *The Complete Works of the Rev. Andrew Fuller: With a Memoir of his Life, by Andrew Gunton Fuller*, ed. Joseph Belcher, D.D..
Fuller, Andrew Gunton, *Memoir* prefixed to Belcher's edition of *The Complete Works of Andrew Fuller*.
Fuller, Thomas Ekins, *A Memoir of the Life and Writings of Andrew Fuller by his Grandson*, J. Heaton & Son, 1863.
Morris, John Webster, *Memoirs of the Life and Writings of the Rev. Andrew Fuller*, 1816.
Ryland, John, *The Work of Faith, the Labour of Love, and the Patience of Hope, illustrated in the Life and Death of the Rev. Andrew Fuller, Late Pastor of the Baptist Church at Kettering and Secretary to the Baptist Missionary Society from its Commencement in 1792*, Button & Son, 1818.

Critical Works concerning Andrew Fuller's System (books and magazine articles)
Dix, Kenneth, *Particular Baptists and Strict Baptists: An Historical Survey*, SBHSB, No. 13, 1976. (A most balanced analysis).
Editorial, *Fullerism*, GS, July, 1993, p. 220.
Editorial, *Fullerism Again*, GS, October, 1993, pp. 327-328. (The GS have remained staunch defenders of the doctrine of the Atonement against modern Fullerite attacks, only to be called 'Hypers' by their attackers.)

Ella, G. M., *The Atonement in Evangelical Thought I-VI*, NF, Vol. 1, No. 01 onwards.

Ella, G. M., *A Gospel Unworthy of Any Acceptation*, Foc., No. 8, Winter 1993/94, pp. 4-6.

Ella, G. M., *Robert Oliver and the Twists and Turns of Historical Revisionism*, Foc., No. 14, Summer, 1995, pp. 8-11.

Foreman, John, *Duty Faith*, The Christian Bookshop, Ossett (Two booklets 80pp & 72pp), 1996. (Expounds covenant truths vital to a sound Christian ministry.)

Jones, J. A., *A Sketch of the Rise & Progress of Fullerism, or Duty-Faith; that Gangrene now Rapidly Spreading in Many Churches*, EV, Sept. 2, 1861. (No comment needed.)

Kennedy, Dr. John, *Preaching the True Gospel Properly*, BRJ, Issues Jan-March, 1995, pp. 33-43. (Not the original title but used to show how John Legg is 'out of step with historic Calvinism and the Westminster standards.')

Kennedy, Dr. John, *The Forgotten Kennedy*, BRJ, April-June, 1995, pp.11-21.

Kennedy, Dr. John, *Man as Evangelised in Relation to God*, BRJ, April-June, 1995, pp. 22-34. (The entire issue is taken up with defining what the proper gospel entails in the face of recent criticisms of Reformed positions.)

Rushton, William, *A Defence of Particular Redemption Wherein the Doctrine of Andrew Fuller Relative to the Atonement of Christ is Tried by the Word of God*, Liverpool, 1831, Primitive Publications reprint, 1973. (When I first attempted to read a few pages of this work, I put it away in disgust, protesting that no Christian could be that heretical! Then I read Fuller and learnt to thank God for Rushton.)

Stevens, John, *Help for the True Disciples of Immanuel: Being an Answer to a Book, Published by the Late Rev. Andrew Fuller, entitled The Gospel Worthy of All Acceptation or, the Duty of Sinners to believe in Christ*, 3rd edit., Simpkin and Marshall, 1841. (A good study-in-depth.)

Wright, George, *Fullerism*, GM, vol. xii, 1877, p. 343. (Worth learning off-by-heart as a protective shield!)

Works Confusing Historical and Biblical Orthodoxy with Hyper-Calvinism (books and magazine articles)

Good, Kenneth, *Are Baptists Calvinists?*, Backus Book Publishers, 1988. (In stooping to pick up all kinds of 'Calvinists', Good inclines to drop orthodox Five Point men.)

Haykin, Michael, *The Early Life of Andrew Fuller*, RT, November, 1995. (An attempt to blacken pre-Fuller Particular Baptists.)

Murray, Iain, *John Gill and C. H. Spurgeon*, BOTM, November, 1995. (An effort to discredit Gill at Spurgeon's expense.)

Murray, Iain, *Spurgeon v. Hyper-Calvinism*, BOTT, 1996. (Emotive scurrility traded as a substitute for sound scholarship and historical accuracy.)

Naylor, Peter, *Picking up a Pin for the Lord*, GP, 1992.

Nettles, Tom J., *Andrew Fuller and Free Grace*, RT, January, 1985.

Nettles, Tom J., *Why Andrew Fuller?*, RT, January, 1985. Nettles is presented as basing the doctrine of free grace on election, without grounding this in Particular Atonement. The author (or perhaps editor) misunderstands Fuller's doctrine of election i.e. the culmination and reward of exercised duty-faith.

Oliver, R. W., *Historical Survey of English Hyper-Calvinism*, F (Engl), 7, 1981, pp. 8-18.

Oliver, R. W., *Significance of Strict Baptists Attitudes to Duty-Faith*, SBHSB, 20, 1993, pp. 3-26.

Sheehan, R. J., *The Presentation of the Gospel Amongst Hyper-Calvinists*, F (Engl), 8, 1982, pp. 28-39

Sheehan, Robert J., *The Presentation of the Gospel amongst Hyper-Calvinists: A Critique*, F (Engl.), 9, 1982, pp. 42-46.

Toon, Peter, *Hyper-Calvinism*, The Olive Tree, 1967. (The best refutation of Naylor's, Oliver's, Sheehan's and Toon's arguments are the 'facts' they bring forward.)

Primary Works of Other Writers and Secondary Literature Dealing with Fuller and the Sources of Fullerism
Brown, John, *Life and Character of the Late James Hervey*, Ogle, Duncan & Co., 1822.
Brown, Raymond, The English Baptists of the 18th Century, BHS, 1986.
Calvin, John, *Calvin's Calvinism*, SGU, trans. Henry Cole, D. D., 1927.
Calvin, John, *Institutes of Christian Religion* (2 vols.), Eerdmans, 1979.
Ella, G. M., *John Gill and the Cause of God and Truth*, Go Publications, 1995.
Ella, G. M., *William Cowper: Poet of Paradise*, Evangelical Press, 1993.
Ella, G. M., *William Huntington: Pastor of Providence*, EP, 1994.
Goadby, J. J., *Bye-Paths in Baptist History*, Elliot Stock, London, 1871.
Grotius, Hugo, The Truth of the Christian Religion in Six Books (Trans. John Clarke, Le Clerc's edition), James and John Knapton, 1729.
Grotius, Hugo, *opera omnia theologica*, Amsterdam, 1679, 3 vols, Faksimile-Neudruck, Friedrich Frommann Verlag, 1972.
Grotius, Hugo, *de iure belli ac pacis*, (translated into German by J. H. V. Kirchmann), Berlin, 1869.
Hervey, James, *The Works of the Rev. James Hervey*, Thomas Nelson, 1837.
Linares, Filadelfo, Einblick in Hugo Grotius Werk vom Recht des Krieges und des Friedens, George Olms Verlag, Hildersheim, 1993.
Nettles, Thomas J., *By His Grace and For His Glory*, Baker Book House, 1990.
Newman, William, *Rylandia: Reminiscences*, London, 1835.
Rippon, John, *Life and Writings of the Rev. John Gill. D.D.*, Gano Books, 1992.
Sell, Alan, The Great Debate: Calvinism, Arminianism and Salvation, H. E. Walter Ltd., 1982.
Stevens, John, *Thoughts on God in the Salvation of His People*, Simkin and Marshall, 3rd edit., 1844.

Dissertations
Heering, J. P., Hugo de Groot als Apologeet van de Christelijke Godsdienst, Stichting voor Historisch Onderzoek, Leiden, 1992. (Shows how Grotius read Socinius whilst in prison and was imprisoned by his views ever since.)
Kirkby, A. H., *The Theology of Andrew Fuller and its relation to Calvinism*, Edin., 1956. (The best defence of Fuller I have ever read by a sympathetic author.)

Magazine Articles Providing Back-Ground Material
Clipsham, E. F., *Andrew Fuller and the Baptist Mission*, Foundations (Am), 10 (1), 1967, pp. 4-8.
Clipsham, E. F., *Andrew Fuller: Fullerism (i-iv)*, BQ, XX, 1963.
Ella, G. M., *John Gill and the Cause of God and Truth*, ET, April, 1994.
Ella, G. M., *John Gill and the Charge of Hyper-Calvinism*, BQ, October, 1995.
Kirkby, A. H., *Andrew Fuller: Evangelical Calvinist*, BQ, XV, 1954, pp. 195-202.
Kuiper, E. J., *Hugo de Groot en de Remonstranten*, NTT, 38 (2), 1984, pp. 111-125.
MacGregor, James, *The Free Offer in the Westminster Confession*, BOTM, 82-83, 1970, pp. 51-58.
Manley, K. B., *John Rippon and Baptist Histography*, BQ, 28 (3), 1979, pp. 109-208.
Nuttall, G. F., *Northamptonshire and the Modern Question*, JTS, NS, XVI, 1965, pp. 101-23.
Parker, T. H. L., *Calvin's Doctrine of Justification*, EQ, XXIV, 1952.

Peski, A. M. van, *Waarom Grotius als Oecumenisch Theoloog Mislukken Moest*, NTT, 38 (4), 1984, pp. 290-297.

Sant, Henry, *William Huntington: Pastor of Providence*, Review Article, Focus, No. 14, Summer, 1995, pp. 15-16.

Stanley, Brian C. H., *C. H. Spurgeon and the Baptist Missionary Society*, BQ, 29 (7), 1982, pp. 319-328.

Young, Doyle L., *Andrew Fuller and the Modern Missionary Movement*, BHH, 17 (4), 1982, pp. 17-27.

White, B. R., *John Gill in London 1719-1729*, BQ, XXII, 1967, pp. 72-91.

Index of Names and Places

Index of Topics

Works Quoted or Otherwise Referred to

Index of Scripture References